SERIOUS SHOPPING

Serious Shopping

Psychotherapy and Consumerism

Edited by

Adrienne Baker

'an association in which the free development of each
is the condition of the free development of all'

FREE ASSOCIATION BOOKS / LONDON / NEW YORK

First published in 2000 by
Free Association Books
57 Warren Street, London W1P 5PA

A catalogue record for this book is available from
the British Library

ISBN 1 85343 482 5 hbk; 1 85343 483 3 pbk

Designed and produced for Free Association Books by
Chase Production Services, Chadlington, OX7 3LN
Printed in the EU by TJ International, Padstow

Contents

Acknowledgements

The writing of this book has had much support and encouragement.

Firstly, I want to thank all the contributors whose chapters, which bring so many extra dimensions to this research, have been written whilst working full time, without the privilege of a six-month sabbatical which I have enjoyed.

My appreciation for the grant of the sabbatical goes to Mrs Gillian Payne, the Director of Regent's College, and to Professor Ernesto Spinelli, the Dean of the School of Psychotherapy and Counselling and, most especially, to my colleagues at the School, who did all my teaching and all my work, giving me time to think and write and edit.

Dr Howard Schaffer, Director of the Division on Addictions at Harvard University Medical School, was enormously generous in giving me many of his own papers on addiction and particularly in provoking my thinking on the subject. Jean Kilbourne of the Stone Center for Research on Women at Wellesley, Mass., provided much food for thought on the power of advertising and the media.

All the participants in this research have shown great courage and insight in talking of their experience of addictive shopping and I thank all of them most sincerely. Especially I want to express my gratitude to Esther Harris who came to London several times to meet me, re-immersing herself in the pain of it all as she pursued her understanding of such a paradoxical addiction.

The patience and critical and constructive comments of my friends and colleagues who have read the manuscript have been much appreciated. I have also valued the interest and encouragement of Trevor Brown and colleagues at Free Association Books.

Most of all, I shall always value the thoughts and inspiration given to me by my daughter, Marion, and my husband, Harvey, whose belief in me has helped me give birth to this book.

Adrienne Baker

Directions Publishing Corp., New York, USA. Reprinted by permission of the University of the South, Sewanee, Tennessee. All rights whatsoever in this play are strictly reserved and application for performance etc. must be made before rehearsal to Casarotto Ramsay & Associates Ltd, National House, 60–66 Wardour Street, London W1V 4ND. No performance may be given unless a licence has been obtained.

Rosalind Minsky would like to thank Polity Press, Cambridge, for permission to include the chapter 'Consuming "Goods"', which was first published in *Psychoanalysis and Culture: Contemporary States of Mind* in 1998

Notes on Contributors

Adrienne Baker is Academic Coordinator and Senior Lecturer in the School of Psychotherapy and Counselling, Regent's College, where she teaches and supervises on the MA and PhD programmes. She is a UKCP registered psychotherapist with her own clinical practice. Her earlier research focused on women in the family and cultural contexts of their lives.

Gemma Corbett is a UKCP registered psychotherapist working with women affected by domestic violence. She also runs her own private practice. Her earlier experience was in education and development work in rural areas in Paraguay and Argentina. Her MA research was on 'Women Religious, Body Image and Dress'.

Simon du Plock is an Associate Fellow of the British Psychological Society, a UKCP registered Existential Psychotherapist and a Chartered Counselling Psychologist. He is Chair of the MA programmes in the School of Psychotherapy and Counselling, Regent's College, and has his own private practice.

Richard Elliott is a Fellow of St Anne's College, Oxford, and Professor of Marketing and Consumer Research in the School of Business and Economics at the University of Exeter. He acts as a consultant to industry, lectures widely overseas and has published over 75 research papers on consumer behaviour.

Mary Harris is Director of the Psychotherapy and Counselling Consultation Centre, Regent's College, and teaches on the MA programme in the School of Psychotherapy and Counselling. She has worked as a psychotherapist and consultant in many settings, including Drug and Alcohol clinics and Family Therapy centres.

David Horne is a psychotherapist and clinical supervisor working in private practice and the voluntary sector. His work has been influenced by existential-phenomenological ideas. Before training as a therapist his career was in the antiques trade.

Rosalind Minsky lives in Cambridge where she teaches psychoanalytic theory to undergraduate and post-graduate students at Anglia Polytechnic University. She has published a range of articles on psychoanalysis and two books: *Psychoanalysis and Gender*, 1996, and *Psychoanalysis and Culture*, 1998.

Fiona Murray, the pseudonym of a therapist practising in the North of England, trained in psychodynamic and subsequently in integrative counselling. Her own experience of addiction inspired her dissertation on addictive shopping. She offers individual and group counselling in the field of addiction.

Rosalind Pearmain is Professional Coordinator and Senior Lecturer in the School of Psychotherapy and Counselling, Regent's College. She is a member of the Guild of Psychotherapists. She has long been immersed in Raja Yoga and is currently working on a doctoral thesis exploring the effects of meditation on perception.

Paula Riddy is a UKCP psychotherapist in private practice. She has previousy written on issues relating to psychology and preventative health behaviour and is interested in links between psychotherapy and society. She is currently training as a Jungian analyst.

Marsha Taylor is a bilingual psychotherapist with a special interest in psychotherapy for the socially disadvantaged. She works primarily with female prisoners, immigrants, refugees and victims of political persecution and torture. Trained initially in Argentina and the US, she holds the MA in Psychotherapy and Counselling from Regent's College and is now working on a doctoral dissertation.

Introduction

Adrienne Baker

Over the time that we have jointly written this book, its subject – when mentioned to outsiders – has often elicited smiles, if not mirth. Well-meaning people have seemed sceptical, as if our viewing shopping as a possible addiction is trivialising the meaning of addiction. For the person who shops addictively, it is a different story.

In the beginning, a tragedy brought me to think about it: the suicide of a young woman whom I knew well. In the dreadful months that followed her death, one of many unanswered questions concerned the plethora of beautiful clothes found in her flat, all unworn. Despair and loss were intermingled with pain and waste. The endless shopping, it seemed, had been a desperate attempt to make herself feel better. But the attempt at comfort had been futile; it had hardly touched the self that she eventually destroyed.

Years later, a boutique owner whom I met at a party observed how many of her customers 'seem to hate themselves'. Discussing this with her made me aware that, in shopping, contradictory things may happen: as if the goods desired were not what was desired, as if the purpose of the quest was not the real purpose.

My final catalyst was a client who spoke of the sense of deprivation which still lingered from an austere childhood. As an adult, she made sure never to need to deny herself anything. But each time she bought whatever it was she wanted, the object became meaningless. This contradiction of emotional emptiness in the midst of material plenty appeared a recurring theme.

Reflecting on this, I recognised how in certain circumstances people can become caught up in a seemingly ordinary behaviour, a behaviour which normally is functional and gives some pleasure. But for people who shop addictively, the behaviour – both qualitatively and quantitatively – becomes increasingly abnormal.

1

It was to understand the meaning to the shopper of this frenzied activity, to fathom something of its origins and to convey the intensity of the experience that this research began.

What is addiction? Horney writes about the

> comprehensive neurotic solution [being] ... a solution not only for a particular conflict but one that implicitly promises to satisfy all the inner needs that have arisen in an individual ... it promises not only a riddance from his painful and unbearable feelings (feeling lost, anxious, inferior and divided), but in addition an ultimately mysterious fulfilment of himself and his life ... No wonder that ... it becomes compulsive. (1950, pp. 23–4)

In researching this book we have struggled with the concept of addiction. In fact, the literature on the subject reflects an ongoing debate. One important perspective sees addictive behaviour as a dysfunctional solution to a developmental wound. Other theorists argue that addictive behaviour is an entity in itself with its own meaning. Whichever understanding seems more relevant, there is always a personal logic, something which makes sense amongst all the confusion.

In discussing any addiction there is always the lure of simple causal explanations and the danger of deciphering the addiction in terms of a preconceived ideology. Understanding the construction of personal meaning is an infinitely more complex task. In studying addictive shopping, we have endeavoured to decode what is implicit in the shopper's unique act of shopping.

Does society's reluctance to recognise addictive shopping as a problem – let alone a serious one – enable us to avoid seeing that an everyday activity may be used as a balm for pain? After all, shopping is so routine and integral to any consumer society that initially it seems incorrect to draw parallels with drug or alcohol abuse. Those involve taking a substance, not socially approved in excess, that is known to be damaging, whereas to 'shop till you drop' arouses only amusement.

D'Astous defines compulsive buying as '... characterized by an incontrollable urge to buy which is impelled by a psychological tension arising from internal factors and which is accompanied by a feeling of relief along with the frustration caused by the addictive nature of the behaviour' (1990, p. 16). As in so many addictions, this initial sense of emotional relief is of great importance in the development and maintenance of an increasingly dysfuntional activity.

The significant factor in shopping which becomes addictive is not the behaviour in isolation: it is the interaction between the person in emotional pain, the perceived 'solution' and the context – past and present – in which this 'solution' is pursued.

Estimates of the prevalence of addictive shopping vary widely. In the USA, Faber and O'Guinn's 1989 and 1992 studies suggest that between 1.1 per cent and 5.9 per cent of the general population may shop addictively, depending upon how it is defined, and Black et al. estimate between 2 per cent and 8 per cent (1998, p. 960). An even higher prevalence is given in Trachtenberg's 1988 study (cited in Hanley & Wilhelm 1992, p. 6) suggesting that 10 per cent of the American population, cutting across all demographic and social strata, may be considered compulsive shoppers. Dittmar et al. (1995) quote a figure of 10 per cent in the UK – although these latter very high figures probably reflect different criteria for inclusion.

Much of the research finds addictive shopping to be more common in women than in men, e.g. Christenson et al. 1994, Schlosser et al. 1994. Their findings also suggest that compulsive buyers are more often depressed and have lower self-esteem than normal spenders. Regarding family histories, Black et al. note that significantly more relatives of compulsive buyers had depression or abused alcohol or drugs than controls (1998, p. 961).

It seems that a chronic sense of personal inadequacy may make a person embrace anything that offers hope. If what has been learned since childhood is that pain can be avoided, albeit at a price, then avoidance may become a way of life. When one 'solution' no longer works, an increase in intensity results – more of the same or an alternative 'solution' is sought.

'An addictive experience is one which absorbs the person's whole consciousness' (Norwood, 1986, p. 23). For a time it relieves the sense of aloneness and detracts from the need to experience other aspects of life, their objective reality and their subjective bleakness. Yet a person trapped in a behaviour which has lost its meaning feels no longer in control of his or her own life. It is as if the possibility of self-definition, indeed even of happiness, is placed in something outside him- or herself. It is as if free will, often fragile, has been extinguished.

In a challenging statement, Peele writes, '... addiction can be considered as an abnormal extension of dependence and of habit ... [it] plays a part in everyone's life – none of us is entirely free of it' (1979, p. 296).

Opinions – and they can only be opinions – are very divided as to whether this extreme form of shopping which becomes totally preoccupying is at one end of a continuum or is a distinct behaviour. Faber and O'Guinn (1989) see compulsive buyers as qualitatively different from ordinary consumers. In contrast, d'Astous (1990) points out that becoming a compulsive buyer is a gradual process and that some who shop compulsively do not do so all the time (indicating an element of choice and restraint). Using the 'compulsive buying scale' developed by Valence et al. (1988) on a sample of 190 consumers, he did not find compulsive buying to be a defining characteristic of any sub-group of shoppers (d'Astous 1990, p. 17).

Certainly for people who shop in this way the relationship with the shopping becomes a love–hate affair, in which there is dependency, isolation and denial. Yet it is a relationship of an intensity never before experienced and one of extremes: desolation and euphoria.

Perhaps in the background there is another question: whether, in labelling, in making someone 'other', we are denying the potential for extreme and frightening behaviour in ourselves.

My own chapter begins the book. In it I pursue the paradox of a person's choosing such an innocent and mundane activity as shopping but, in investing it with almost magical potential for reparation from hurt, being destined for disappointment. I suggest that what the person wants in the object sought is not what he or she really wants. The yearning, which the shopping cannot bring, is for the ever hoped-for relationship – past, present or future. As Buber writes: '... we long for things which cannot help us, and we know it ... But actually ... it is something within ourselves that we long for' (1970, 73).

Whilst there are parallels with other addictive behaviours and these behaviours are often themes running though both personal and family life, shopping which becomes addictive is distinguished from other addictions in that there are things, objects, involved. Much of the psychoanalytic literature depicts significant relationships as objects within the internal world (Gomez 1997). That these inner objects, or the lack of them, may be transposed onto concrete objects is suggested in many of the narratives. The shopping, for the emotionally needy person, becomes an attempt at consoling the self with acquisitions from the external world. The objects fulfil, and then fail to fulfil, a purely symbolic function (Lawrence 1990). But also there is a relationship with the things themselves: they carry the poignancy, the tragedy, the longing, the despair, the emotional intensity of human relationships.

As with all defences, the addictive shopping tells of loss and the difficulty in facing and grieving the reality of the loss. It exposes the inadequacy of the relationships that have been and, almost inevitably, of all other relationships. Most of all, it conveys the relationship with a very fragile self.

Rosalind Minsky further considers the fragile identity. Looking at contemporary society, she notes the extent to which traditional ways of identity confirmation, especially through the family, have been undermined. Shopping, she suggests, has unconsciously become a means of reducing anxiety and the sense of not-belonging. Drawing on Freudian and object relations theory she argues that, in consuming goods, we narcissistically seek out substitutes for the perfect idealised self we phantasised about when still merged with mother. But, because it confuses phantasy and reality, this attempt at self-transformation can only ever be ephemeral.

Turning to a different group of 'shoppers', Marsha Taylor, a psycho-therapist working with women who shoplift, sees the pervasiveness of similar emotions – anxiety, depression, despair – as are present in women who addictively shop. In a culture in which possessions have such a defining role, she suggests that the woman with no money, for whom addictive shopping is not an option, may express – and thus intensify – her sense of worthlessness in shoplifting.

Two existential chapters follow. Simon du Plock discusses an existential therapy with a young man who obsessively buys gifts. Considering the gift-buying as a possible defence against death anxiety du Plock suggests that, by the therapists's attending carefully to the client's meaning world, the client became able to face his fears about being an adult and surviving the death of his parents. Du Plock critiques therapeutic approaches which view such difficulties as 'symptoms' of an 'illness' called 'addiction', arguing that both client and therapist may be freed from the pathologising process by seeking an understanding of the personal meanings implicit in a client's behaviour.

David Horne then discusses the meaning and power of shopping as a primary and significant relationship to the world, a contained and predictable world as opposed to one of uncertainty and meaningless-ness. Using clinical and personal experience he suggests that shopping provides an identity and a way of constructing a self and may be used as a defence against anxiety and guilt, thus denying the existential void or lack of self.

Considering clothes shopping, Gemma Corbett asks whether women use this to mitigate feelings of dissatisfaction with their bodies. She suggests that women's frequently felt low self-esteem and poor body image are derived from cultural messages about beauty and desirabil-ity and that effective therapy should aim to decode these and enable women to value themselves more authentically.

Rosalind Pearmain then asks what it is that we experience when we go shopping. Are we attracted more to the sensory-affective aspects of the evironment, the perceptions of space, refuge and coherence, rather than to the acquisition of goods? Are there transformational aspects within the shopping experience? The subjective, embodied life of shopping, intertwined within daily routine, has often been marginalised within economic and post-modernist theories. Her exploration encompasses a feminist view of architecture and space.

Paula Riddy discusses the distinction between collecting and addictive shopping. She explores the meaning of addictive shopping in the context of a family framework suggesting that, in families with poor communication, the behaviour conveys a complex message about unmet needs.

Richard Elliott then focuses on the social context of addictive consumption and the dynamics of power and control between men and women. Noting the dysfunctional aspects of addictive behaviour, his research indicates its possible positive functions: not only can it leaven depression, it may also allow for the discharge of revengeful emotions in 'spoiling' relationships.

Mary Harris's chapter explores the dilemma of addiction as perceived solution. When it fails to resolve the source of distress, relief is sought in another addiction, thus compounding the original problem. She considers families with several generations of addictive behaviours, looks at gender issues and choice of addiction and discusses addictive shopping as one option within a cluster of addictive behaviours.

These themes become only too real in Fiona Murray's chapter, set in the context of loss and emotional deprivation over four generations of women. From her personal experience and with great courage, she reflects on how money, presents and clothes were seen as substitutes for maternal care and how, later, alcohol became the link to her father. Subsequently, shopping became the panacea to end all ills. Finally, she describes the struggle through therapy to understand the seduction of addiction and eventually to give a deeper meaning to her life.

For all of us, it has been an extraordinarily compelling book to write and a painful one. At times I have felt quite defensive, as if we must justify both the writing and the shopping as not an indulgence. I hope we have respected the enormous trust placed in us by all the people who came forward and talked and tried to make sense of their shopping.

REFERENCES

Black, D. W., Repertinger, S., Gaffney, G. R. and Gabel, J. (July 1998) Family History and Psychiatric Comorbidity in Persons with Compulsive Buying: Preliminary Findings. *American Journal of Psychiatry* 155 (7), 960–3.
Buber, Martin (1970) *Ten Rungs: Hasidic sayings*. New York, Schocken Books, p. 73.
Christenson, G. A., Faber, R. J. and de Zwaan, M. (1994) Compulsive Buying: Descriptive Characteristics and Psychiatric Comorbidity. *Journal of Clinical Psychiatry*, 55, 5–11.

d'Astous, Alain (March 1990) An Inquiry into the Compulsive Side of 'Normal' Consumers. *Journal of Consumer Policy*: vol. 13, no. 1, 15–31.

Dittmar, H., Beattie, J. and Friese, S. (November 1995) Shopping – Necessity, Entertainment, or Addiction? *Newsletter of the Economic & Social Research Council on Economic Beliefs and Behaviour*, 1, 6–7.

Faber, R. J. and O'Guinn, T. C. (1989) Classifying Compulsive Consumers: Advances in the development of a diagnostic tool. *Advances in Consumer Research*, 16, 738–45.

Faber, R. J. and O'Guinn, T. C. (1992) A Clinical Screener for Compulsive Buying. *Journal of Consumer Research*, 19, 459–69.

Gomez, Lavinia (1997) *An Introduction to Object Relations*. London, Free Association Books.

Hanley, A. and Wilhelm, M. (1992) *Journal of Economic Psychology*, 13, 5–18.

Horney, Karen (1950) *Neurosis and Human Growth: The struggle towards self-realization*. New York, W. W. Norton.

Lawrence, Lauren (1990) The Psychodynamics of the Compulsive Female Shopper. *The American Journal of Psychoanalysis*, 50, no. 1, 67–70.

Norwood, R. (1986) *Women Who Love Too Much*, London, Arrow Books.

Peele, S. (1979) Redefining Addiction 11. The meaning of addiction in our lives. *Journal of Psychedelic Drugs*, 11, 289–97.

Schlosser, S., Black, D. W., Repertinger, S. and Freet, D. (1994) Compulsive buying: Demography, Phenomenology and Comorbidity in 46 subjects. *General Hospital Psychiatry*, 16, 205–12.

Valence, G., d'Astous, A. and Fortier, L. (1988) Compulsive Buying: Concept and Measurement. *Journal of Consumer Policy*, 11, 419–33.

1

'Even As I Bought It I Knew It Couldn't Work'

Adrienne Baker

[It] ... seems to have rescued her the way morphine rescues a cancer patient, not by eradicating the pain but simply by making the pain cease to matter. It's almost as if she's accompanied by an invisible sister, a perverse woman full of rage and recrimination, a woman humiliated by herself, and it is this woman, this unfortunate sister, and not Laura, who needs comfort and silence. Laura could be a nurse, ministering to the pain of another. (Cunningham 1999, p. 149)

In his novel, *The Hours*, Michael Cunningham movingly portrays the sense of being somehow alienated from the self. It is a feeling only too familiar to the person shopping addictively. The enigma is that to shop and shop is an attempt to get better without involving others, an attempt that never works. Yet, almost always, the painful process is repeated.

Listening to the stories of women and men who shop addictively, I glimpse something of their rawness. Their desperation, sometimes masked, comes with them into the room. As they describe their experience it feels as if deep inside, alongside an aching sadness, there is a voice that drives them on and that deceives. It is like a siren but it is part of the self. Over and over again, it seems to offer balm: buying, it says, will ease the pain. But the opposite happens, as if something seeping from a wound inside pollutes the purchases. Then another, equally powerful, voice chastises them for such terrible waste.

In a way I have been privileged because, hearing that I am interested in the subject, people who see themselves as shopping addictively have chosen to talk about their understanding of what they are doing. But there is a huge responsibility: the researcher, like the therapist or counsellor, invites vulnerable persons to re-immerse themselves in feelings that seem to inhibit any joy in living. The feelings often convey such a sense of loss, like a mourning for a lost self, but a mourning with no end. Yet, as in therapy, although the process of talking allows insights to emerge, the awareness alone feels not enough; it remains 'stuff in the head'. For those whose very selves feels fragile it is a struggle to begin to feel that they matter, that they have worth, that they can have desires and dreams. It requires a response at the deepest emotional level. Often it seems that their needs are insatiable – after all, they themselves have tried to feed their hunger in the only way they know how, and failed.

To listen, whether as therapist or researcher, to the addicted person's feeling of being trapped in an ever-repeated cycle, is to be confronted with emotional pain. Perhaps that is why many of the analyses of addiction seem distant from the phenomenon. This chapter, within the framework of an academic study, conveys something of the despair of people with an addiction, their endeavour to present to the world a competent self, the futility of their 'solution' (in this case, shopping) – which they recognise as useless – and the self-hatred which results.

There is an irony in focusing on shopping for we are constantly exhorted to shop; it is an expected and an acceptable activity and no one is hurt by it. How can something which is usually functional and is sometimes seen as a way of lifting one's spirits become a bad thing? The subjective reality is that the badness is perceived as internal; it defines the self and the mood which needs lifting is hopelessly submerged in the badness.

> I'd go into boutiques when I was so raw, just looking and grabbing. (Woman, 62)

The insights given by people who shop addictively are central to this chapter. They come from interviews with men and women who responded to newspaper and journal articles inviting participants in the research and from long-term clinical work with one male client. The research is qualitative and, in striving for subjective meanings, uses a phenomenological approach (Burns 1979; Hollway 1989).

In using these personal narratives, I am aware of the danger in generalising from them. Each person's route through their darkest hours is unique. Yet in each account there are hints of the meaning behind the addiction and there are links, both to others who shop addictively and to possible theoretical understandings. As a therapist, working with insights from both psychodynamic and family therapy thinking, I hear the client's struggle to survive emotionally. Every addiction concerns this struggle, together with an awareness that the addiction may be only a strategy, that mere survival is not enough. Communication about any addiction is difficult, yet in this type of research something happens in the coming together of the story, the teller and the listener, which allows the pain-filled compromises to be shared. The addiction remains personal and private, but speaking about it gives words to the anger and loss and longing.

This chapter therefore begins by considering some of the under-standings of addiction, the insidious way in which the activity becomes compelling and the 'choice' of shopping.

It continues with an attempt to understand the inner world of the addictive shopper and to depict the sense of craving and unfulfilled need. In this context, the shopping is both functional and dysfun-tional.

There follows a description of the shopping experience: its intensity – 'the frantic acquiring' – and the seemingly inevitable process through climax to denouement. Themes explored include the symbolic meaning of spending and possible parallels between addictive shopping, binge-eating and bulimia and compulsive gambling. Finally, there is discussion on co-existing addictions, on the concept of 'moveable pathology' and some thoughts on approaches to therapeutic work.

ADDICTION

Can the definition of addiction be applied to an activity not dependent on biochemical change? Shaffer suggests that 'anything can be addictive which powerfully and quickly and predictably changes how you feel' (personal communication, May 1999). He writes:

> Addictive behaviors typically serve the addict in the short run at the price of longer-term destructiveness. Physical dependence is not a requisite for addiction. ... addictive behaviors organize the addict's life. All of life's other activities fit in the gaps that the addictive behavior permits. (Shaffer et al. 1989, footnote to p. 7)

The addiction can be to a substance or an experience; shopping, gambling or eating (or abstaining from eating) could equally fulfil this definition – a view similar to that presented by Marks (1990) and contested by Jaffe (1990), who believes there is a risk of 'trivializing dependence' by such parallels. Marks points out that 'We have no universally accepted use of terms like addiction, craving and compulsion' (ibid., p. 1391). Yet there is a need for some sort of framework within which to understand addictive behaviour, a task in which many clinicians are engaged (e.g. Miller 1980; Peele 1985 and 1989; Orford 1985; Marks 1990; Jaffe 1990; Shaffer 1991). Drawing on current definitions of substance dependence, pathological gambling and eating disorders, Walters suggests that addiction may be defined as 'the persistent and repetitive enactment of a behavioral pattern' which includes:

1. progression (increase in severity)
2. preoccupation with the activity
3. perceived loss of control
4. persistence, despite negative long-term consequences

(Walters, 1999, p. 10)

Discussion on addiction is characterised by much dissent and different conceptual models. For example, until relatively recently, the addiction-as-disease model has had considerable influence in the study of addictive behavior, although with many critics (e.g. Szasz 1971; Orford 1985; Peele 1989). Being a medical model, it is persuasive: it offers a diagnosis, a definition, a pathology. Also, it appears to relieve the person with an addiction of responsibility. Yet it cannot convey 'a topography of personal distress' (Shaffer et al. 1989, p. 25).

Another influential model is that of 'the addictive personality' (discussed in Jacobs 1997; Nakken 1988). It notes the many similarities among people who adopt addictive behaviours, particularly 'a childhood and adolescence marked by deep feeling of inadequacy, inferiority, and a sense of rejection ...' (Jacobs ibid., p. 172). The addictive behaviour lifts them out of a chronically depressed state. But critics (e.g. Walters 1999) ask whether the fact that some people engage in several addictions necessarily proves the existence of an addictive personality. There may be a third variable mediating between the person's emotional state and his addictive involvement. Also, in labelling the addicted person psychiatrically ill as well as addicted he becomes doubly stigmatised. Moreover, the major problem with both of these models is that they erode the sense of choice and the hope of recovery.

The question of personal choice is all-important. Emphasising this, Walters offers an alternative to the addiction model. His 'lifestyle model' explores how the host (the person) interacts with the agent (the substance or activity) and the environment and how each affects the other. The significant difference with his model is its belief '... that people *choose* to engage in addictive patterns of behaviour, although they do not understand the full ramifications of their choice' (1999, p. 15).

How self-defined addictive shoppers understand their own behaviour gives insight into the perception of gradual loss of control. It seems as if initially there is an element of choice about whether or not to 'indulge' in the activity which subsequently becomes chronic, by which time there is a quality of insatiability.

> I needed to get out into that shopping environment which totally consumed me. (Woman, 56)

> There is a desperation about it, a 'must have' like the infant's need for instant gratification. (Woman, mid-40s)

> It terrifies me how it's got out of hand. I went through the £10,000 that we made from the change-over of houses very quickly. A year ago we couldn't pay off anything towards the credit cards. We still owe about £25,000. Yet I've spent nearly £1,000 in four weeks on forty to fifty separate transactions. When a new book or video comes out on a subject I'm interested in, I must have it on day one. (Man, 40)

Kaufman, discussing male substance abusers, suggests that they cherish the illusion 'that they can control their use of these substances' (1994, p. 6). But, in relation to addictive shopping, Krueger writes,

> The shopping binge is experienced as [an] uncontrollable and totally consuming urge. It 'has to be done' ... as a bridge to sanity, the only way to feel real and alive inside rather than emotionally dead or empty. It is a desperate, almost disintegrative anxiety, centering on a single hope, 'grabbing onto something tangible, real, in order to feel'. (1988, p. 580)

It may be that whether or not a behavioural addiction can be likened to a chemical dependence is less important than the central question: why and how profound is the need for relief from existing feelings?

IMPULSIVE, ADDICTIVE AND COMPULSIVE SHOPPING

The earliest writers on 'buying mania', Kraepelin (1915) and Bleuler (1924) – cited in McElroy et al. 1995 – stressed the impulsive features of the condition although it took decades for interest in the subject to be re-ignited. There are many parallels between the three conditions and possibly the distinction is a purely academic one. They are all undoubtedly maladies of the affluent society and relevant to particular cultures with an emphasis on acquiring and possessing. In terms of the emotional state of the shopper, low self-esteem is nearly always significant (Rook 1987; O'Guinn and Faber 1989; d'Astous 1990; Faber and O'Guinn 1992; Dittmar et al. 1996; and others) – a finding with obvious implications for therapy.

Studying impulse buying, Rook (1987) sees it as 'fundamentally a problem of failing to delay gratification' (cited in Baumeister et al. 1994, p. 224). As a result, the person makes unintended purchases, disregarding long-term consequences. The shopping represents an 'acquisescence in self-regulation failure' but the descriptions also suggest a total preoccupation, similar to that of the addictive shopper, and often a sense of being 'mesmerised by the object'. As with addictive shopping, its potential for mood change is important and, typically, guilt follows the splurge. The paradoxical effect of such behaviours is that, whilst an element of hope motivates the person as he or she buys, the results of the activity in real life – mounting debts, family conflict – further erode an already fragile self-esteem.

Compulsive and addictive shopping – much more fully explored in what follows – equally represent a craving to buy. The shopper is caught up in an activity both frantic and irresistible, often driven by an unacknowledged need to relieve a gnawing depression and emptiness. But the objects bought fail to fill the abyss and self-hate nearly always results.

WHY SHOPPING?

The distinction between addictive shopping and collecting is explored in Paula Riddy's chapter. In this chapter the focus is on the individuals' own (usually very frightened) acknowledgment of themselves as shopping addictively. Whilst some of the research participants speak of their having had a previous addiction, as Fiona Murray describes in her chapter, yet to become addicted to shopping is understandable. In our affluent consumer society we are bombarded by images which entice, implicitly promising compensation for a pervading sense of lack or even the possibility of a transformational experience. There are huge vested interests urging us to buy.

Jean Kilbourne, exposing the pernicious effectiveness of advertising in the USA (a $130 billion a year industry), discusses the extent to which products are portrayed as having sexual attributes, as if they were lovers: 'The ads sell a great deal more than products. They sell images and concepts of success and worth, love and sexuality' (personal communication, May 1999).

Shopping which gradually becomes addictive is, arguably, only an extension of what we all do. Its social acceptability has great relevance, together with the comforting perception that it is not self-destructive or hurtful to others. But this is at a conscious level. Unconsciously, it seems, there is a constant yearning for something lost or never given. It cannot, of course, be replaced but there is the illusion that, with enough (objects, things), it can. For a while, elements of hope and illusion free the emotional energy trapped in depression as the searched-for object is invested with almost magical powers to transform the person into someone who feels loved.

Many of Krueger's patients (1988) addicted to shopping had also had bulimia (a parallel discussed later). He suggests that

> the emotional significance of spending and acquiring possessions had been underscored by their parents who bestowed possessions or money, as well as food, substituting physical comfort for emotional nurturance. The individuals ... came, in part, to use compulsive shopping ... as a substitute for love. There is a component of aggression ... by forcing parents or spouses to supply money to make up for the emotional support they had failed to provide ... [However] for this to develop into a compulsive-shopping pattern, a significant degree of underlying developmental arrest must be present, an arrest with its roots in earliest development. (1988, p. 575)

The Inner World

Ian McEwan, in his novel on obsessive love, writes 'There are always antecedent causes. A beginning is an artifice, and what recommends one over another is how much sense it makes of what follows' (1997, pp. 17–18).

Khantzian (in Kaufman 1994) similarly warns, 'Addiction develops in context ...' He stresses the complexity of the matrix in which self-destructive behaviour develops. The family of origin is often '... enmeshed in addictive substances or addictive behaviors and dysfunction ...' (p. vii).

There is a curious irony that, in everyday conversation, we may caustically describe someone preoccupied with shopping and style as narcissistic, meaning self-loving. Yet, as Liz Good writes, 'the word narcissism comes from the Greek "Narka", to deaden' (in Cooper and Maxwell 1995, p. 148) – a process which does, indeed, take place whilst addictively shopping: pain is deadened.

Narcissism

> I shop feeling bleak inside. It's as if I'm immersed in a charade, searching for something that I know won't make any difference to my life. As in all

charades, I pretend to be what I'm not: confident and with self-esteem. Then, when I go to pay, I smile at the shop assistant, as if she's the one who needs reassurance that what I've bought will make me happy. (Woman, mid-50s)

From Freud onwards, theoretical discussions on narcissism indicate the enormous complexity of the subject. Of recent works, Symington presents a gentle and humane study, exploring the ever-present tension stemming from our earliest need of intimate relationships. 'We aspire to be whole, but it is always a struggle because we are battling against something' (1993, p. 23). He makes what is for me a very important point: that there are elements of narcissism in all of us and that, the more we intellectualise, the more likely it is that we want to avoid our own painful insights.

Risking that insight, my own fragilities resurface: an easily aroused sense of inadequacy (here intensified by the encounter with a concept I know to be relevant). But the fragility must be hidden and so I cloak it in a façade of self-sufficiency and competence. The act works but the self within stays vulnerable.

For many of the participants in this study, aspects of the 'impoverished narcissist' depicted by Cooper and Maxwell seem to describe their experience: 'Even when they do achieve, they cannot feel supported by their accomplishments. They appear not to be able to incorporate anything good because they have nowhere to put it' (1995, p. 18). It is as if good feelings have no fertile soil in which to take root.

Cooper and Maxwell (ibid., p. 17) movingly cite Levin (1993): 'Narcissistic wounds are special kinds of hurts ... They are the hurts that go to the core'.

In Cooper and Maxwell (1995, ch. 13) Liz Good summarises current thinking on narcissism as having two main perspectives. One views '... narcissistic disorders as stemming from an intense vulnerability in the self ... ' resulting from an inadequate maternal response. The mother, often herself depressed, contributes to the child's sense of not being really loved: she is withdrawn, inconsistent, withholding. An alternative understanding notes 'the crucial role of aggression in the aetiology of narcissism'. This view, drawing on Klein's work, suggests that 'all feelings of dependency upon someone elicit negative feelings' (ibid., p. 149).

Addiction, Good suggests, develops as a narcissistic defence allowing the illusion of being in control, of not needing others. It frequently begins in adolescence, a time of particular vulnerability when issues of separation are central and the young person struggles with giving up and mourning the significant early relationships. Looking particularly at drug-taking, she sees addictive actions (and delinquency) as 'usually related to the search for a love object ... [They] also offer escape from loneliness, isolation and depression ...' (ibid., p. 150) – a sort of temporary equilibrium. Yet 'addiction as a narcissistic defence is paradoxical': whilst initially the action gives an illusion of control both of painful feelings '... and, in phantasy, the primary object' (ibid., p. 150), it shortly leads to loss of control and in itself produces the painful feelings it aims to avoid.

To draw a parallel with addictive shopping, the shopper may pursue a seemingly insatiable need for a good inner object without having to relate in any meaningful way with the person who provides the good things. Yet after every splurge it is not long before he or she feels submerged in depression, guilt and remorse. It is as if the source and possibility of gratification must be denied. Certainly the buyer may not benefit from the object bought, because it represents a new kind of dependence.

It's as if I can't define myself, as if the dislike of myself, wanting to punish myself is always there ... and the shopping is a way of somehow courting disaster. (Woman, mid-40s)

Drawing on Symington's point (1993, p. 10) that narcissism exists within organisations, it seems reasonable also to suggest its presence within troubled families.

ENVY

Most people seem to have something more productive to do with their lives. I know I'm very selfish and I hate myself for it. I'm a failure in many ways. For many years I've not had a satisfactory sexual or social relationship. I'm bored with my job, with my life. If you were to sum up my life in a phrase, it's 'wasted opportunity' – and then I despise myself for not doing anything about it. (Woman, mid-50s)

I look at other women and I can see those who love themselves. I don't. (Woman, mid-30s)

Several of the research participants expressed envy – maybe one of the most primitive emotions. The sense that others have something which one lacks, although in this context thought of in terms of material possessions, suggests a cavernous emptiness. The yearning is undefined but corrosive and there is a continous comparing of the self with others. Envy is self-destructive because it can never be satisfied and, as Minsky points out, it '... spoils the inner world as well as the outer'

(1996, p. 96). Gomez similarly suggests that, 'Envious external relationships lead to envious internal relationships, wreaking havoc on a
sense of clear identity and basic self-worth ...' (1997, p. 40).

> If I'd been offered your job, I'd have gone straight out and bought five suits.
> I keep thinking that the right feathers might make me feel alright, but it
> doesn't matter how much I buy, it doesn't satisfy the need. How could it?
> (Woman, 40)

Central to this study is the view that the objects bought stand in for
relationships desired. The object relations perspective, with its
emphasis on internalised relationships, therefore has particular significance. For example, Klein's essay on envy suggests that the primary
love object, the mother (felt to the infant as the mother's breast), '...
forms the core of the ego' (1957, p. 180). If that earliest mothering feels
inadequate and the infant remains unrequited, a sense of insatiable
need produces '... the angry feeling that another person possesses and
enjoys something desirable ...' (p.181). According to Klein, '... greed,
envy and persecutory anxiety ... are bound up with each other ...' (ibid.,
p. 187). The envy makes one want '... to spoil what is good because it
is outside the self' (Gomez 1997, p. 40) and because it is needed. That
which is longed for feels elusive as if it has always been withheld, so the
person wants what the other has.

Being ill-equipped to define themselves, such people constantly seek
the confirmation of others but, even if given, it is never enough. The
endless shopping attempts 'to restore a depleted self' (Krueger 1988, p.
581), to mend the damage to the self resulting from a long-ago
inadequate or severed relationship to the person whom Symington
(1993) calls the lifegiver. Also, Krueger suggests, the addictive shopper
strives to repair a distorted body image: the developmental arrest is 'of
body self as well as psychological self' (1988, p. 581).

WOMEN AND SHOPPING

All the studies of addictive shopping suggest that it is more prevalent
with women than with men (Christenson et al. 1994; Schlosser et al.
1994; McElroy et al. 1995; Dittmar et al. 1996). Even allowing for the
possibility that men who shop excessively have usually been seen as
'collectors' (a point pursued in Paula Riddy's chapter), women's
addictive activity is more likely to include shopping. Traditionally,
shopping carries with it the image of 'women doing women's work in
a women's world'. The stereotype presents women – usually not in

valued paid employment or careers – as spending significant amounts of time in shopping. Whilst dated, both image and stereotype retain a kernel of truth.

Women who shop addictively cover the gamut of experience; their need to shop is unrelated to age, income or background. They may or may not be in relationships; they may or may not be mothers.

Much research on female development considers the girl's fragile sense of self. The young girl's mother has central importance in how her daughter becomes (a point later discussed in relation to eating disorders). If, as a result of her development within a culture of male-defined values, the mother has a poor self-image, it is difficult for the young girl to resist similarly developing a low self-esteem. Feeling of little worth, the daughter strives to prove herself and one of the time-honoured ways to do so is to make herself attractive. She becomes captive: lured to fashion and products that promise beauty. Clothes, the right clothes, might allow her to feel good – and this is the focus of Gemma Corbett's chapter.

In his *A Theory of Shopping*, the anthropologist Daniel Miller writes that many of the women in his study '... still reflect the condition of femininity which Coward (1992) calls "the desire to be desired". Their primary ambition, notwithstanding their commitment to a career, is for a satisfactory relationship based on *love* ... for most of these women ... love returns as almost the sole arbiter of happiness or despair ...' (1998, p. 121). The act of buying '... expresses a relationship between the shopper and a particular other ... either present ... desired or imagined' (ibid., p. 12).

For those women who are mothers, much of the early feminist writing gives insight into the fragile sense of self which is relevant, too, to the addictive shopper – although I am not suggesting any significant connection (e.g. Scarf 1980; Rossiter 1988). Especially women who are mothers, immersed in domesticity, learn to put other people's needs first. Even when children leave home, the habits of a lifetime remain and depression lurks in the wings as a possibility. Bart, for example, observes from her clinical work that the 'adjusted' woman, who finds meaning in her life by carrying out culturally defined tasks – caring for others – and whose sense of worth comes from other people, 'is left with an empty shell in place of a self when such people depart'(1971, p. 53). If, now, the shell is filled with shopping, it would be an understandable but belated attempt to meet her own needs.

There is another aspect to the prevalence of women as shoppers. Looking historically, Nava (ch.3 in Falk and Campbell 1997) notes how 'the everyday lives of ordinary women [were] massively affected by the culture of consumption as symbolised by the advent of the department store' (1997, p. 64). But, considering the activity of shopping and the real and symbolic offerings of this 'culture of consumption', she continues: 'that anonymity and desire can be re-read more negatively as loneliness and dissatisfaction' (ibid., p. 72).

A significant gap in the literature on women and shopping concerns lesbians. To date I have found only two references. Some of the contributors to Dunne's (1997) book recall recognising in late childhood that they were different from other girls, for example in resisting their mothers' attempts to dress them in more 'feminine' clothes. From a quite different perspective, Mort remarks that much less advertising is directed towards lesbians than to male homosexuals because of 'perceptions of their low spending power' (1996, p. 180).

MEN AND SHOPPING

Throughout the consumer literature there are far fewer men involved in addictive shopping, yet the male participants in Paula Riddy's and my own study spoke of similar emotions to those expressed by women shoppers: the desire to prove themselves as somebody worthy of love and the seeming forlornness of the hope.

In what is still generally seen as a society conducive to men's self-determination, what is the source of such insecurity? One possible understanding comes from psychoanalytic theories of male development which suggest that the boy '... must repress and deny the intimacy, tenderness and dependence of the early bond with the mother if he is to assume a 'masculine' identity' (Segal 1990, p. 79). Inevitably, in repudiating the feminine, there remains something unresolved: his longing for mother. Yet, if the little boy may no longer identify with her, by implication he must also reject all she does and represents.

Equally relevant in attempting an understanding of why shopping has traditionally featured so little in the lives of men, is a consideration of the development of gender roles. Shopping in this context would be seen as women's realm. For example, in relation to clothes shopping, Mort points out that in the early 1950s Burton's, the men's outfitters, took great care in creating a particular image of its clients: 'Significantly, the term "shopping", with its more feminine and potentially more chaotic connotations, was never used by the firm' (1996, p. 138).

Mort suggests that it is younger men who are more drawn to the role of consumer. He also points to the differences between heterosexual and homosexual cultures, each with their distinctive stance on the role of commodities for men (ibid., p. 193).

However, in the absence of more research on male consumer activity it seems possible to hypothesise that, just as men's expression of depression is expressed differently from women's, so is their choice of addictive behaviour.

THE SHOPPING EXPERIENCE

> I was driving home and feeling so bleak. There was a familiar sense of emptiness, pointlessness, inside me. Then I saw myself turn the car round and drive to the shops, as if it wasn't of my own volition. It was as if I was an observer of myself. A tension had built up inside me and only buying myself something could release it. I searched for shoes and bought them and thought I've got off cheaply this time. But even as I was paying I knew they wouldn't make me better and as I drove home the desperation came back. (Woman, 60)

There is a repeated process in the shopping experience which has frequently been described. It begins with an inner feeling of tension and a gnawing preoccupation with the need to buy. At a cognitive level, the awareness is there that 'it won't work' and that the negative feelings which follow a splurge are as bad as the tension which requires release. The search itself offers a temporary relief: it substitutes a more realistic tension, to find the thing pursued, and may even contain an element of self-respect at the skill and tenacity of the hunt. Like a hunt, the excitement builds up to a frenzy. Finding and purchasing are the climax, a fleeting pleasure. There follows the all-too-familiar depression and guilt.

Aspects which seem common to all the descriptions are the intensity of the experience, the lack of control and the need to be alone. The shopper does not want to be accompanied – another person would be an interference – and even other shoppers and sales assistants are felt to be peripheral. Regardless of whether the shopping takes place in a large store, specialist shop or jumble sale, the shopper shops trance-like, in a changed state of awareness.

For some, perfectionism may be superimposed on the search:

> If it's a gift, I go to endless trouble to get something just right for that person. If it's for myself, I don't give up, I'm obsessional. For example, if I'm going to a meeting I'll displace some of the anxiety into finding the right shoes or bag or jacket. If I see what I think I need, but in the wrong size or colour or material, I'll persist till I find the right one. It becomes a quest for a holy

grail. Then I don't wear it; I don't want to get it spoiled. I like things to stay pristine. (Woman, mid-60s)

The see-saw effect of hope raised then hope lost may bring back memories of childhood experience. Gomez (1997, p. 181) sees addiction as a safer alternative to relationships, needing no reciprocity. Guilt and shame, frequently denying the possibility of using or wearing the things bought, are a function of the underlying depression. One does not deserve these things. Atonement is needed. Perhaps not to admit to oneself that the buying has become out of control, and certainly to hide it from others, secrecy develops and the goods bought are stowed away.

The guilt, in fact, sets up its own cycle, described in relation to her drug addiction by Linda Schierse Leonard:

> Guilt was my constant companion ... the addiction fed off incessant guilt ... it was very important to understand this vicious circle ... Feel guilty about wanting to use. Feel guilty about spending money to use. Feel guilty about using. Feel guilty about the after effects of using. Feel guilty about lying about using. The only cure – use more! (1990, p. 30)

THE SYMBOLIC MEANING OF SPENDING

Money as power when emotionally the person feels fragile is relevant.

> I've discussed with my husband what it feels like for me to go into a shop, see something very expensive and say 'Yes, I'll take two'. He's always had money; I haven't. Ironically, I know that it was growing up without money that made me strong ... When I think about my mother ... I feel she was judged. It hurts me for her. I keep needing to remind myself what the humiliation feels like. (Woman, late-30s)

Krueger (1991) discusses the futile attempt at narcissistic gratification. He looks at the mourning process when that which should have brought happiness does not do so. It is the loss of illusion: that, in buying, one can achieve acceptance and esteem from others. But the reality is that no amount of external recognition can ever be enough. Although money and its use may initially represent freedom, they do not free the individual: an unfulfilled dependency remains.

Alongside this is the endlessly renewed hope that possessions, if enough of them can be acquired, will somehow compensate for the emotional emptiness. Whether the money for these purchases is generated by oneself or by another is, of course, of significance (and

Richard Elliott, in his chapter, considers 'revenge spending'), but the purpose of the spending is an attempt at self-restoration. The shopping represents a defence against the awareness of loss and a desire to retrieve an early relationship which was never adequate. In the '... absence of a stable internal self-image ... these individuals must turn to external sources' (Kohut 1977, in Krueger 1991, p. 222).

As with other addictions, addictive shopping is a cry for help and attention, a need for someone to care enough to set limits. Krueger describes this in one of his clients: 'She recalled feeling depressed all the time and wanting someone to hold her, to wrap her in enveloping boundaries' (1991, p. 215). He writes, 'Many behaviours regarded as impulsive, addictive, or unrelenting are designed to evoke or establish boundaries' (1988, p. 583).

SOME SIMILARITIES WITH BINGE-EATING DISORDER AND BULIMIA NERVOSA

In some ways there is a parallel with bulimia nervosa. Orbach, writing on therapy with bulimic women, suggests that, 'We need to help her find out why she cannot keep something first perceived as good and comforting ... to understand what it is about a potentially soothing experience that invariably contains its opposite ... what it is about taking in good feelings that turns them poisonous so fast' (1993, p. xvii, footnote 3).

McElroy et al. (1995) see comparisons between compulsive buying, binge-eating disorder, and kleptomania – the latter discussed in Marsha Taylor's chapter on shoplifting.

Neither compulsive buying nor binge-eating disorder are classified in *DSM IV* as mental disorders, although binge-eating is included as a defining component of bulimia (*Diagnostic and Statistical Manual of Mental Disorders*, 4th edn, 1994, American Psychiatric Association). Where it differs from bulimia is that 'compensatory behaviours', such as purging to prevent weight gain, are not undertaken. Yet aspects of both binge-eating disorder and bulimia nervosa mirror addictive shopping: the excessive amount consumed (bought) in a discrete period of time, the feeling of lack of control, the sense of urgency, the aloneness and secrecy of the activity and the subsequent feelings of shame, guilt and depression (McElroy et al. 1995, p. 20). The impulse is irresistible, the 'high' is craved, the 'crash' inevitable.

Discussing theories of causation, Mc Elroy et al. first quote social theories. Noting the higher incidence of these conditions in women than in men they point to the availability of merchandise and women's traditional role as shoppers. They then consider psychodynamic theories which suggest, 'that these conditions reflect defenses against, or the symbolic enactment or gratification of, unconscious or unacceptable impulses, wishes, conflicts or needs ...' (1995, p. 23). They consider narcissistic injury as relevant in the aetiology of eating disorders and compulsive shopping.

Many feminist and feminist psychoanalytic writers portray women's development as intricately bound up with their own mother's sense of self (e.g. Eichenbaum and Orbach 1986; Coward 1992; and many others). Recognising how the young girl both internalises and identifies with her mother, it is not surprising to see the transmission through the generations of a low self-image. This is formed as a result of internalising 'how we are perceived, what we are told, what feelings and attitudes are conveyed by the primary caretaker', who is almost always the mother. But if the mother has a low self-image, the daughter becomes 'the recipient of her mother's wounded narcissism' (Menaker 1982, in Dowling 1989, p. 172). The mother, herself needy, undermines her infant's sense of self.

Orbach, discussing bulimia, could equally have been depicting addictive shopping: ' ... the symbolic meanings contain with them the tortuous conflict between desire and denial ... plenitude clashing with impermissibility ...'. She continues: '... the breaking through of longing and the vigilance ... that surrounds longing encapsulate the woman's relationship to need and desire ... The feelings of emptiness inside induce such guilt about wanting, having or getting ...' (1993, pp. xix and xx).

As Orbach similarly writes about eating disorders, the shopping itself is not the problem, it is a 'solution' to the problem.

COMPULSIVE GAMBLING

In some ways, compulsive gambling is closer to addictive shopping than binge-eating or bulimia in that it does not involve chemical dependence. Yet both compulsive gambling and addictive shopping produce a rush of adrenalin and, in fact, gamblers who have stopped gambling report withdrawal symptoms similar to those of drug addicts, suggesting some sort of biochemical arousal and dependence (Wray and Dickerson 1981, in Shaffer 1989, p. 7).

Rosenthal, discussing understandings of pathological gambling, could be writing of addictive shopping: it '... serves multiple defensive functions. There is an illusion of power and control as a way of defending against depression and loss ... It may be utilized as a method of self-cure in the struggle to maintain a precarious sense of identity' (1997, p. 209).

Orford (1985) warns that the label 'compulsive gambler' may become a kind of 'master status'and stresses the multi-factorial origins of all excessive behaviours. Bearing his warning in mind, it is useful to look at parallels between the behavioural aspects of compulsive gambling and addictive shopping. Just as with excessive eating, the actor in the obsessional scenario 'finds his own behaviour alien and tries to resist it' (Moran 1975, in Orford ibid., p. 37). Moran describes the 'pathological' gambler as feeling:

1. Concern ... about the amount of gambling, which is considered excessive
2. An overpowering urge to gamble ... preoccupied with thoughts of gambling ... tension relieved only by further gambling
3. The subjective experience of the inability to control the amount once gambling has started ... (Orford ibid.)

It is, of course, worth considering whether the impact of any excessive behaviour is relative to the socio-economic context in which it takes place (a point developed in Marsha Taylor's chapter). Cornish, 1978 (in Orford 1985), suggests that: '... an individual is more likely ... to define his behaviour as ... a problem in some circumstances than others. The heavy gambler with plenty of money and spare time ... will be considerably less likely to view his behaviour with anxiety than a similar person less fortunately placed ...' (in Orford ibid., p. 40). Whilst this may be partially true, my sense is that it fails to capture the fear and despair which accompany any sort of behaviour where one feels out of control.

In promising understandings, the theories seem so often to give only labels. For example, the defining label of 'addictive personality' has a decisiveness about it that leaves little room for hope. Whether as researcher or therapist, I feel less able to learn from a client's perception of reality if I am influenced by a perspective that defines the client for all time.

What is so striking over and over again is the person's own desire to regain control: there is bewilderment and frustration, shame and anguish, but rarely does the person abdicate responsibility.

CO-EXISTING ADDICTIONS

Acting addictively is, in a strange way, purposeful. It has two aims: to lessen pain and to find a solution to pain. If, or when, one possible way of trying to heal oneself fails to work – or the harm felt is so great – another remedy may be tried.

It is very understandable for it to be part of a family script. Hoffman writes, 'I think it is particularly helpful for the therapist to think of problems as stories that people have agreed to tell themselves' (1990, p. 3). Maybe 'solutions', however ineffective, are similarly shared. That other addictions are part of their lives is in many of the accounts:

> I'm not able to acknowledge myself as I am. Clothes are only one aspect; abortive dieting is another aspect. I don't like the way I look. (Woman, 62)

The co-existing and previously existing addictions may be in the family of origin, in the current relationships or in the self.

Certainly much of the research (Valence et al. 1988; McElroy et al. 1995; Black et al. 1998) indicates that a person who shops addictively is not unfamiliar with addictive behaviour.

> My mother would buy things that she'd never use. She lived in a sort of fantasy world. (Woman, mid-60s)

Paula Riddy in her chapter writes of addictive shopping as a covert form of family communication and Richard Elliott suggests that a workaholic can provoke addictive shopping in a partner as a form of revenge.

My own clinical work illustrates the possibility that addictive behaviour passed from parent to child may even represent an unclear but tacit agreement to share pain:

> James, a long-term client who fears that his profligate spending is destroying his marriage and his family, talks of his nineteen-year-old daughter, a university student. She eats compulsively but, despite weighing twenty stone, denies that she has problems. He says: 'She hates me ... She is very close to her mother. My wife overcompensates to her. I get even less attention because Ann wants to make the world alright for her.' As our work progresses, the question 'who is doing what for whom' seems very relevant and I suggest some family sessions which he, his wife and their children accept. During our first meeting, the daughter talks of her anger, 'He's ruining our lives.' But in later sessions she acknowledges her own ability to sabotage herself. Whilst hating her father she seems to have internalised something of his pain and suffering, in this way carrying it on to the next generation. (Names and identifying features have been changed)

A question which arises in considering any form of addictive behaviour in the family context is whether it has a homeostatic value. Kaufman (1994) suggests that often there is a high degree of interdependence with fear of success and separation.

Ironically, in families with problems there is often a desire not to upset a precarious equilibrium, even though that equilibrium is bought at the cost of one member's carrying the family's distress. In James's family, two members share this task. This is not to suggest that the 'task' is thrust upon an unwilling family member: it is more that a fragility within the parent or child allows him or her to assume the 'identified patient' role. Sometimes the collusive quality of family relationships will result in the family's maintaining the very behaviour about which they feel such concern – parents or partner will over and over again pay the unpaid bills or overlook the endless unused, unneeded and quickly hidden away purchases.

THERAPY

Although there is a considerable body of literature on therapy with people who are addicted to drugs and alcohol, to date little – if anything – has been written about therapy specifically with addictive shoppers. Partly, I suspect, this is because the addictive shopper, seeing other addictions as self-destructive and therefore as *real* addictions, fears that this one may not be taken seriously. They fear that it is somehow too trivial to present as a valid problem for therapy.

Even if a person is in therapy, that he or she shops addictively may be mentioned almost casually. One client, whom I have been seeing for two years, revealed early in the therapy her shame that she is binge-eating. She is a successful businesswoman in her mid-fifties, in every way 'larger than life', but her exuberance hides intense loneliness and self-disparagement. Only recently though (and not knowing that I am researching it) has she begun to talk of her compulsive shopping – of holidays when she shops and shops and of late-night shopping when she buys 'lots of young, fun things'.

As a therapist, my thinking might involve certain connections: the recognition that addictive behaviour comes about because of need, that the need is a deep one reaching far back to childhood, that it concerns impoverishment. From this, I may extrapolate: that the addiction serves a purpose, that its promises are false, that the behaviour – instead of replenishing – has further depleted the self. There follows what is perhaps the core belief of every therapy: that the therapeutic relationship can go some way towards restoring a person's sense of his or her own real worth.

For the client there are different considerations; these concern the fear of losing something that has had meaning, however pointless that meaning has become. 'What else can I do with my life?' – although not expressed – may well underly some of the shoppers' ambivalence about declaring their despair. Therefore, whilst consciously wanting to change there is simultaneously resistance; defences, especially denial, come to the fore and there are risks. There may result a 'flight into health' or the emergence of an alternative pathology.

Shaffer emphasises that 'Addictive behaviors serve while they destroy' (1994, p. 423). There is a real ambivalence about relinquishing something in which hope still resides. It worked once to ease the pain. Now, the tension of wanting to stop and simultaneously fearing the void can become almost unbearable. It certainly communicates itself strongly to the therapist.

However, just as there is no one cause of addictive behaviour, similarly no one treatment approach can claim fully to understand what might bring about change in the client's sense of self, for the one common theme in the lives of addictive shoppers is low self-esteem.

> My mother would never accept that I was depressed. Her attitude was, and still is, 'shake yourself and get out of it'. I've never had any praise from my parents and I need it. I've only ever seen myself as inadequate ... My wife is my rock and she holds me in place. When I have a 'spend-up' she becomes very angry and says I'm punishing her. Then I recoil because I know she's right. I get very frightened that when I spend she's going to explode and disappear ... I've tried suicide once in the past two years and thought about it many times more. I tried to die. I left a note and went off. I wanted to throw myself over a bridge and then I didn't have the bloody guts to do it. (Man, 40)

Kaufman (1994) and Shaffer (1994) outline the genesis of addiction, a consideration with implications for therapy. The most crucial stage in its becoming a way of life is the initial repeated experience of positive consequences. The motivation to change can be mobilised only when the imbalance between positive and adverse consequences becomes a life crisis. There also has to be the acceptance of personal responsibility for what has been and for the struggle and the loneliness to come, for there *is* loneliness: in a strange way the shopping has been like a fickle lover in whom one goes on believing. As with other addictions, for the client who addictively shops there is real fear in recognising that the object loved has betrayed the self.

Essentially the need is to work not just with the overt symptoms but with the heart of what is being brought, the diminished self. Scherhorn writes,

> Objectively, he (she) could ... face the circumstances ... which burden his (her) life with desperate frustration ... and seek out ways of changing them.

Subjectively this task may be associated with feelings of ostracism and punishment, threat and terror, fear and inferiority that he seems not able to overcome. (1990, p. 37)

Given the depth of the wound which brings a person to addiction, a therapeutic approach must help the client explore the sense of impoverishment and emptiness reaching back to earliest childhood. Apfel writes:

Rather than seeing emptiness as an irreducible state, the psychodynamic approach would probe into the process of emptying ... would help the person ask why (s)he has a need to make the self into a shell ... what rage or fear or other feeling had to be emptied ... (1996, p. 314)

However, just as the child's early parental relationships are significant in the complex aetiology of addictive behaviour, so, too, are the current relationships in which it is maintained. I am suggesting that, to be productive, therapy should ideally work with the individual – with the memories, perceptions and feelings of childhood as they are struggled with in adult life – and with the client in the context of his or her current family relationships.

Kaufman (1994) gives a comprehensive discussion of the many cognitive behavioural and Twelve Step programmes and group work undertaken with people who are substance abusers. Whilst recognising the possible relevance of some of these to the predicament of the addictive shopper, my sense is that they are not enough.

For a person who feels inadequately loved and therefore unlovable there has to be space for reflection, a space in which the distorted thinking about the self can be challenged, not only at a cognitive level but in the deepest recesses of the heart. Manic shopping as a strategy had fleetingly obliterated the sense of 'not mattering', yet that feeling had returned. I believe that only within a therapeutic approach in which there is trust and in which the relationship is a pivotal part of the process can there emerge a gradually changing attitude to the self.

Alongside individual therapy, and if resources allow, family therapy is important. It is, after all, in the intimate world of the family that the person's addictive behaviour has grown and developed meaning. The family, too, is in pain; the family is the patient. Often it is a family in which secrecy, denial and adaptation have seemed the only options. The scenario offers each member his or her role, possibly as rescuer, possibly as alternative symptom bearer.

With the client with whom I work both individually and as family therapist, his profligate spending is mirrored by his daughter's binge eating. For both of them, objects, once gained, become toxic and bring shame. But Mother is also in the dance: the competent one who makes all alright again. In a strange, sad way her needs too are met as, to the outside world, they continue to play at happy families.

Whatever the approach, for therapy to be of any help it should be a process of understanding a unique person in a particular life situation. Ideally it bestows a sense of hope and, ultimately, of joy. Although perhaps unexpected in a study of addictive shopping, William Styron's account of his recovery from depression says so much:

> ... I knew I had emerged into light. I felt myself no longer a husk but a body with some of the body's sweet juices stirring again. I had my first dream in many months, confused but to this day imperishable, with a flute in it somewhere, and a wild goose, and a dancing girl. (1991, p. 75)

THE THERAPIST

Winnicott's seminal paper, 'Hate in the Counter-Transference' (1949), pursued the possibility that this may take place in psychoanalytic work. In relation to addiction, Shaffer writes of the therapist's malice and aversive impulses when the therapy fails to work: 'Blaming patients for failing to thrive in treatment is a sophisticated form of displaying clinical hate ...' (Shaffer 1994, p. 429). In my own work with the client referred to earlier, conflicting emotions pulled: at one level, I wanted to work maternally; he seemed a sad little boy, just that, not a husband, father or professional man. At another level, I was disturbed by my anger at his having no 'fire in the belly'. I wanted to mobilise him, to breathe life into him.

Kaufman, in similar vein, warns of the development of a co-dependent relationship between therapist and client. It is an aspect of 'therapist overinvolvement ... when patients and/or their outcomes become overly important to therapists' own psychological well-being' (1994, p. 167).

There is another consideration: the therapist's personal history. Whilst this is not necessarily of addictive behaviour, it is noteworthy how easily one can become an addictive helper. The concept of the 'wounded healer' (Holmes, 1991) is especially relevant. It suggests that the patient's suffering is communicated to the therapist for whom it has personal meaning. In the re-evoking of his or her own struggles, the therapist finds both the capacity and the desire to heal. For me, too, there are resonances in this work: I recognise what underlies addiction: the search for love and confirmation.

The sages of old tell us that when God wishes to punish a man, He grants him all his desires. Our wishes need restraint; they must be tempered always by awareness of our responsibility to live a life for good in the world. To be given all we think we want is to be as a child, overwhelmed.

Yet to shop addictively is to yearn, although the true object of desire is unclear. To the casual observer, the addictive shopper is a person buying an object, seemingly undertaking a fairly ordinary activity. To the shopper herself, the activity feels like a nightmare, one from which she cannot emerge.

In the final part of this chapter, there are three ideas I want to explore: alienation, the split and possession (the furies within). Although the theories offer explanations, there is something elusive which they fail to capture.

ALIENATION

We may be alienated by or from someone or something. Cross-cultural work and feminist writings, from their different viewpoints, indicate how the individual may feel alienated from and by the dominant culture. Family therapists similarly draw attention to the sense of alienation which may be experienced by one member within a family.

Discussing free will, Scherhorn writes, 'self-estrangement prevents him from realizing that he has a choice' (1990, p. 38). Whilst both addictive and compulsive behaviour share a sense of loss of control, Scherhorn suggests that there is a distinction: 'Addictive behaviour runs out of control because of an overpowering but initially welcome desire; compulsive behaviour, on the other hand, is controlled by an unwelcome pressure which the person experiences as alien to himself.' To be addicted is '... to be driven by an irresistible urge which one experiences as one's own want or need' (ibid., p. 34). Yet the addict 'cannot see himself as the author of his actions ... [his] behaviour appears to be choiceless' (ibid., p. 40).

Laing (1960) depicts the ontologically insecure person's fragile identity and his struggle to preserve a sense of self. He lacks the 'act of confirmation' to affirm his being. Perhaps a similar feeling of inner alienation as that described by Laing haunts the person who becomes addicted. He or she feels extreme inner loneliness and a pervading sense of loss. The pain has a relentlessness to it and invokes an awareness of life slipping away.

THE SPLIT

Throughout my discussion of addictive shopping there is the hypothesis that, underlying the shopper's insatiability, is the need somehow to make reparation to the self for what is still – even in adulthood – felt to have been inadequate. At an extreme, the parent may indeed have neglected or abused the child – and the sequelae of this in adult life are much documented. But often, although the objective reality is of competent parental care, the subjective reality, the memories and perceptions of childhood, is of an absent parent: not physically absent, but preoccupied, depressed or otherwise unavailable. The resulting sense of rejection nearly always engenders rage – a rage against the parent which by now is futile. Instead, it is split off and turned against the self.

In the scenario of addictive shopping, the rage has its original source – that of felt parental inadequacy – and is then further fuelled by the self's futile attempt at compensation.

The concept of splitting in psychoanalytic theory traditionally draws on Klein's (1946) discussion of the paranoid-schizoid position in which good and bad are polarised. At the extreme of this, and in relation to the addictive shopper, what seems to occur is that the self attacks the suffering part of the self, leading to fragmentation (Gomez 1997, p. 38). It is a complex split, between desire and superego. The desire, though, is not just an anarchic id: it has within it the wish to heal the self. Yet the shopping is merely an external act, its gifts are meaningless and it invites the wrath of the superego. Vengeance is provoked and directed inwards.

The task of therapy is, therefore, a fundamental one and involves helping the client to develop compassion for herself 'through modifying the ruthlessness of [her] inner judgements' (Gomez 1997, p. 48).

> But, ineffably, psychotherapy heals. It makes some sense of the confusion, reins in the terrifying thoughts and feelings, returns some control and hope and possibility of learning from it all ... Psychotherapy is a sanctuary; it is a battleground; it is a place I have been ... despairing beyond belief. But always it is where I have believed – or have learned to believe – that I might someday be able to contend with all of this. (Redfield Jamison 1995, p. 89)

POSSESSION: THE FURIES WITHIN

As in any addiction, the parts of the self are locked in battle and the person is split between controller and controlled. But the question of choice is ever-present.

71914

The notion of possession is deep in mythology and in the belief systems of many non-Western cultures. In our own culture, as Ussher writes, '... prior to the regulation of society through scientific discourse', the person who acted in any way deemed as deviant by the defining authorities was believed to have been '... invaded by evil spirits' and required exorcism to be rid of them (1991, pp. 44–5).

For the individual, the sense of there being diminished freedom of choice is a frightening one. The task of trying to understand it involves a search for meaning: the meaning of that particular addiction to that particular person, its relevance within the family's way of relating and its significance within a society which lures and then judges.

In Marks and Spencer's my mother became, for a brief moment, a proper person again ... When she shopped she existed in the here and now of that engagement with dresses and cardigans and shoes and hats and handbags. Her fractured life slipped away for a moment and she was whole once more. (Grant 1998, p. 218)

REFERENCES

Apfel, R. J. (Winter, 1996) With A Little Help from My Friends I Get By: Self-help books and psychotherapy. *Psychiatry* 59, 309–22.

Bart, P. B. (1971) Depression in Middle-Aged Women in V. Gornick and B. K. Moran (eds) *Woman in Sexist Society*. New York, Basic Books.

Baumeister, R. F., Heatherton, F. F. and Tice, D. M. (1994) *Losing Control: How and why people fail at self-regulation*. San Diego CA, Academic Press.

Black, D. W., Repertinger, S., Gaffney, G. R. and Gabel, J. (July 1998) Family History and Psychiatric Comorbidity in Persons with Compulsive Buying: preliminary findings. *American Journal of Psychiatry* 155 (7), 960–3.

Burns, R. B. (1979/1986) *The Self Concept: Theory, measurement, development and behaviour*. Harlow, Essex, Longman.

Christenson, G. A., Faber, R. J. and de Zwaan, M. (1994) Compulsive Buying: Descriptive characteristics and psychiatric comorbidity. *Journal of Clinical Psychiatry* 55, 5–11.

Cooper, J. and Maxwell, N. (1995) *Narcissistic Wounds: Clinical perspectives*. London, Whurr.

Coward, R. (1992) *Our Treacherous Hearts*. London, Faber.

Cunningham, M. (1999) *The Hours*. London, Fourth Estate.

d'Astous, A. (March 1990) An Inquiry into the Compulsive Side of 'Normal' Consumers. *Journal of Consumer Policy* 13 (1), 15–31.

Dittmar, H., Beattie, J. and Friese, S. (September 1996) Objects, Decision Considerations and Self-image in Men's and Women's Impulse Purchases. *Acta Psychologica* 93 (1–3), 187–206.

Dowling, C. (1989) *Perfect Women: Hidden fears of inadequacy and the drive to perform*. London, Collins.

Dunne, G. A. (1997) *Lesbian Lifestyles: Women's work and the politics of sexuality*. London, Macmillan.

Eichenbaum, L. and Orbach, S. (1986) *Understanding Women*. London, Penguin.

Faber, R. J. and O'Guinn, T. C. (1992) A clinical Screener for compulsive Buying. *Journal of Consumer Research* 19, 459–69.

Falk, P. and Campbell, C. (eds) (1997) *The Shopping Experience*. London, Sage.

Gomez, L. (1997) *An Introduction to Object Relations*. London, Free Association Books.
Grant, L. (1998) *Remind Me Who I Am, Again*. London, Granta Books.
Hoffman, L. (1990) Constructing Realities: An art of lenses. *Family Process 29*, 1–12.
Hollway, W. (1989) *Subjectivity and Method in Psychology: Gender, meaning and science*. London, Sage.
Holmes, C. (1991) The Wounded Healer. *Society for Psychoanalytic Psychotherapy Bulletin 6* (4), 33–6.
Jacobs, D. F. (1997) A General Theory of Addictions: A new theoretical model: ch. 9, pp. 166–83, in D. L. Yalisove (ed.), *Essential Papers on Addiction*. New York, New York University Press.
Jaffe, J. H. (1990) Commentary: Trivializing dependence. *British Journal of Addiction 85*, 1425–7.
Jamison, K. Redfield (1996) *An Unquiet Mind: A memoir of moods and madness*. London, Picador.
Kaufman, E. (1994) *Psychotherapy of Addicted Persons*. New York, Guildford Press.
Klein, M. (1946) Notes on Some Schizoid Mechanisms in *Envy and Gratitude and Other Works 1946–1963*, London, Virago.
Klein, M. (1957/1988) *Envy and Gratitude and Other Works 1946–1963*. London, Virago.
Krueger, D. W. (October 1988) On Compulsive Shopping and Spending: A psychodynamic inquiry. *American Journal of Psychotherapy XLII* (4).
Krueger, D. W. (Summer, 1991) Money Meanings and Madness: A psychoanalytic perspective. *Psychoanalytic Review 78* (2).
Laing, R. D. (1960) *The Divided Self*. London, Pelican.
Leonard, L. Schierse (1990) *Witness to the Fire: Creativity and the veil of addiction*. London, Shambhala.
McElroy, S. L., Keck, P. E. and Phillips, K. A. (1995) Kleptomania, Compulsive Buying, and Binge-Eating Disorder. *Journal of Clinical Psychiatry 56* (4), 14–27.
McEwan, I. (1997) *Enduring Love*. London, Cape.
Marks, I. (1990) Editorial: Behavioural (non-chemical) Addictions. *British Journal of Addiction 85*, 1389–94 and 1429–31.
Miller, D. (1998) *A Theory of Shopping*. Cambridge, Polity Press.
Miller, W. R. (ed.) (1980) *The Addictive Behaviours*. Oxford, Pergamon Press.
Minsky, R. (1996) *Psychoanalysis and Gender*. London, Routledge.
Mort, F. (1996) *Cultures of Consumption: Masculinities and social space in Late 20th century Britain*. London, Routledge.
Nakken, C. (1988) *The Addictive Personality: Roots, rituals and recovery*. Center City MN, Hazelden.
O'Guinn, T. C. & Faber, R. J. (1989) Compulsive Buying: A phenomenological exploration. *Journal of Consumer Research 16*, 147–57.
Orbach, S. (1993) *Hunger Strike*. London, Penguin.
Orford, J. (1985) *Excessive Appetites: A psychological view of addictions*. Chichester, John Wiley.
Peele, S. (1985) *The Meaning of Addiction: Compulsive experience and its Interpretation*. Lexington MA, Lexington Press.
Peele, S. (1989) *Diseasing of America: Addiction treatment out of control*. Lexington MA, Lexington Books.
Rook, D. W. (14 September 1987) The Buying Impulse. *Journal of Consumer Research*, pp. 189–99.
Rosenthal, R. J. (1997) The Psychodynamics of Pathological Gambling: A review of the literature: ch. 10, pp. 184–212, in D. L. Yalisove (ed.) *Essential Papers on Addiction*. New York, New York University Press.
Rossiter, A. (1988) *From Private to Public: A feminist exploration of early mothering*. London, The Women's Press.
Scarf, M. (1980) *Unfinished Business: Pressure points in the lives of women*. New York, Doubleday.
Scherhorn, G. (1990) The Addictive Trait in Buying Behaviour. *Journal of Consumer Policy 13*, 33–51.

Schlosser, S., Black, D. W., Repertinger, S. and Freet, D. (1994) Compulsive Buying: Demography, phenomenology and comorbidity in 46 subjects. *General Hospital Psychiatry 16*, 205–12.

Segal, L. (1990) *Slow Motion: Changing masculinities, changing men.* London, Virago.

Shaffer, H. J. (1991) Toward an Epistemology of 'Addictive Disease'. *Behavioral Sciences and the Law, 9* (3), 269–86.

Shaffer, H. J. (1994) Denial, Ambivalence and Countertransferential Hate, in J. Levin and R. Weiss (eds), *The Dynamics and Treatment of Alcoholism.* Northdale, New Jersey, Jason Aronson.

Shaffer, H. J., Stein, S. A., Gambino, B. and Cummings, T. N. (eds) (1989) *Compulsive Gambling: Theory, research and practice.* Lexington MA, Lexington Books.

Styron, W. (1991) *Darkness Visible.* London, Cape.

Symington, N. (1993) *Narcissism: A new theory.* London, Karnac Books.

Szasz, T. S. (1971) The Ethics of Addiction. *American Journal of Psychiatry 128*, 541–6.

Ussher, J. (1991) *Women's Madness: Misogyny or mental illness?* Hemel Hempstead, Herts., Harvester Wheatsheaf.

Valence, G., d'Astous, A. and Fortier, L. (1988) Compulsive Buying: Concept and Measurement. *Journal of Consumer Policy 11*, 419–33.

Walters, G. D. (1999) *The Addiction Concept: Working hypothesis or self-fulfilling prophesy?* Needham Heights MA, Allyn & Bacon.

Winnicott, D. W. (1949) Hate in the Counter-Transference. *International Journal of Psycho-Analysis 30*, 69–74.

2

Consuming 'Goods'

Rosalind Minsky

One of the intriguing aspects of the word 'consumption' in the setting of psychoanalytic theory is that it seems to refer back directly to the baby's earliest experience of consuming the mother so that it can survive not only physically but also psychically. Along with the nourishment contained in the mother's milk, the baby also takes in a pleasurable primitive sense of identity, of having what Winnicott calls a 'real' existence. In this psychoanalytic context, pleasurable cultural experiences of many kinds, though in different degrees, may be seen as symbolising our earliest experience of the 'good breast'. Symbolically, we may 'consume' or incorporate other people, ideas or material objects into ourselves as a means of psychical survival.

The increasing availability and consumption of consumer 'goods' has been a defining characteristic of post-war culture in western countries. Intrinsic to this process, has been both the massive development of science and technology and the marketing of these 'goods' in terms of meanings with which individuals, by means of mass advertising, have been invited to identify. As many writers have observed, the second half of the twentieth century has seen the steady development of the marketing of desire in the form of symbolic goods which represent longed for aspects of ourselves that we unconsciously imagine we can acquire from the external world. Advertisers have tried to persuade us that we can buy whatever we want to be. They have also been able to define the particular commercial forms our unconscious wishes might take so that cars or beer, Coca-Cola or a pair of Nike trainers may come to represent, for example, sexual wishes, power, status, security, comfort or a sense of belonging. The success of this marketing enterprise and the mass consumption of an increasing quantity and diversity of goods as they become available, as well as the concepts of fashion and style which persuade us that we constantly need to re-invent the meanings of ourselves in specified ways, can be understood only in terms of a combination of historical, cultural and psychical factors.

In the latter half of the twentieth century there has been unprecedented technological and economic development and the intensification and globalisation of the capital and power required to make financial profit out of these developments. In western countries, and increasingly further afield in developing nations such as those in the Pacific rim, this has resulted in jobs, higher wages and an increased surplus available for spending on consumer goods among many people despite low wages and unemployment among significant minorities in many places. In the last twenty years the gap has widened significantly between the haves and have nots, both globally and within individual countries. But the success of the modern phenomenon of consumerism and shopping as a major source of pleasure and identity for many people, cannot be explained only by technological and economic development. A psychoanalytic perspective suggests that millions of individuals' pleasure in consumption and their willingness to invest so much of themselves in consumer commodities, often working long hours in unrewarding work in order to pay for them, is directly related to the erosion of other sources of identity which used to be more readily available within culture. For many, the painful experience of living under communism in Eastern Europe seems to have been intensified by the absence of consumer goods as a pleasurable means to ease the burden of so many assaults on identity and meaning.

Fragmentation, dislocation and an increasing sense of disconnection from others have been seen as characterising contemporary culture by both modernist and post-modernist writers. Central to this fragmentation have been at least three major social changes. One of these has been the gradual, post-war decline and break-down of old, stable communities which, without idealising them, frequently provided large numbers of individuals with many of the positive experiences in their lives (even though they were also sometimes experienced as suffocating and inhibiting). Such communities provided many people with a secure basis for the development of a sense of identity through nurturing feelings of belonging, of being known and recognised, of being an insider rather than an outsider, and through a sense of shared meanings, solidarity and mutual support in times of hardship and ill-health. Such communities, often based on extended kinship, with their network of identifications and social affiliations, have declined for many complex reasons but particularly because of the increase in job mobility, developments in communication and, in many cases, mass-housing schemes which have dispersed and isolated people onto vast estates on the edge of cities away from the more intimate, if old-fashioned, inner-city neighbourhoods. Together with these kinds of attacks on urban and rural communities, and on the sense of identity and continuity they helped to provide, there has also been further fragmentation in an unprecedented increase in family break-up in the last three decades of the twentieth century. In Great Britain one in three families now split up.

All other things being equal (in the sense that there has been no significant physical, sexual or emotional abuse, and even sometimes when there has), family break-up causes emotional trauma. It means that individual identities may also break up as a result of unbearable feelings of grief and loss. Psychoanalytic perspectives suggest that the child's identity is made up of the internalisations of both parents, however imperfect one or both may be. When a family breaks up this identity is suddenly split down the middle. This may mean there are two competing halves associated with mother and father respectively pulling in two different directions, with all the associated feelings of loss, disorientation, guilt, anger, anxiety and helplessness. Psychoanalytic approaches suggest that, apart from feelings of loss of part of their identity when a parent leaves, children often tend to feel that the break-up is their fault, that it is because of their 'badness', whether it is in terms of guilty desire or angry feelings. But divorce and break-up of the micro-community of the modern, relatively isolated nuclear family is usually experienced by parents as well as children as a major assault on identity.

Another source of significant cultural change in Western Europe and America has been a political assault on what has been seen as welfare dependency. In the last fifteen years, for ideological as well economic reasons, there has been a sustained attack on the post-war concept of the socialised community supported by taxation and national insurance which, via the state, accepts the responsibility for caring for people during times of economic hardship, unemployment or ill-health. Many people had grown accustomed to this post-war idea of social nurture and responsibility based on the sense of social cohesion generated in the wartime years. Recent high unemployment, job insecurity, increasing tendencies to employ people on short-term contracts justified by the need for a flexible response to the exigencies of the global market, and the rapid removal of much of the social fabric of welfare and health provision, have been other recognisable factors in widespread feelings of anxiety, insecurity, disconnection, lack of self-esteem and helplessness.

In the kind of cultural context outlined above, psychoanalytic knowledge suggests that the consumption of consumer 'goods' may play a central role in encouraging, if not creating, escapist or narcissistic forms of identity. For some of the two-thirds of the population who are economically in a position to take an active part in it, this may help, temporarily, to plug the psychical gap left by early unresolved experiences of loss and separation and also by other nurturing sources of identity within culture based on fulfilling, sustaining networks of relationships in the family, community or society more generally. Kleinian theory, in particular, suggests that certain experiences and deprivations brought about by cultural experience provoke high levels of anxiety which in some more vulnerable people cause primitive defence mechanisms to resurface as a way of defending a sense of meaningful identity. Freudian theory suggests that shopping and the purchase of consumer goods which are symbolically laden with longed-for aspects of ourselves, may, in the short term at least, be one reliable form of gratification in the context of rapid social change and frag-mentation. Even for those in work, long working hours, bureacratic and hierarchical line-management work structures, high levels of general stress including, for women in particular, that involved in combining work and family commitments and the easy availability of credit facilities, may all contribute to the attraction of consumer goods. Shopping offers a form of active power which many may feel they lack in other areas of their life and, for some, may act as a defence against feelings of culturally or psychically induced emptiness and meaning-lessness. Indeed, it could be argued from this perspective, following Lasch, that contemporary culture encourages us to substitute infantile forms of gratification for emotional integration (Lasch 1980). From a Freudian perspective, consumer goods may evoke childhood phantasies of achieving a state of bliss and completion with the mother whereas from a more Winnicottian perspective, they may evoke comfort, closeness and security also associated with early, pre-Oedipal experience. The car may often symbolise phallic power and sexuality but also the comfort, security and containment associated with the womb. Such unconscious symbolic meanings may well be a factor in the reluctance to exchange the car for public transport, even if the latter were to become cheap and frequent. Of course, conscious factors such as convenience, economy and environmental considerations are interwoven with unconscious meanings, but psychoanalytic theory suggests that for many, the unconscious meanings are likely to be the most salient.

Let us look now, in more detail, at some of the unconscious processes which may be involved in cultural consumption of a variety of kinds including the consumption of romantic fiction, films, videos, TV programmes and celebrities. This involves looking particularly at the psychoanalytic meaning of consumption or 'taking in' which is embedded in concepts such as incorporation, identification, narcissism, the ego-ideal, projection and introjection and projective identification.

ORAL 'INCORPORATION'

For Freud, the consumption of the mother's milk is the baby's first way of relating to itself and the outside world – it almost literally eats or incorporates the mother. As we have seen, in the highly pleasurable 'taking in' of the mother's milk the baby not only gains nourishment but also its first sense of having a real existence or identity, at that time still merged with the breast. Through this process of the baby's identification with or incorporation of the mother, the breast represents both its physical and psychical survival. In his *Three Essays on Sexuality* Freud describes this process of incoporation of both milk and a primitive sense of identity as the oral phase of sexuality, followed by and overlapping with the anal, phallic and genital phases (Freud 1905, p. 31). Freud suggests that as adults we all carry vestiges of this kind of oral behaviour in the need, sometimes, to incorporate or consume substitute forms of the symbolic 'good breast'. In states of anxiety or boredom we may seek the comfort associated with the breast by smoking, drinking, taking drugs, eating chocolate and comfort-eating generally, kissing, having conversations in which we consume a lot of space and time, soaking up television or the sun, or going on a shopping spree. Afterwards we may feel temporarily better, or more substantial, like the baby after a good feed because we now have something in our inner world which acts as a substitute for the meaning of the 'good breast'. These activities evoke memories of our earliest experience of the breast as a source of pleasure, comfort and identity.

However, Freud argues that if a baby experiences difficulty or trauma during the oral stage of its infancy, its future development as an adult may be particularly unconsciously preoccupied with the idea of incorporation as a means of gaining access to a sense of identity. There may be a feeling that nothing and no one is ever enough to fill an overwhelming psychical hunger. In close relationships such an individual may be experienced as very emotionally demanding. In extreme forms, and particularly in situations which provoke anxiety and feelings of helplessness, adult oral behaviour may involve, for example, excessive drinking and greedy eating which may involve eating disorders such as bulimia and drug addiction. The pleasure of incorporation or 'taking in' may be achieved through the mouth, nose, ears or eyes, skin, intravenously or through 'greedy' shopping and the appropriation of large quantities of consumer objects (an extreme example would be Imelda

Marcos's consumption of over 3,000 pairs of shoes). All these forms of 'consuming' behaviour may enable an individual to achieve a fragile, but temporary, sense of identity which, in early infancy, was the only basis for identity available to the baby. Some extreme forms of adult oral behaviour involving, for example, alcohol or drug abuse, are often regarded by therapists as an attempt at self-medication, as a temporary way of boosting confidence and obtaining a sense of psychical substance and identity in order to obliterate a yawning sense of emptiness and isolation. Therapeutic groups such as Alcoholics Anonymous often seem to be effective because they offer the possibility of forming meaningful relationships with whole people rather than a part-object (the breast). These are based on shared experience and objectives and mutual support which offer the potential for other less destructive, less dependent, emotionally richer, more integrated forms of identity to begin to emerge.

NARCISSISM AND THE EGO-IDEAL

Freud's theory of narcissism and the idea of the ego-ideal and Lacan's concepts of the Imaginary and ideal ego have been widely used in the analysis of culture and particularly in the analysis of consumerism. These concepts seem to suggest why desires or needs and their temporary satisfaction can be so easily constructed in consumer societies. Let's look first at Freud's theory of narcissism.

Freud first used the term narcissism in 1910 when he was trying to explain why homosexual men choose a lover who is the same as rather than different from themselves. He came to the conclusion that they take themselves as their sexual object, narcissistically, and therefore seek partners who resembles themselves. This means they can then love their lover as their mother loved them. Later, in his paper 'On Narcissism' written in 1915, Freud suggests that narcissism is a transitional stage between what he calls the baby's auto-eroticism or desire for pleasure from its own body and its desire for an external object, seen as a whole rather than part object (initially the mother and later other objects) but with whom its identity is still merged (Freud 1914, pp. 65–97). In the narcissistic phase the baby projects its own body onto the mother whom it then loves as itself. In this way the baby forms a phantasied but satisfying, coherent image of its self reflected back to it by the mother's behaviour. Previously, in the *Three Essays on Sexuality*, Freud had seen this identity as being made up entirely of pleasurable sensations. So the baby is given what Lacan calls an Imaginary sense of a free-standing 'self' or ego (Lacan's Mirror-stage) even though it still shares an identity with the mother. So the baby, and later narcissistic adult, projects its 'self' onto an object in the external world and then internalises this external relationship with the object as its self while imagining itself to be separate and independent from this external object or idea. This may happen in heterosexual as well as homosexual relationships when individuals often choose someone very like themselves.

Freud distinguished between two types of love: narcissistic love characterised by the desire to be loved (to be given idealised reflections of the self) and anaclitic love characterised by the desire to love. Freud thought some narcissistic types of relationship conformed to the kind of love characteristic of heterosexual relationships, and falling in love with the ideal of a perfect partner. (He also thought it was involved in some women's wish to be worshipped and adored.) In romantic love we often fall in love with our self projected onto the other. We speak of finding our 'other half', our self in another. This might explain a sensation characteristic of the initial stages of falling in love, what I call 'kissing into infinity'. During the kiss we project our self onto the other – all our phantasies and desires – and then, in the process of psychical incorporation, we feel a sense of oneness and what Freud described as the 'oceanic feeling' which may turn our legs to jelly with the sheer weight of what we have momentarily invested in the other person, sometimes on the basis of very flimsy evidence! Freud's theory of narcissism suggests we're actually kissing our phantasised self merged in the other. Traditionally, popular ballads about romantic love refer to the sensation of head-spinning dizziness, of 'walking on air', of having someone 'under our skin', references to a powerful feeling of unreality and identification. But as we get to know the person better and gain a more realistic view of him or her, we usually lose these sensations because we have to deal with a 'real' person who cannot, realistically, carry all our phantasies. The movements associated with the computer-generated, non-stop drumbeat of the dance music played at raves, whether or not combined with drugs, seems to induce the same kind of 'head-spinning' trance-like sensation of bondedness with others, of oneness with the universe. This again may be a psychical return to the 'oceanic feeling' reminiscent of our once merged, bonded existence with the mother. As well as the feeling of being in love, this seems also to be associated with deeply held religious feelings and experiences. In the context of relationships with consumer 'goods', we may fall in love in a similar way with the idea of a holiday, a car, a pair of boots or even a glistening, new, white fridge. Freud's theory of identification suggests that the new fridge reflects back to us a transformed, pristine, immaculate self ready to embark on a new life. The first scratch or stain, the first piece of plastic trim which falls off, the first hint of perished rubber and our phantasies of it and ourselves begin to dissolve as the reality of real fridges in everyday use sets in. Both we and the fridge have to sink back into the imperfect, stained mundanity of the real world and we have to abandon our self-idealisation. This phenomenon may help us to explain the lure of the spotlessly new in many other contexts which seems so intrinsic to marketing, fashion and the need to keep up to date. These are used to justify the need for continuous consumption of commodities for the purpose of refuelling our identities as well as satisfying the needs of a capitalist economy.

As we saw earlier, Freud thought the love of parents for their children was another form of loving ourselves in the other so that children are experienced by their parents as a psychological as well as a physical extension of themselves. He also thought love for a much younger partner was another form of narcissistic love which involves the idea of loving the 'self' we used to be or would have liked to have been, that is, a feeling of renewal. Freud argued that although we normally eventually transfer our narcissistic love from the narrow confines of a relationship in which our identity is fused with someone else's (at first the mother's) to a love-object we experience as separate, we always retain some potential for love based on narcissism. The problem with relationships based on narcissism is that part of our unconscious identity is projected onto someone or something else in the external world which, in making us very psychically dependent on them, makes us very vulnerable if that person rejects us, leaves us, or dies. It seems clear that narcissism or love of the same can express itself in both het-erosexual and gay relationships since 'masculinity' and 'femininity' or difference may exist in an infininite number of mixes, in male or female bodies.

Freud's notion of the ego-ideal is central to narcissism in both its normal and pathological forms. In his paper 'On Narcissism' he suggests that the love which was originally fixed on our self in its merged state with the mother is, after the separation and loss of the mother at the end of the Oedipal crisis, turned inwards onto a mother who we have now internalised as an inner object. Freud argues that when we abandon or lose an object we don't just leave it behind us. Instead, we internalise the idea of the loved object so that it lives on inside us and contributes to who we are. In this sense we are made up of abandoned love objects. Having internalised the lost mother so she becomes part of who we are, we then turn the full beam of our love inwards, which since she is now a part of us, means onto our selves. The ego-ideal then, represents an unconscious strategy for returning to the earlier state of merged dependence on the mother through the installation of her as an idealised object, part of our self, in our internal world. It seems to refer specifically to the internalisation of the bonded 'oneness' between the mother and baby and our attempt to hold onto this idea of completion with the mother for ever. In contrast, the superego (also an internalised object) is linked to three people; the father who represents culture and the reality beyond the mother and baby couple (Frosh 1991, p. 82). The ego-ideal in the adult, therefore, is best understood as representing the pursuit of narcissistic nirvana with a substitute for the mother, the pre-Oedipal pursuit of oneness, a pre-social time where the self and the mother are still merged, where incest has not been recognised, where there is no father, no difference and no structure (Frosh 1991, p. 82). It therefore represents an attempt at recovering the baby's sense of omnipotence and the reinstatement of illusion or phantasy. In contrast, the superego or symbolic father represents restriction, boundary, constraint, the recognition of symbolic castration, that is 'reality' or culture and adult forms of pleasure and sexuality. As Frosh puts it 'In a nutshell, the ego-ideal represents escapist imagination, the super-ego reality' (Frosh 1991).

Freud's powerful idea of the ego-ideal has been clarified and helpfully elaborated by Janine Chasseguet-Smirgel.

> The violent end to which the primary state of fusion is brought by [the baby's] helplessness obliges the infant to recognise the 'not me'. This seems to be the crucial moment when the narcissistic omnipotence that he is forced to give up is projected on the object, the infant's first Ego-Ideal, a narcissisic omnipotence from which he is henceforth divided by a gulf that he will spend the rest of his life trying to bridge. (Chasseguet-Smirgel 1985, pp. 6–7)

This first overwhelming loss, the gap between what we are and what we want to be, as Lasch and others have suggested, then underlies all other cultural forms of alienation, for example, historical myths of a golden age, of the first expulsion from paradise or primary fall from grace which are central to many religions. However, as Frosh, argues, as well as inspiring nostalgia for an idealised past, a need for oceanic experience, the desire for states of trance, it also inspires a search for reunification which can underlie the motive for art as well as 'regressive longing' (Frosh 1991, p. 84). But Frosh distinguishes between the narcissism involved in creativity and regressive narcissism which involves our seeking an idealised self in, for example, a new car or a new partner. Frosh sums up the crux of the argument.

> creativity, like mental health in general, is concerned with facing reality, with acting upon it, transforming it, expressing, repairing, re-generating it,

and the emotions it produces. Narcissism, embedded structurally in the attempt of the ego to merge with the ego-ideal, is the denial of difference in favour of an imagined land in which there is no separation and loss, no unmet desire, and indeed no work. The ego-ideal, even though it fulfils a reality principle function, by establishing the existence of plans and hopes (i.e. post-ponements of pleasure) holds out a seductive promise of return to the longed for early state when ego and non-ego were merged; it is, therefore, more a carrier of regressive rather than creative urges. (Ibid.)

One of the central emotional 'truths' at the heart of psychoanalytic knowledge is that in order to remain creatively rather than regressively in touch with our inner world we have, at the same time, to be able to recognise loss, frustration, uncertainty and contradiction.

Chasseguet-Smirgel argues, importantly, that it is not the ego-ideal itself that is regressive, but the striving for the ego-ideal without the mediation of reality, without the acceptance of separation, symbolic castration, the recognition of loss and difference, in fact everything that results from a relatively successful resolution of Freud's Oedipal crisis, Lacan's transition to the Symbolic, Klein's depressive position or Winnicott's transitional space.

So Chasseguet-Smirgel argues, following Freud, that the pursuit of pleasures or ideals, whether in the form of consumer goods, political causes, religions, belief systems in the form of 'grand narratives', may be, but is not always, a regressive desire for an escape from the need to face reality. But she suggests that a rigid adherence to anything: nationalism, communism, fascism, the market, psychoanalytic theory or any other belief which argues that it alone represents the 'truth' is a failure to face up to the reality of difference and is based on the desire for merged perfection with the mother. But this does not mean, as some post-modernists such as Lacan want to argue, that we have to give up all values and sense of moral purpose. There are causes we may want to defend but when we embrace these values, psychoanalysis generally suggests that we need to do it within a context of being able to separate escapist phantasy from reality. We have to live with the reality that life is full of uncertainty, ambivalence, conflict and contradiction which we can never omnipotently control, but it is this realisation which allows us access to emotional growth and creativity.

Psychoanalysis generally, then, suggests that if we consistently unconsciously confuse the meaning of ourselves with objects outside ourselves in the external world, we remain potentially very fragile. By refusing the difference between our self and the meanings the object has outside as a 'not me' object, we cannot relate to the world beyond the projections we make onto it. Although we may gain short-term pleasure, it is always at the expense of an underlying sense of meaninglessness. From within an object relations perspective, Winnicott argues that extreme forms of narcissism result from early maternal deprivation. This may result in varying degrees of what he calls a false self which is alienated from a self which remains undeveloped and in hiding. This false self remains in a state of undifferentiated fusion with the mother who is then confused with objects in the external world which we mistake for ourselves.

Lacan, building on Freud's ideas, defines narcissistic identifications as the realm of the Imaginary. Here we are beset by a hall of mirrors which represents a dead-end consisting of images which we misrecognise as a coherent identity. For Lacan, this blinds us to our essential de-centredness, filling the gap in our being where desire, loss and longing are permanently installed. The difference between Freud's and Lacan's conception of identity is that Lacan takes the self or ego to be entirely in the illusory sway of the Imaginary, distinguishing it clearly from a precarious subjectivity which we can obtain only in language. In contrast, Freud sees the ego or consciousness as an identity which may be constructed more or less narcissistically but which may equally well become relatively emotionally integrated. For Lacan, identities in both the Imaginary and the Symbolic are unstable in different ways whereas for Freud, consciousness can remain relatively undisturbed by unconscious eruptions. Kenneth Wright, writing from a Winnicottian perspective, distinguishes between the gap or absence left by the loss of our mothers which we fill by the process of symbolisation and the gap with which some of us are left because we failed to have 'good enough', 'non-impinging' mothering (Wright 1991). This means we never had the fundamental bedrock ingredients for a primary sense of self or what Winnicott calls the feeling of being 'real' rather than of just existing. This reassuring feeling continues to occupy the psychical centre of the child whose mother could be 'good enough' even though it has had to relinquish her.

In the context of the particular form of the 'taking in' or identification with public figures and celebrities known mainly through the media, let us consider for a moment the massive public response to the death of Diana, Princess of Wales in 1997 and what may be its significance in unconscious terms. Contrary to the view of some commentators at the time, that Diana was being narcissistically consumed as an idealised, dehumanised icon of perfection and saintliness, for the most part, much of the public reaction seemed eminently realistic. The stunned mourning of her death seemed to centre on the perception of her as an imperfect mixture of qualities rather than as the embodiment of goodness and truth. As Klein's theory emphasises, phantasy in the form of idealisation (and denigration) often prevents us from perceiving what is real and distinctive about individual human beings and the contradictions, ambiguity and ambivalence which exist in all of us. The public response to Diana's death suggested that she reflected a complicated mixture of vulnerability, insecurity, impulsiveness, humanity, humour and an intuitive capacity for spontaneous emotional generosity in relating to others, albeit in a glamorous, privileged setting. In the context of the increasing experience of social fragmentation and isolation mentioned earlier in this chapter, many people also seemed to find comfort in a transient sense of community and collectivity with others while they testified with their flowers and messages to their sense of identification with her. Through ordinary rather than narcissistic identification, her loss seemed to contain something of themselves as the loss of most things we value or love inevitably does.

The public's response to Diana's death may represent a major cultural turning-point in the sense that the public allied itself uncompromisingly with the spontaneity and intuition associated with the 'feminine' but importantly, blended with the activity and assertiveness associated with cultural 'masculinity'. In other words, Diana represented a blurring of rigid gender boundaries. Put in Kleinian terms, there was a public alliance with the realism and creativity associated with the depressive position and the beginning of emotional integration. What the public mood challenged was the rigidity of what Klein describes as the paranoid-schizoid position or Winnicott's false self encapsulated in the control and unreality of patriarchal 'masculinity' and authority. This was symbolised, in the public perception, in the monarchy. In his powerful funeral tribute, Diana's brother, Earl Spencer, referred directly to Diana's intuition. 'Your greatest gift was your intuition ... your instinctive feel for what was really important in all our lives.' This echoes the language of Winnicott. Diana's death seems to have reinforced a huge and growing national longing for emotional growth, integrity, creativity and imagination in public life and an end to what people perceived as the sterility of control, rigidity and denial. This may have begun with the landslide Labour victory four months before. The public may also have intuitively recognised the unconscious womb-envy implied in the ambivalence or hostility of much of the media and the palace. Diana, for all her narcissism, seemed to represent the intuitive, emotional world associated with the mother but she was also beautiful and becoming increasingly articulate and potent. This could do her no good in many quarters. As a result of her death, the public (men as well as women), many suprised by the depth of their feelings, seem spontaneously to have been struck with a collective deluge of emotional insight provoked by their powerful feelings of loss.

Contact with these feelings seemed to complete what looked like a public transformation of consciousness through the emergence of a valuable kind of intuitively derived 'truth'. Whether this was temporary or more enduring remains to be seen.

Finally, in this section, let us look at the meanings of a new car as an example of a less healthy narcissistic muddling of ourselves with material objects in the external world. Most of us are concerned about the design for practical and aesthetic reasons. We think about the engine and the size and shape of the body of the car in terms of economy, reliability, comfort, security and the overall appearance. Many people are also concerned with the image and, in particular, whether the car looks 'sexy' or 'muscular'. These terms would imply real or imagined levels of power, agility and performance. It is often important that the capacity for high performance connoted by fuel injection or turbocharging, for example, is symbolised literally in the car's presentation in the form of 'badging'. In BBC 2's intriguing and often moving television documentary series about motoring, *From A–B* (BBC 2 1994) a company sales rep tells of how he and his wife sat at home one evening and wept after the discovery that his company had allocated him a smaller car than he had expected and without the coveted 'i' after the car type number, indicating petrol injection. The man identified his car with himself and he felt his entire 'masculine' being had been humiliatingly called into question by the incident. In telling the story he showed all the signs of feeling himself to be a castrated and broken man. The loss of the 'i' represented the loss of himself. His experience is not so suprising if we recall the number of times we have seen advertisements for large, powerfully built cars caught almost 'in flagrante' with beautiful, desirable women. Of course, many modern advertisements, most recently for jeans, beers and perfumes, sell identities, sexual and otherwise, in much more subtle ways but the mechanism through which we are seduced to invest ourselves in these meanings remains the same.

IDEALISED AND DENIGRATED CONSUMER GOODS

Klein's theory also suggests that consumer consumption is about the projection of our idealised selves onto consumer goods as well as other individuals, ideas and causes. We subsequently re-introject these idealised objects as ourselves (projective identification). In the context of what many see as a culture dominated by infantile longing, such ideas are very illuminating. Both Klein's concept of projective identi-fication reminiscent of the rigidity and over-simplification of the paranoid-schizoid phase and Freud's victim/victimiser remnants of symbolic castration allow us to detect the presence of idealisation and denigration in relation to consumer goods as well as people. We idealise those goods with which we identify and denigrate 'others'. Through a process of denigration we may turn consumer objects, like people, into rejected 'others' on the basis of their perceived difference from ourselves. This seems very like Foucault's 'dividing practices' as they apply to consumer commodities. We create certain consumer objects, as well as people, groups, ideas and causes as symbolic others, that is like inanimate lepers, criminals, deviants or 'defectives'. Fashion and style play a major role in allowing us to constantly bolster our sense of who we are by indicating how we can renew ourselves by continually creating new arrangements of objects as psychical vehicles for idealisation or denigration. We may redefine our selves and create new others on the basis of objects being 'in fashion' or identified with a group with which we want to be associated. Fashion thus allows us to continually recreate our selves whether in relation to cars, clothes, lager or anything which has been commodified. We sometimes express this matter of taste and style in the quite passionate terms of love and hate. We may say we 'wouldn't be seen dead' in some item of clothing, or a particular car or describe something we don't 'fancy' as 'rubbish'. Perhaps the idealisation of the self made possible by the acceptance of some goods and the denigration of others is most obvious in adolescents who, in the throws of trying to gain a viable sense of identity, often make passionate identifications with certain kinds of clothes, music, football teams or lifestyles generally which involve equally impassioned rejections of others, often to the point of fighting it out. Adults may be doing something similar when they identify with one particular way of thinking or theory to the exclusion of all others, thus closing off vast tracts of insight and possibility. It seems likely that a primitive need to maintain a sense of identity on the basis of idealising some things and denigrating others may form the basis of the desire to compete rather than co-operate in many areas of life.

So both Klein and Freud seem to suggest, within different conceptual frameworks, that primitive means of establishing a fragile form of identity may pervade many of our relationships with consumer objects as well as individuals and groups perceived as 'other'. (This might help us to explain why consumer consumption has been so stunningly successful.) To what extent does the political ideal of consumer 'choice' depend on this 'productive' sado-masochistic dynamic based on competition?

Let us look now at a more Winnicottian view of the unconscious meanings of consumption.

THE TRANSFORMATIONAL ROLE OF CONSUMER OBJECTS

Christopher Bollas, like Kenneth Wright, builds on Winnicott's central idea of the transitional object. He emphasises the transformational role of the mother for the baby's psychical development. Elaborating on Winnicott's idea of the transitional object (often a small piece of torn-off blanket or rag which the baby carries around with him or her) he suggests that the baby's creation of what he calls a transformational object is the baby's displacement of the transformational process with the mother onto this object and later innumerable objects in the outside world as the baby evolves from the experience of a process to what Bollas calls 'the articulation of experience'. It finds symbolic equations which stand in for and compensate for the loss of the mother. Bollas argues that the search for transformational objects continues in adult life. For some, religion offers the chance for a meta-morphosis of the self echoing the earliest experience of a bond with the mother within a mythic structure. For many others, in secular life, hope is invested in new objects: a new car, consumer goods, job, move to another country, holiday, change of relationship. Bollas says all these can be seen as a request for transformation and signify the experience of transformation first experienced in the process of the baby's development with the mother. Advertising actually promises that a product will alter the subjects' external environments and therefore change their internal mood. This is in contrast with Freud and Lacan's theories which suggest that these objects signify the nar-cissistic or Imaginary search for total, unending bliss and completion with the mother and therefore evoke false, unjustified hopes for a unity of being which can never be possible. Bollas takes a different view. He argues that these signifiers evoke the promise of transforma-tion because they chime with pre-verbal memories of a self or ego. They evoke our unconscious response not by offering us the illusion of wholeness and completeness but by putting us back in touch with very early experiences with the mother which have never been symbolised in thought or language. But Bollas also points to aesthetic moments when an individual feels a deep, subjective rapport with an object: a painting, poem, symphony, landscape or love song. They too usually chime with a pre-verbal ego memory. However, Bollas argues that some people may seek negative aesthetic experiences which refer back to early negative ego experiences and manifest the particular negative structure of their personal unconscious or what Bollas calls 'unthought known'. This is very similar to Freud's repetition compulsion in which individuals repeat traumatic situations because, through them, they remember how they came into being existentially, not cognitively.

But Bollas asks, drawing on Winnicott, what happens to people who fail to be disillusioned by, for example, consumer goods or other perceived transformational objects failing to live up to expectations? He argues various disturbances emerge from such failure such as the compulsion to gamble, the criminal who seeks the perfect crime to repair unconsciously defects in his/her identity and, externally, bring wealth and happiness. In addition, Bollas gives the example of the search for the perfect partner. All constitute a deficiency in our experience of having an identity or, as Michael Balint put it, they offer the chance to repair the 'basic fault' (Balint 1984). As an example of a failed maternal relationship, Bollas cites the mother who makes her child into a mythic object for her and itself (for example, the 'special' child whose extraordinary gifts will transform the fortunes and standing of the family) rather than looking after its needs as a child rather than her own. As the 'golden larvae' the child experiences no psychical space as its own. Its inner space exists for and belongs to the mother. 'As an adult the child's existential despair is flung into a mythic narrative in an order where the real is used to populate the fantastic' (Bollas 1991, p. 20).

So Bollas argues that the search for transformation is perhaps one of the most widespread, archaic ways of relating which is not desire or craving or longing as Lacan insists it is. It arises from the idea that the object will deliver change and have the capacity to rescusitate memory of early change and transformation but this is existential, pre-verbal memory, not cognitive memory. Bollas cites extremest political movements as examples of not so much a wish to consume or re-merge with the mother but of the belief that they will affect a total transformation which will deliver everyone from a whole spectrum of 'basic faults' – social and moral. The certainty of the revolutionary, he argues, which is striking to the observer, is not based on desire but on the longing for change and delivery from a perceived deficiency in the self. For Bollas, transformation is not the search for gratification in the Imaginary as Lacan suggests but emerges out of some people's frustration about ever being able to achieve emotional insight and growth through other means. Similarly, Bollas reminds us, 'aesthetic moments are not always beautiful and wonderful but sometimes ugly and terrifying but none the less moving because they tap an existential memory' and put us in touch with ourself (Bollas 1991, p. 27).

CONCLUSIONS

Psychoanalytic approaches suggest that shopping, which seems so much a part of our external, social existence, often refers back to our internal world. Shopping frequently provides a pleasurable but temporary substitute for a sense of identity. We may shop as a means to repairing and transforming unacceptable aspects of our identities or to the delivery of longed-for aspects of the self.

REFERENCES

Balint, M. (1984) *The Basic Fault*, London, Tavistock and Routledge.
Bollas, C. (1991) *The Shadow of the Object: Psychoanalysis of the unthought known*, London, Free Association Books.
Chasseguet-Smirgel, J. (1985) *The Ego Ideal: A psychoanalytic essay on the malady of the ideal*, London, Free Association Books.
Freud, S. (1905), *The Three Essays on the Theory of Sexuality*, Pelican Freud Library, Vol. 7.
Freud, S. (1914) 'On Narcissism', Pelican Freud Library, Vol. 11.
Frosh, S. (1991) *Identity Crisis: Modernity, psychoanalysis and the self*, London, Macmillan.
Lasch, C. (1980) *The Culture of Narcissism*, London, Sphere Books.
Wright, K. (1991) *Vision and Separation*, London, Free Association Books.

3

From Harrods to Holloway: When Compulsive Shopping is Not an Option

Marsha Taylor

A WORLD AWAY FROM HARRODS

I get nice things for myself – nice designer clothes, like. If I don't go to Harrods one Saturday and get something, I feel really bad in the middle of the week and I'm like: 'Let's go! Let's hurry up and get there!'

This description of feelings about what might be routine Saturday shopping sprees comes from a strikingly attractive British-born woman of non-European ethnic origin who appears younger than her twenty-nine years. The visits to Harrods, which 'Sara' – not her real name – describes as an almost weekly feature of her life since late adolescence, now take place only in memory. For the time being, Sara must recall these regular outings to 'get nice things' from a cell in Her Majesty's Prison Holloway, where she serves a six-month custodial sentence for shoplifting: 'I see things that I want, things that I could never afford, and I take them.'

HMP Holloway, the largest women's correctional facility in western Europe, sprawls over several acres of land in north-central London – geographically little more than a short taxi ride from the glittering and perfumed halls of Harrods but metaphorically a world away. Bits of the Holloway buildings – as well as the plumbing, staff sometimes suggest in jest – date back to Victorian times. To add modern amenities including a computer room, gymnasium and swimming pool, much of the complex has been refurbished or rebuilt. A central courtyard with its tree-shaded garden of flowering plants tended by inmates acts in fine weather as an open-air recreation area.

52

Mod cons and blossoms embellish but do not conceal the reality of prison: barbed wire tops every external wall, and iron bars cast shadows across each outside window. Along Holloway's seemingly endless corridors, painted and repainted in institutional replication of the old saw about the Forth Bridge, sets of barred and locked iron doors block movement at intervals of twenty to thirty metres or less. Mingled odours of cooked food and pine disinfectant linger in each passageway. A range of sound – raucous laughter and irate shrieks, voices raised perhaps in command or anguished argument – swirls round corners, easily deceiving the ear as to the location of the source.

The Prison Service designates HMP Holloway primarily as a remand facility for women awaiting trial. At least four thousand unsentenced women now pass through annually, and the prison must strain at the seams most days to squeeze in over five hundred. Once sentenced, inmates may be moved on rapidly to other prisons to make room for arrivals. Faces new and old appear or disappear daily, each dragging the few permitted belongings in and out in bin liners. There may never be time to get names right: an inmate must learn quickly to respond to her number – perhaps TJ4271 or RB2647.

In most respects Sara represents a rather typical Holloway inmate since, like her, about two in three are aged between twenty-one and thirty-nine, over three in four hold British nationality and one in five enters Holloway for crimes involving theft and handling of stolen property, the category that takes in shoplifting and other property offences classed by law as less serious than burglary or robbery. Sara is unusual, however, in that she has no involvement with drugs: one inmate in three now comes to Holloway accused of drugs-related offences, the fastest-growing category of crimes committed in the United Kingdom by females.

The elements of Sara's life – such as broken family, childhood abuse, poor education and, above all, poverty – that may seem to explain, if not to justify, her actions appear unfailingly in the lives of most inmates in Holloway. 'Psychological situations which may lead to crime and antisocial actions are deeply associated with sociological, cultural and historical conditions', explain forensic psychotherapists Welldon and van Velsen (1997, p. 4). 'Many offences have roots which go back into the structure of society and/or the earlier experiences of the mentally disordered offender. There is always a complex interaction between personality and environment.' Yet, identical elements – poverty and the deprivation, neglect and abuse that may be concomitant – also mark the lives of countless others who manage to remain on the right side of the law or, at the very least, are not found out on the wrong. 'Why are individual differences so great?', Welldon and van Velsen ask rhetorically. 'Why do some survive environments better than others?' (1997, p. 4).

Thus the story of what moves Sara from Harrods to Holloway is both representative, delineating elements from the culture of poverty common to many others, and unique, as all lives are unique, taking a strand here and a strand there to weave the psychopathological fabric of a cluster of excessive behaviours.

Sara comes from the Midlands, the third child amongst five born to a family of recently arrived immigrants from outside Europe. Seemingly without the network of supportive relatives and contacts in Britain that members of some immigrant communities can count on, the father struggled to provide for the family whilst the mother held a traditional stay-at-home role. Possibly because of the family's straitened financial circumstances, Sara – the only girl – was taken at the age of four to the family's country of origin and left by the father with his parents. She received no explanation for what she experienced as abandonment.

> Every day I would say: 'When are my parents coming to get me?', and [my grandmother] would always tell me: 'Tomorrow, tomorrow'. But they didn't come 'tomorrow'. They didn't come until I was eight.

By then Sara had suffered repeated sexual abuse by young male relatives who gave her sweets in exchange for silence. Reunited with her birth family back in Britain, she disclosed the abuse to her mother and was not believed. Coming to view the abuse as her own fault, she became withdrawn and tearful. School seemed difficult, with poor marks and few friends. With growing frequency, she consumed large amounts of food – especially sweets and chocolates stolen from shops. Weight-gain inevitably followed. Chided by various members of her now-broken family, she followed each episode of overeating by quantities of laxatives.

Surprisingly good results in Sara's school-leaving examinations seemed to mark the start of a newly positive period. Leaving the Midlands and her family conflicts behind, she came up to London where she got a job, began a business studies course and met her first – and only – boyfriend. But, in a seemingly natural and uncomplicated progression from stealing sweets as a child, shoplifting came to provide her with otherwise unaffordable clothing and treats.

A career in modelling to capitalise on unusual height and lovely face evaded her grasp: Sara failed to keep down her weight. As her dreams of modelling faded, bouts of overeating followed by laxatives and vomiting slowly spiralled out of control. The binge–purge syndrome spilled into the workplace. She lost two jobs in rapid succession and went on the dole, dropping her course and being dropped in turn by her boyfriend. Regular shoplifting expeditions sometimes ended in detection, with each successive arrest followed by a caution until at last she received a custodial sentence.

Sara accepts her time in Holloway rather philosophically, noting that at least the prison environment prevents her from overeating and taking laxatives. However, contact with other shoplifters makes her sense for the first time that what may underlie her shoplifting somehow differs from the 'professional' norm.

> When I walk out with something, I feel really clever. But half the time I take stuff I don't want and I just give it away. I see other girls here that have taken twice as much stuff as me, and they've sold it all on and made thousands of pounds. Now I feel really stupid. I do this just for fun. Well, not fun. It's not fun any more. I don't know why I do it, really. It's just that ... nothing is ever enough. Not food, not clothes, nothing. Nothing is ever enough.

From Market to Department Store

The market predates recorded history. Here individuals came, in what most probably were the earliest beginnings of peaceful human intercourse, to barter with one another, bringing whatever they were able to make or produce in excess in order to seek out useful complements in the goods made or produced by others. Thus, with barely four thousand years to its name, money is a relatively recent innovation compared to barter but one which transformed definitively the nature of markets. No longer did buyer and seller stand perplexed, trying to decide how many oranges a pair of sandals might be worth or how to proceed if the sandal-maker wanted lemons. Money, the newcomer to the marketplace, made it possible for goods to change hands swiftly by providing a standard of value and a means of payment (Davies 1994).

Over the centuries, flourishing accordingly as money gained widespread acceptance, markets and fairs established themselves in Britain in or near villages and locations such as crossroads and river fords that buyers and sellers could reach easily on foot, by cart or on horseback. Markets offered more than trade in goods: for most social strata, 'market day' became synonymous with an outing, the marketplace acting as a central point in which to meet others and find entertainment. For the extremely poor, trapped on the margin of the lively market trade, there was a ready, albeit risky, remedy: thievery, a commonplace happening to which no market could remain immune.

As the population grew, markets grew in tandem with them and one market day sometimes stretched into several – often a daunting prospect in all weathers.

The need for permanent and fixed locations where merchants could trade throughout the week rather than just on one day led to the growth of shops in the eighteenth and nineteenth centuries. Specialised shops could thrive in major towns, supported by the local population and clientele who would travel greater distances to obtain particular goods, while the general stores catered for the broader needs of a smaller population in rural areas (Couch 1989, p. 3).

The rise of the English shop, specialised or general, changed the nature of the buying and selling experience: shopping became compartmentalised. No longer did one location provide goods, companionship and entertainment. For many segments of society, a visit to a shop soon became a less engaging – and thus less frequent – occurrence. Today, when shopping is more commonplace, 'it is easy to forget that in the early part of Victoria's reign many rich and middle-class people went to the larger stores, but did not go in: they expected the proprietor to bring to their carriage door goods' from which to choose (Baren 1998, p. 6). The butcher, baker, candlestick-maker and other provisioners called in order to show their wares to the cook or housekeeper at the servants' entrance to the better homes. Working poor seldom went shopping because they were obliged to buy most goods from the mill or factory owner's shop, where little choice and poor value for money were the norm. 'Even lower down the scale the very poor lived from hand to mouth and would only rarely be able to shop. They could not afford new clothes and their diet was very basic' (Baren 1998, p. 6).

Thus, in the mid-nineteenth century, the marketplace seemed ready for a further radical transformation: the rise of the department store, where appealing goods displayed in an atmosphere of elegance sought to entice the shopper inside. The lead in this retail revolution was taken by Paris, where Au Bon Marché – growing from four departments in 1852 to a multistorey edifice on an entire city block thirty-five years later – reigned as the world's largest department store until after the First World War. London – with its own Bon Marché opening in Brixton in 1877 and small specialist shops such as Harrods grocery rapidly expanding lines of goods traded – Bath and Edinburgh in Britain as well as New York, Philadelphia and Chicago in America also made room for the retail leviathans (Adburgham 1964).

In the opulent surroundings created by the new temples of the retail trade, goods, companionship and entertainment also came together

once again: akin to 'magnificent stage settings ... department stores
were more than just places where merchandise was bought and sold,
... [also being] visited ... as tourist attractions – as monuments to
modernity – for the interest and pleasure they afforded in themselves'
(Nava 1997, p. 66). Gordon Selfridge summed it up when he astounded
London in 1909 with his purpose-built neo-classical emporium on
Oxford Street: the function of a department store, said Selfridge, was as
'a social centre, not a shop. Later his slogan was "Why not spend the
day at Selfridge?"' (Adburgham 1964, p. 276).

The department store shopper was permitted, even encouraged, to
indulge in behaviour that seemed alien and unwelcome in the small
shop: not merely to look but to touch the goods on offer – with no
subsequent obligation to buy. Often touch itself seemed almost
magically to seduce the shopper. The smiling and helpful shop
assistants meanwhile exerted another form of subtle pressure, and the
obligation to buy also became a moral one (Adburgham 1964).

In *Au Bonheur des Dames* (The Ladies' Paradise or Ladies' Delight), a
novel set against the seductive backdrop of colour, light and mirrors
that the fictional Paris department store of the same name creates, Zola
describes the array of goods:

> Silks, satins, and velvets [lay] fanned out in profusion in a supple, vibrant
> range of the most delicate flower tones: at the top, velvet – deep black, white
> as milky curds; below that, satin – pinks and blues, with bright folds fading
> into pale shades of infinite subtlety; at the bottom, silk – all the colours of
> the rainbow, pieces moulded into shell shapes, folded as if round a drawn-
> in waist, brought to life by the skilful hands of the shop assistants
> (1980[1883], p. 32).

Depicting with some prescience the femininisation that subsequently would characterise shopping in the twentieth century
(Campbell 1997), Zola (1980 [1883]) suggests that the department store
phenomenon also achieved a degree of democratisation, extending
access to luxury goods beyond 'ladies' of the upper classes to those of
the middle and lower-middle classes – precisely the group targeted in
London by Selfridge. These ladies

> might equally well afford to spend a day at Harrods, and would find the
> amenities equal to those that Selfridge was offering to them, if not better –
> but they were shy of strolling into Harrods just to have a look round and
> use the public services. In contrast, when they walked along Oxford Street,
> they were irresistibly sucked into Selfridges (Adburgham 1964, p. 276).

But in the ladies' paradise that the department store seemed to offer, there was trouble from the start: even as something like upper-class luxury spread through these stores to the middle and lower-middle classes, it remained well out of the financial reach of women of the lower classes – including the shop assistants who daily worked amidst luxury without earning enough ever to partake of it. At least, legally. In-store theft by employees, which today continues to account for about half of all retail losses through theft worldwide (Couch 1989), seems to have put in an appearance early on: praising a complex system of sales invoices, receipts and counterfoils devised by the owner of Au Bonheur des Dames to control stock that otherwise might drift out of the store in shop assistants' bags, a management colleague chortles with satisfaction: 'Now less will be stolen from us' (Zola 1980[1883], p. 68).

Beyond the structural malaise of theft by shop assistants, trouble in paradise also loomed from an external source: in the closing pages of *Au Bonheur des Dames*, Zola recounts the humiliating ordeal of a lady shopper discovered by store detectives to have concealed about her person 'Alençon lace frills, twelve metres, ... a handkerchief, a fan and a scarf' (1980[1883], p. 516). A shoplifter is unmasked. Certainly, it will not be the last time: the department store and shoplifting 'are two phenomena intimately linked to each other. As department stores were established around the world, they automatically brought shoplifting in their wake' (Fredriksson 1997, p. 131).

To Steal by any other Name

The philosophical and psychological nature of the human will to acquire and to possess – the wish to hold things as property – sparks a rich tradition of intellectual inquiry that extends back in time at least as far as Pythagoras in the sixth century BC, and broadly across disciplines at least as disparate as economics and psychoanalysis. Acquisitiveness and possession are viewed variously – and sometimes simultaneously – as utilitarian in response to need, innate in response to instinct, or cognitive in response to 'socially induced mental representations determin[ing] which objects are valued for possession' (Rudmin 1990, p. 312).

From a psychoanalytically informed perspective on anthropology, Roheim concludes that property constitutes 'the introjection of part of the external world into the self' (1927, p. 153). In the self-perception possessions become an integral part of the self (Litwinski 1951). The individual who possesses objects feels him- or herself to come alive through them (Benjamin 1973). When possessions assume such a preponderant defining role in individual identity, those without ready monetary resources may feel themselves obliged to resort to acquiring goods – and perhaps thereby, to acquiring an identity – by the only means that they perceive as available to them: if not shopping, then shoplifting.

In considering the shoplifting phenomenon, it is important to note that the concept of shoplifting is a social and/or legal construct and thus differs from one society to another. The *Oxford English Dictionary* classifies the word 'shoplifting' as 'origin obscure'; thus, coined in English rather than derived from another language. In fact, in such major modern European languages as French, German, Italian, Spanish and Swedish, there is no single word for 'shoplifting'; instead, the concept is expressed by phrases equivalent to 'stealing from shops'. The psycholinguist will point out that the presence in a language of a single word to describe a phenomenon is likely to correlate directly with the degree of interest that the phenomenon awakens in the society speaking the language.

Shoplifting is simply a form of stealing – so classified by law in Britain – and inquiry into motivations for stealing may help to shed light on motivations for shoplifting. Following on from early psychoanalytic writers such as Abraham, Alexander, Fenichel and others who sought to uncover the factors underlying the 'antisocial conduct ... [of] stealing', as Tiebout and Kirkpatrick (1932, p. 114) call it, the two authors note that

> the child starts with an innate desire to take things he wants. This we do not label stealing because we appreciate the fact that the child unless so taught, senses neither the distinction between that which is his and that which is not, nor does he realize that things which are not his belong to someone else who has a prior claim on them (p. 115).

Emphasising the socially created nature of the stealing concept, Tiebout and Kirkpatrick add that 'children have to develop both a sense of property and then a respect for it before their primitive impulses are completely and satisfactorily socialized' (1932, p. 115). When these external prohibitions become a part of the child, 'a process which the psychoanalysts call introjection, ... there will be set up within [the child] a conflict between such responses and [the] desire to take things' (p. 115). If an individual fails to develop an adequate property sense – usually through inadequate instruction by parents and other authority figures – or, having developed it, fails to accept it as a check on behaviour, stealing will result. In the latter case, Tiebout and

Kirkpatrick suggest, two sets of factors may 'overwhelm the already developed resistances: ... (1) those which are centered around the acquisition of the object, and (2) those which arise from the commission of the act' (p. 117).

In those individuals for whom possession of the object itself 'seems to be the reason for the theft, there is always a feeling of deprivation' (1932, p. 117) which the article taken is felt to satisfy, the two authors explain. The deprivation may be physical – that is, when an individual is hungry or cold, the theft of food or clothing – or emotional – that is, when an individual feels emotionally bereft, the theft of an object 'stolen not for what it is but for what it symbolizes ... as a representative of a loved person who is felt to be lost' (pp. 118–19) (in the latter case, an object also may act as fetish although this is thought to be rare).

In those individuals for whom 'the object taken appears to be of little or no importance ... the stimulation for and satisfaction from the stealing arises from the commission of the act itself' (1932, pp. 119–20), Tiebout and Kirkpatrick say. They mention as examples, firstly, those who steal in order to be punished to relieve pre-existing guilt feelings, a psychopathology originally outlined by Freud (1916) in the brief monograph 'Criminals from a Sense of Guilt'; secondly, those who steal for the thrill such as groups of adolescents; thirdly, those who steal to take revenge on others, usually parents; and finally those who steal compulsively to relieve inner tensions. Tiebout and Kirkpatrick underline two essential points. On the one hand, 'every act of stealing has multiple determining factors' which, on the other hand, in the same individual 'may shift from time to time' (p. 121). Thus, in their view, 'it becomes necessary to individualize not only the delinquent but each individual act of the delinquent' (p. 123) before an understanding of the psychiatric factors involved can be attained.

Woddis (1957–58) expands Tiebout and Kirkpatrick's categories for those who steal motivated by the wish to commit the act itself, suggesting that 'states of depression and tension appear to be precursors of theft, and sometimes the stealing appears to be an integral part of a depressive psychosis' (p. 89). In the essay on stealing as a defence, Allen expands on the notion that 'acts previously thought of as pure impulse expression are now recognized as having defensive functions' (1965, p. 572). In cases in which the individual may experience a strong need 'to reject underlying dependent strivings, stealing primarily represents an ego defense against anxiety', Allen adds.

Thus stealing – in the form of shoplifting or any of its other manifestations – may be perceived as causally linked to both anxiety and depression.

A CRIME OF POSSESSION

I needed some new blue jeans so I nicked a pair and got 'done' straightaway.
I were only out a day – outside, I mean. Out of Holloway. I been in here lots
of time before. Can't remember how many, but I got 27 – maybe it's 28 by
now – well, 27 or 28 of them whadjacallits: not convictions exactly, but like
that. Offences, maybe. That might be the word they said in court. For
shoplifting mostly. I been shoplifting since I was thirteen. I used to nick stuff
to sell, 'cuz I was doing drugs, but then I found another way of making
money – dealing drugs, I mean – so I just nick stuff I want for meself. That's
all I do now in the stores.

'Harriet' – a pseudonym – is now twenty-one. Never in one place long
enough even to obtain a minimal legal income by going on the dole,
shoplifting is to her what shopping is to the countless young women
who choose to live within the law: a way of life. Time in Holloway
forms an integral part of her eked-out existence.

Yet Harriet also may embody something of a historical tradition.
Studies of crime in English-speaking countries dating back to the
fourteenth century show an astonishing stability in patterns of
women's lawbreaking: until the rapid rise of the drug culture amongst
females in the last two or three decades, most women arrested were
accused of minor property or morals offences, but seldom of serious
property crimes, such as burglary and robbery, or crimes of violence
(Chesney-Lind 1997). Minor offences against property, Chesney-Lind
contends, often are 'closely tied to women's economic marginality and
the ways women attempt to cope with poverty' (pp. 95–6). Thus, as
both shoplifter and drug user, Harriet appears to sum up all that is both
old and new in female patterns of lawbreaking.

If shoplifting serves as the illegal counterpart to shopping, perhaps
its apparent feminine character mirrors the femininisation of shopping
characteristic of the twentieth century (Campbell 1997). Indeed, at first
glance, this might seem to be the case: in a psychiatric study of
shoplifting in Britain carried out more than forty years ago – still the
most detailed ever attempted in this country on the motivations for
the phenomenon – Gibbens and Prince (1962) state that 'shoplifting
differs from many other offences in that the majority of convicted
adult offenders are women' (p. 6), though boys predominate among
juveniles. However, note must be taken of the word 'convicted': the
authors refuse to contend that shoplifting is the quintessential
feminine offence, emphasising the difficulties inherent in drawing that
conclusion from data available.

Moving on from a North American study of shoplifting in
Philadelphia department stores in 1937, which showed that those

prosecuted and convicted accounted for only four in one hundred thefts detected by the stores and thus an infinitesimal number of overall thefts in stores, Gibbens and Prince emphasise that arrested and convicted shoplifters generally make up only a small percentage of the individuals who shoplift. Factors such as detection by the store and arrest 'intervene between the commission of the offence and the appearance of the offender in court' (1962, p. 5), they add. Women may simply be detected and charged more frequently than men, the two suggest.

In Sweden an investigative report prepared in 1968 for the Ministry of Justice bolsters this view: the real number of instances of shoplifting 'is substantially greater than the number of discovered cases, ... [and] shoplifters who get caught do not necessarily have the same characteristics as the shoplifters who do not' (Fredriksson 1997, p. 130).

Gibbens and Prince decry the fact that the psychiatrist with an interest in trying to understand 'the psychology and motivation of the individual offender ... is apt to see [only] small numbers' (1962, p. 6) of shoplifting cases selected in regrettably haphazard fashion: beyond the impossibility of evaluating the undetected shoplifter and the improbability of evaluating the shoplifter whom a store chooses not to prosecute, court recommendations for evaluation tend to vary. One court may mandate psychiatric evaluation only for first-time offenders but not for recidivists, they say, whilst another may favour the reverse. Most courts also seem to recommend psychiatric evaluation more frequently for females than for males who therefore tend to be under-represented in data available.

With these caveats, and stressing that 'as elsewhere in the psycho-pathology of crime, it is futile to look for a specific cause of any particular' offence (1962, p. 78), Gibbens and Prince draw out some common themes regarding a group of over five hundred convicted female shoplifters – of whom only one in ten considered themselves to be shoplifting 'professionals' – from three London courts during one twelve-month period. Psychosis, neurosis or apparent psychosomatic illness presented in one in five. Fewer than one in ten had significant physical ill-health or addiction to alcohol or drugs. However, what the authors describe as 'a sense of inferiority, of whatever origin, is common' (p. 75) to almost all of them, and a majority also presented depression, with a substantial number experiencing concomitant anxiety and tension. A striking commonality emerged in that shoplifting usually seemed to be 'more often carried out by women who would never steal from any individual' (p. 89). 'A surprising number' (p. 59) were said to come from Social Classes I and II but no break-down was given.

In a comparison sample of two hundred convicted female shoplifters – of whom a higher proportion, or about one in four, saw themselves as shoplifting 'professionals' – serving custodial sentences in HMP Holloway during a second twelve-month period, serious mental disorder presented more frequently; that is, in about one in three. Rates of physical ill-health, as well as alcohol and drug addiction, were also higher at about one in five. No information was given on links with depression and anxiety, but the Holloway sample seemed to indicate that no demonstrable connection existed between shoplifting and pre-menstrual tension. Amongst the Holloway sample food was stolen to satisfy hunger in fewer than 1 per cent of cases. No information was given on social class (Epps 1962).

In New Zealand, psychiatric evaluations were carried out amongst fifty convicted thieves – half of whom were shoplifters – 'prompted by the recognition of stealing as a symptom of depressive illness' (Medlicott 1968, p. 186). Medlicott quarrels with frequent 'emphasis upon theft as a symptom of the menopause … [since] it is not the menopause as such but the high incidence of depressive episodes in the late forties, fifties and sixties which is probably the important factor' (ibid.). With females predominating amongst the shoplifters, excepting only 'the shoplifting of books which appears largely a male prerogative' (p. 187), Medlicott found in his summation of the psychiatric evaluation results that depression resulting from losses of various types was the most important single factor which might be viewed as a common motivation.

In Canada, fifty convicted shoplifters were evaluated psychiatrically after sentencing in a further attempt to determine if shoplifting might be driven by a specific psychiatric syndrome: Bradford and Balmaceda (1983) subsequently disputed the frequent psychiatric assumption that 'females shoplift more than men … although more female shoplifters present for a psychiatric examination' (p. 251). Unfortunately, what might prove to be recurrent psychopathology in shoplifters of either gender usually will be missed, they contend, since recidivist shoplifters – either 'professionals' or the mentally disordered – seldom get referred for psychiatric examination. Shoplifting 'is not a specific psychiatric syndrome', they conclude, 'although psychiatric illness is clearly a factor in the shoplifting behaviour of a certain group of adult females' (p. 253).

In the United States – specifically in New York City, where the rate of drug addiction is high – James et al. (1979) found that the majority of almost three hundred females imprisoned for theft had shoplifted in order to get money for drugs. In a larger sample of almost five hundred women in prison in New York State, seven of ten were drug users who had shoplifted or worked as prostitutes or both in order to buy drugs.

Drug culture may have changed dramatically the patterns of those who shoplift, at least among those arrested and convicted of the offence (James et al. 1979).

In Britain during the latter part of the 1980s, criminal statistics from the Home Office seemed to indicate a substantial decrease – by over one-third – in the number of recorded shoplifters, Farrington and Burrows (1993) explain. Analysing and further investigating the data, in the face of insistence from retailers that shoplifting actually continues to rise unchecked, the authors conclude that, apart from what also may be a sharp drop in detection of offences, the main reason for the apparent decrease lies in the treatment of shoplifters after apprehension. Retailers and police alike show growing reluctance to record an offence by those under seventeen or over sixty, and the Crown Prosecution Service seems increasingly unlikely to suggest to the court custodial sentences for first-time offenders or those who have stolen items of minimal value. Those receiving custodial sentences may tend to be recidivists, many of them drug users, and the apparent 'steep decline in the number of recorded shoplifters must have been caused almost entirely by the actions of the police and/or the Crown Prosecution Service' (Farrington and Burrows 1993, p. 67).

Thus the multiple drug-related offences which have led Harriet to Holloway 'lots of times' fit the pattern now common to many convicted shoplifters serving custodial sentences in Britain. Her story will speak for those of many.

Born in an impoverished urban setting in the north, the eldest child of an uneducated teenage mother, Harriet cannot remember her father. When she was two, her mother moved in with a man who was able to provide a limited but steady income from criminal activity. Harriet recalls this period as happy and peaceful with few material wants.

> He were good to me. I call him my real dad, even though, he isn't ... Me mam was good to me, too. I think she spoilt me when I was little. She give me everything I asked for.

Life changed radically when Harriet was six. Her mother and 'father' split up. Tough times followed: there were no more treats and sometimes even basics were lacking. The mother soon went to live with Harriet's stepfather, and a baby sister was born when Harriet was seven. Financial problems persisted since the stepfather worked only occasionally and often spent his wages on drink. Angry and abusive at home when money ran short, he would hit Harriet's mother who would cry 'but not do nothin' – just take it'.

In contrast to what Harriet viewed as her mother's inaction stands her own behaviour. With no little glee, she describes herself as 'a tearaway, really bolshie. Always in trouble, one scrape after another. Hated school, sassed the teachers. I never learnt nothing there.' On the street, however, Harriet learned a great deal: she started taking drugs at the age of twelve, and shoplifted to feed the growing habit. At thirteen, she became the target of repeated sexual abuse by her stepfather but refuses to blame the abuse for her drug-taking which, she points out, started earlier. When she felt as a sixteen-year-old that she could no longer stand to be in the house with her stepfather, she moved to London to live. She did not run away, she emphasises, and her mother would have her back 'anytime'.

> The good thing is me mam believes me about me stepdad. She's always believed me, never said I made it up the way some girls' mams do. But she stays with 'im, like, so I don't have nowheres to go. I been in Holloway heaps of times, but then they chuck you out and there's nothing to go to. I live rough or in a squat. I go for a hit right away and in a few days I'm hooked again. I do 'em all. At first only E's and things, but now crack, H – whatever's going ... I shoplift to get money for drugs or sometimes stuff I need. I know what I'm doing. I'm not one of them what can't stop the'selves nickin' any old rubbish.

'THEM WHAT CAN'T STOP THE'SELVES NICKIN' ANY OLD RUBBISH'

Harriet may never have heard the term 'kleptomania', but she manages to give a clear and colourful description of the shoplifters that she has met in HMP Holloway who might fulfil the criteria for this diagnostic category. She – and, indeed, the 'kleptomaniac' shoplifters themselves – probably would be surprised to discover that two of history's notable kleptomaniacs were kings: Henri IV of France in the sixteenth century and Vittorio Emanuele I of Sardinia and Italy in the nineteenth century.

The kleptomania concept emerged early in the intellectual struggle to unravel the mysteries of the human mind. 'In the first astonishingly fertile period of psychiatry in Paris at the end of the 18th century', Gibbens and Prince (1962) recount, 'Pinel described what he called "mania without delirium" as a disease of the will-power, ... [an] illness of moral will-power shown in some cases of theft and homicide' that in 1810 Rush thought also might be similar in a psychological sense to 'the involuntary movements of convulsions' in the physiological arena (p. 68). Esquirol soon expanded further on Pinel's theorising, himself conjecturing that there could be a link between what he called the '"instinctive monomanias" – alcoholism, fire-setting and homicide –

where the patient "acts without passion or motive but only under involuntary instinctive impulse"' (ibid.).

The 'small but distinct subgroup of thieves (who) impulsively or compulsively steal worthless or unneeded objects, or objects easily obtainable by legitimate means ... was first described by Matthey in 1816 under the name "klopemanie"' (McElroy et al. 1991b, p. 93), including it in 'a list of manias that took in dipsomania (alcoholism), pyromania (fire-setting) and dromomania (running away)' (Gibbens and Prince 1962, p. 68). In 1838, in a case study published with Esquirol entitled 'On a case of suspected madness in a woman accused of theft', Marc became the first to refer to 'kleptomania', suggesting it *ex post facto* as a diagnosis for what might have ailed Henri IV and Vittorio Emanuele I (Gibbens and Prince 1962). The definition of 'kleptomania' conceived by Marc in 1838, as rendered by Wimmer in 1921, is 'a conscious urge to steal occurring in an individual in whom there is no ordinary disturbance in consciousness. The individual concerned frequently strives against this urge, but by its nature it is irresistible' (quoted in Aggernæs 1961, p. 1). Recalling the Rush conjecture on a physiological substratum for the behaviour, Wimmer added that in his view 'unconscious organic instincts may motivate kleptomania' with hunger, sexual excitement and pregnancy-related disturbance respectively playing a part in three cases that he treated (quoted in Aggernæs 1961, pp. 1–2).

In 1922, Stekel undertook a review of almost a century of medical literature on cases of kleptomania, adding insights gleaned from work with three cases of his own as well as two cases seen by assistants. A pupil of Freud, Stekel concurred with Wimmer in claiming that unconscious and ungratified sexual instinct is the 'driving power behind the thefts' (Aggernæs 1961, p. 3). However, as Aggernæs notes, it seems 'scarcely coincidence that the interest in the possible sexual genesis [of kleptomania] awoke approximately simultaneously with ... publication' (ibid.) of major works by Freud on libidinal theories of neurosis. From the five cases that Stekel presented, he concluded that in kleptomania there exists a sexual psychogenesis with homosexuality possibly latent; that the act of theft takes place in a state of 'clouding of consciousness' (p. 4); and that the impulsive thefts constitute a 'repetitive compulsion' (ibid.). Beyond the sexual psychogenesis theory of kleptomania – also favoured by Fenichel (1996[1945]) – Stekel emphasised 'how numerous the motives may be for the kleptomaniac's behaviour', Aggernæs notes (p. 5). There is no suggestion that he felt kleptomania to be exclusive to females or the middle and upper classes.

Yet, the figure of the well-to-do kleptomaniac female seized by irresistible sexual urges beyond her control, as presented in the Marc and
Esquirol case study, seemed to take hold in the creative consciousness
rather more readily than did the notion of kleptomaniac kings (or, for
example, Stekel's stolid village spinster who stole pairs of military socks,
a bag of sugar and a bull that she could not pay for but also did not need
or want). Madame de Boves, the kleptomaniac shoplifter created by Zola
in *Au Bonheur des Dames*, is depicted as 'ravaged' by the will to rob:

> For a year she had been stealing like this, ravaged by a furious, irresistible
> need. The attacks had got worse, increasing until they had become a
> sensual pleasure necessary to her existence, sweeping before them all
> prudent reasoning ... [S]he was stealing with pockets full of money, stealing
> for stealing's sake, ... spurred on by desire, possessed by the neurosis which
> her unsatisfied appetite for luxury had developed within her when
> confronted by the enormous, brutal temptation of the department stores
> (1980[1883], p. 516).

In a less sensationalised fashion than in Zola's overblown and overtly
sexual prose, the kleptomaniac shoplifter – who was both female and
able to pay for the goods taken – did indeed emerge in the early days
of the department store. Documented in *When Ladies Go A-Thieving*, a
study of shopping and shoplifting in turn-of-the-century America,
Abelson (1989) suggests that in that historical time of transition in
much of the industrialised world, society could more readily accept the
seemingly mystifying behaviour of these affluent but larcenous ladies,
if able to place the behaviour firmly within an illness model. In this
way, says Abelson, 'neither the excesses of the institutions nor
consumer capitalism were indicted. The fault lay within the women
themselves' (p. 12).

Kleptomania and shoplifting may be viewed more appropriately as
concentric circles that coincide partially but not completely: as Tiebout
and Kirkpatrick (1932) note in their review of motives for theft that
includes the compulsion to steal, some shoplifters but not all are kleptomaniacs, and some kleptomaniacs but not all are shoplifters since
the former steal not only from shops or stores but also from other
individuals, libraries, museums, private homes and workplaces.

Although taking root in public perception as synonymous with
kleptomania, the stereotypical well-to-do female represents only one
among many who may present the syndrome. In the comprehensive
review of medical, psychoanalytic and psychological literature on
kleptomania that Aggernæs completed in 1961, he concludes that the
common theme in most cases is neither gender (since both males and
females are represented in the cases examined) nor socio-economic

class (since those unable to pay for what they have stolen also manifest kleptomaniac theft), but, rather, what Stekel had called '"a condition of clouded consciousness" or altered consciousness' at the moment of the theft (Aggernæs 1961, p. 5). In Aggernæs's own work with nine cases of kleptomania seen between 1953 and 1957, both men and women as well as all classes of society were represented.

Gender and economic circumstances are not the only areas of disagreement associated with the kleptomania concept. Lack of unanimity extends even to spelling, with Fenichel (1996[1945]) and others preferring 'cleptomania'; to whether the term best describes the syndrome, with Socarides (1954) suggesting 'pathological stealing ... [since] "cleptomania" is neither a form of mania nor a clinical entity' (p. 246); and, as Socarides states, to whether kleptomania should exist as a separate diagnostic category, with Antheaume (1925), Abelson (1989) and others supporting Socarides's view (cited in McElroy et al. 1991b).

However, the *Diagnostic and Statistical Manual of Mental Disorders (DSM IV)*, published by the American Psychiatric Association, and the *International Classification of Diseases (ICD 10)*, put out by the World Health Organisation, list kleptomania as a clearly defined diagnostic category. The *DSM IV* (1994) places it, together with intermittent explosive disorder, pathological gambling, pyromania and trichotillomania, under 'impulse control disorders not elswhere classified'. McElroy et al. (1992) suggest that 'members of this ... category [also may] include repetitive self-mutilation ..., compulsive shopping ["oniomania"] ..., compulsive sexual behavior ..., and compulsive facial picking' (p. 318)). Kleptomania's essential feature is 'recurrent failure to resist impulses to steal objects not needed for personal use or their monetary value; the objects taken are either given away, discarded, returned surreptitiously, or kept and hidden'; the individual 'experiences an increasing sense of tension' before theft, 'pleasure or relief' during it but then 'signs of depression, anxiety and guilt about the possibility or actuality' of detection (*DSM IV* 1994, p. 322).

Keutzer (1972) noted that, in spite of the frequency with which kleptomania appears in the relevant literature, treatment modalities seldom are discussed. From a behavioural perspective, Keutzer recounts her own successful treatment of a single case by operant conditioning, while Glover (1985) reports successfully using aversive conditioning (covert sensitisation) in a single case. From a psychodynamic perspective, Fishbain (1987) suggests that, in the case of a patient who stole compulsively and masturbated during or immediately after theft, recalling a similar case reported by Fenichel (1996[1945]), kleptomania seemed to be 'a risk-taking response to depression and therefore can be thought of as a symptom-relief mechanism' (1987, p. 603); the patient was treated successfully in a psychodynamic way combined with medication.

In a study of twenty patients with kleptomania, strictly diagnosed according to the criteria in *DSM III-R* (the 1978 precursor of *DSM IV* and identical to it as regards kleptomania), McElroy et al. (1991a) looked at a group including both males and females (no information is given as to socio-economic class). The researchers say that most patients 'found the urges [to steal] senseless, intrusive and ego-dystonic, some reported pleasurable feelings during the act of theft, variously described as "a rush", "a thrill", "high", "euphoric", or "manic". All patients stated that they considered their stealing to be wrong' (1991a, p. 654). Other disorders associated with kleptomania in patients in this sample were 'bulimia nervosa with or without anorexia nervosa, obsessive-compulsive disorder, and alcohol abuse or dependence. Most of the bulimic patients stole food as well as items other than food' (McElroy et al. 1991a, p. 654). (A significantly higher incidence of kleptomania amongst diagnosed bulimics than amongst the general population already had been noted by Casper et al. (1980).)

As a result of this work, McElroy et al. (1991a) conclude that kleptomania 'may represent an underdiagnosed disorder' (p. 657) far more common than previously supposed, and further emphasise that it 'is an inadequately studied disorder' (McElroy et al. 1991b, p. 106). They hypothesise (1991b) that 'a relationship exists between kleptomania and obsessive-compulsive disorder, eating disorders and major mood disorders, raising the possibility that these four diagnostic categories are members of an extended family of disorders' (1991b, p. 105) which the authors term 'affective spectrum disorder' – all responding positively to similar types of mood-altering medication. Noting that kleptomania and other impulse control disorders such as pathological gambling 'may be related to mood disorders, alcohol and psychoactive substance abuse and anxiety disorders [especially obsessive-compulsive disorder]' (1992, p. 318), McElroy et al. point out that these impulse control disorders 'might be better conceived as addictive disorders ... [since] the irresistible impulse to steal or gamble resembles the urge to drink or use drugs' (p. 323).

McElroy et al. (1994) further note, in a study of twenty cases of oniomania or compulsive buying, features similar to those of kleptomania such as the self-reported experience of an 'irresistible or uncontrollable' urge, an altered state of awareness during the act 'variously described as "a 'high' like taking cocaine", "a buzz", "a rush", or "like taking a narcotic"' (p. 243) and subsequent feelings of shame and guilt.

Kleptomania and compulsive buying also share the condition of 'secret disorders', concealed insofar as possible from family and friends (McElroy 1994, p. 246). These two disorders, together with binge-eating, 'have received little systematic study and remain poorly understood' (ibid.), perhaps making up a 'family of compulsive-impulsive spectrum disorders, which in turn may belong to the larger family of affective spectrum disorder' (McElroy et al. 1995, p. 14).

The 'middle-aged woman of blameless reputation who has stolen for quite unexplained motives some object of little value which she could easily have afforded to buy', noted frequently by Gibbens and Prince (1962, p. 5) amongst the recorded shoplifters of two generations ago, today has largely disappeared from the ranks of those imprisoned for shoplifting offences. With cheque books and credit cards to hand, even when spending more than can reasonably be afforded, the middle-class individual seems to play out the same pathology in a different way in a different setting: compulsive buyers report that 'having access to credit cards, money, shopping catalogs, or home shopping television programs seemed to "enable" their compulsive buying' (McElroy et al. 1995, p. 18).

For those compulsive individuals so far down the socioeconomic ladder as to have no access to the instruments of the legal money economy, instruments that would 'enable' them to shop either normally or compulsively, choice is severely restricted. Kleptomaniac shoplifting may be the recourse used when compulsive shopping is not an option.

'Olivia', a thirty-two-year-old drug dealer serving a sentence in HMP Holloway for a single shoplifting offence because of a prior record of drug-related crimes, has never had a cheque book or credit card. Her own behaviour puzzles her deeply.

> I dunno why I did it. For nothing, for kicks, I guess, I dunno. I only took a fucking pair of socks. Can you believe it? Banged up in this place for a fucking pair of socks?! Wasn't nothin' goin' through me mind. Can't remember nothin'. I must have been out of me skull, off me head. Dunno why I did it. It wasn't even fun. And I never wear socks anyway.

A WORLD AWAY FROM HOLLOWAY

'Pilar' literally trembles when she says the word 'Holloway'. Yet, with several recorded offences and cautions by magistrates' courts behind her, she knows that another arrest for shoplifting inevitably will mean a custodial sentence there. In desperation, she seeks psychotherapeutic help for a lifelong pattern: shopping and shoplifting to obtain goods that she does not need or want.

A middle-class immigrant from Latin America, Pilar – not the name by which she is known – came to London more than a decade ago. Leaving behind a fragmented family – a mother who died when she was an infant, a remarried father and an unyielding stepmother who relegated Pilar and her younger sister to a dreary convent school – she immigrated in order to learn English well and study for a career in a medically related profession such as nursing or midwifery. Neither goal has been achieved. She works as a live-in housekeeper for a well-to-do family, earning a good salary which she is free to spend as she wishes.

> I buy what I like for myself. I like to buy. If I want face cream, then face cream; if I want a pair of shoes, then a pair of shoes. I feel satisfied when I buy something nice.

In a continuation of behaviour that began when she started taking small items that belonged to her hated stepmother and later to the convent sisters, Pilar also takes things without paying.

> I feel so good when I get something. I see beautiful things and I want them for myself. I like brand names – the best things going – a Moschino dress, for example. I only go to Harrods or Harvey Nichols ... Then I come home and look at my room. I have so many things sitting around – things of no use to me. I look at them and ask myself: why so many shoes, why so many dresses. They don't do anything for me once I've got them home. Why, I hardly ever go out! I want to stop getting so many things but I just can't.

REFERENCES

Abelson, E. (1989) *When Ladies Go A-Thieving*. Oxford, Oxford University Press.
Adburgham, A. (1964) *Shops and Shopping*. London, George Allen and Unwin Ltd.
Aggernæs, M. (1961) A Study of Kleptomania with Illustrative Cases. *Acta Psychiatrica et Neurologica Scandinavica* 36 (1), 1–46.
Allen, A. (1965) Stealing as a Defense. *The Psychoanalytic Quarterly* 34, 572–83.
Baren, M. (1998) *Victorian Shopping*. London, Michael O'Mara Books Limited.
Benjamin, W. (1973) *Illuminations*. London, Fontana.
Bradford, J. and Balmaceda, R. (1983) Shoplifting: Is there a specific psychiatric syndrome? *Canadian Journal of Psychiatry* 28, 248–54.
Campbell, C. (1997) Shopping, Pleasure and the Sex War. In P. Falk and C. Campbell (eds) *The Shopping Experience*, London, Sage Publications.
Casper, R., Eckert, E., Halmi, K., Goldberg, S. and Davis, J. (1980) Bulimia: Its incidence and clinical importance in patients with Anorexia Nervosa. *Archives of General Psychiatry* 37, 1030–46.
Chesney-Lind, M. (1997) *The Female Offender: Girls, women and crime*. London, Sage Publications.
Couch, D. (1989) *Retailing*. London, Penguin.

Davies, G. (1994) *A History of Money*. Cardiff, University of Wales Press.

Diagnostic and Statistical Manual/Fourth Edition (1994). Washington DC, American Psychiatric Association.

Epps, P. (1962) Women Shoplifters in Holloway Prison. In Gibbens, T. and Prince, J. (1962) *Shoplifting*. London, Institute for the Study and Treatment of Delinquency.

Farrington, D. and Burrows, J. (1993) Did Shoplifting Really Decrease? *British Journal of Criminology* 33 (1), 57–69.

Fenichel, O. (1996[1945]) *The Psychoanalytic Theory of Neuroses*. London and New York, Routledge.

Fishbain, D. (1987) Kleptomania as Risk-Taking Behaviour in Response to Depression. *American Journal of Psychotherapy* XLI, 598–603.

Fredriksson, C. (1997) The Making of Swedish Department Store Culture. In P. Falk and C. Campbell (eds) *The Shopping Experience*, London, Sage Publications.

Freud, S. (1916) Some Character-Types Met With in Psycho-Analytic Work: (III) Criminals from a sense of guilt. *The Standard Edition of the Complete Psychological Works* Volume XIV, translated and edited by J. Strachey, London, Hogarth Press and the Institute of Psycho-Analysis, 1953–1974.

Gibbens, T. and Prince, J. (1962) *Shoplifting*. London, Institute for the Study and Treatment of Delinquency.

Glover, J. (1985) A Case of Kleptomania Treated by Covert Sensitization. *British Journal of Clinical Psychology* 24, 213–14.

James, J., Gosho, C. and Wohl, R. (1979) The Relationship Between Female Criminality and Drug Use. *International Journal of Addiction* 14 (2), 215–29.

Keutzer, C. (1972) Kleptomania: A direct approach to treatment. *British Journal of Medical Psychology* 45, 159–63.

Litwinski, L. (1951) Toward the Reinstatement of the Concept of the Self. *British Journal of Psychology* 42, 246–9.

McElroy, S., Pope, H., Hudson, J., Keck, P. and White, K. (1991a) Kleptomania: A report of 20 cases. *American Journal of Psychiatry* 148 (5), 652–7.

McElroy, S., Hudson, J., Pope, H. and Keck, P. (1991b) Kleptomania: Clinical characteristics and associated psychopathology. *Psychological Medicine* 21, 93–108.

McElroy, S., Hudson, J., Pope, H., Keck, P. and Aizley, H. (1992) The DSM-III-R Impulse Control Disorders Not Elsewhere Classified: Clinical characteristics and relationship to other psychiatric disorders. *American Journal of Psychiatry* 149 (1), 318–27.

McElroy, S., Keck, P., Pope, H., Smith, J. and Strakowski, S. (1994) Compulsive Buying: A report of 20 cases. *Journal of Clinical Psychiatry* 55 (6), 242–8.

McElroy, S., Keck, P. and Phillips, K. (1995) Kleptomania, Compulsive Buying and Binge-Eating Disorder. *Journal of Clinical Psychiatry* 55 (56/suppl. 4), 14–26.

Medlicott, R. (1968) Fifty Thieves. *New Zealand Medical Journal* 67 (248), 183–8.

Nava, M. (1997) Modernity's Disavowal: Women, the city and department store. In P. Falk and C. Campbell (eds) *The Shopping Experience*, London, Sage Publications.

Roheim, G. (1927) Primal Forms and the Origin of Property. In E. Borneman (ed.) *The Psychoanalysis of Money*, New York, Urizen Books (1976[1973]).

Rudmin, F. (1990) The Economic Psychology of Leon Litwinski. *Journal of Economic Psychology* 11, 307–39.

Socarides, C. (1954) Pathological Stealing as a Reparative Move of the Ego. *The Psychoanalytic Review* XLI, 246–52.

Tiebout, H. and Kirkpatrick, M. (1932) Psychiatric Factors in Stealing. *American Journal of Orthopsychiatry* II, 114–23.

Welldon, E. and van Velsen, C. (1997) *A Practical Guide to Forensic Psychotherapy*. London and Bristol, Pennsylvania, Jessica Kingsley Publishers.

Woddis, G. (1957–58) Depression and Crime. *The British Journal of Delinquency* VIII, 85–94.

Zola, E. (1980[1883]) *Au Bonheur des Dames*. Paris, Editions Gallimard.

4

Gifts of Life: An Existential Approach to Shopping Addiction

Simon du Plock

He bought presents for everyone, overhauled his room, wrote out resolutions ... How foolish his aims had been! He had tried to build a breakwater of order and elegance against the sordid tide of life without him and to dam up, by rules of conduct ... the powerful recurrence of the tides within him. Useless. From without as from within the water had flowed over his barriers: their tides began once more to jostle fiercely above the crumbled mole. He saw clearly too his own futile isolation. (Joyce 1992, pp. 104–5)

The study and treatment of addiction has been one of the fastest growing areas of psychotherapy over the last decade. Addiction constitutes a major success story and testing ground for therapists since it is almost universally perceived as a social evil as much as an individual tragedy, and our work has been of considerable importance in the increasing willingness of society and individuals to view this condition as a quasi-medical problem rather than one of personal morality; the addict, then, is the victim of an illness rather than a misfit or criminal.

As our perception of addiction has changed it has become more widely acceptable and even fashionable. The entry of a relatively less negative concept of addiction seems to have provided an answer for a large number of people who wish to arrive at an understanding of their own repetitive or destructive behaviour. People routinely describe themselves as addicts of any number of substances; it is, in fact difficult to imagine anything which can be consumed in any way which could not now be considered the object of an addiction. Indeed, in popular usage repetition of, or even the wish to repeat, an activity is taken as adequate evidence for addiction. This is a considerable distance from the *DSM IV* definition of addiction with which therapists are familiar; this change may, perhaps, be linked to a more general shift in our perception of ourselves as consumers. We talk of ourselves as consumers of all aspects of living (it is probably only a matter of time before we begin to view ourselves as consumers of death too), and it logically follows that we can be addicted to sex, food, exercise, television, the internet ... There is no single activity of life (including consuming psychotherapy and counselling) which remains outside this circle of potential addiction, as the title of this book indicates. It is hard to find many references to shopping addiction prior to 1990, and even four or five years ago the suggestion that such a phenomenon existed would probably have met with incredulity if not derision.

We need to ask whether, when the concept of addiction has become so transmuted, it any longer has any essential meaning at all: are we, perhaps, adopting the attitude of Humpty Dumpty and saying that when we use a word it means exactly what we want it to mean? We need also to consider whether the broadening of the concept of addiction might not lead, indeed may already have led, to a trivialising of an experience which can, for some people, be intensely distressing.

It is worth recalling, though, that incredulity and derision have often been the initial reactions to conditions which have gone on to be widely acknowledged and do not necessarily indicate more than a defensive reaction against a new idea. In any case if books have been written on the subject then it seems to follow that it must exist. By writing about it we invent it. It is a fact that relatively large numbers of people describe themselves as shopping addicts. They would have described themselves differently before the term 'shopping addict' became available to them. What is of interest, and the approach to this situation which perhaps provides the greatest opportunity for therapeutic work, is to discover what it is that the individual is experiencing when he or she refers to a phenomenon using the convenient and relatively socially acceptable rubric of 'shopping addiction'. It is also important to view the individual as active in this process and to ask what the function of the 'addiction' is for them, and what their life would be like were the 'addiction' to be in some way removed. Alongside this, we should also ask what therapy would look like if the concept of addiction were viewed in this way; what the function of addiction is for psychotherapy is as pertinent as the question of what the function of psychotherapy is for the addict.

To summarise, then, just as it is important to know how the meaning of addiction has changed, so it is important to arrive at an understanding of its meaning at the level of the individual client. If we take this meaning as the focus of therapy and its understanding as the locus of therapeutic change we will also affect a shift in the way in which therapy is delivered.

INTRODUCTION

When I was approached with the idea that I might contribute to a text on 'shopping addiction' my initial reaction was to be intrigued by the idea, but also nonplussed. It should be clear from even my outline of the existential-phenomenological approach below that existential psychotherapists generally eschew placing labels on their clients or putting them into categories. We are often criticised for this as if it were rooted in misguided liberalism, lack of an appreciation of the horrors which can attend on mental illness, or both. The idea seems to be that we cannot hope to work successfully with the clients whom we have not designated according to the strictures of the *Diagnostic and Statistical Manual*. In fact few, if any, qualified existential therapists are ignorant of such instruments; their critiques of such diagnostic aids have been influential in refining them for the general good.

Our wish to avoid labels cuts, in fact, to a basic premise of existentialism, namely that human beings, rather than having a 'fixed' or essential nature like a tree or a stone or a table, are constantly in process, are constantly choosing themselves. In Sartre's well-known formulation, '... man first of all exists, encounters himself, surges up in the world – and defines himself afterwards' (1943, p. 290). Existence, then, preceeds essence. So it is that, as Warnock (1970) has noted, existential philosophers have been wary of describing themselves as existential philosophers since labels attempt to fix what is process, and to limit its freedom. Clearly then, the notion of writing about shopping addiction, with its implicit assumption that I could identify one or more of my past or present clients as a sufferer of this particular 'condition' was problematic. Nevertheless the concept of addiction itself raises interesting questions for the existential therapist.

Existential therapists are, in general, extremely sceptical about the notion of 'addiction' because it appears to run counter to something fundamental about being human and, therefore, also to a fundamental tenet of their approach, that is, the freedom which we all have to make decisions about our lives. Much has been written on freedom by existential philosophers and therapists and I do not propose to go in any detail into this area. Few existential therapists, though, have written about addiction *per se* since they do not categorise their clients as addicts. To do so would be to view meaning-making clients as less autonomous and more restricted than they are. This view, which may appear at first sight to fly in the face of reason, is not limited to existentialists. Drew, a critic of the disease concept of addiction, writing in the *Drug and Alcohol Review* in 1990, stated

> Those of us who have contributed to the literature about models of drug dependence, have indulged in irrelevancies. We have pursued an absolute scientific course rather than responding to existential needs. We have produced a psycho-bio-social model of drug dependence that excludes the essence of human existence – options, freedom to choose and the centrality of human values. (pp. 207–10)

I would agree with Bergmark and Oscarsson (1987) that 'repetitive behaviour signifies a decision to relinquish choice'. For me the most useful thing for the therapist to do is to enable clients to clarify the meaning of their behaviour to themselves. Existential therapists are not, of course, a homogeneous group; of those who have written on this issue, Wurm (in du Plock 1997), discussing a client's use of alcohol, is particularly useful. He agrees, in his work with clients, that repetitive behaviour is about deciding not to exercise control. Writing about a particular client Wurm says that he was concerned to look at the fundamental issue of what makes life meaningful for him. The client

> ... was then able to reflect on the choices he had been making, and the possibilities available to him in the future. I remember asking him what he liked about drinking, but not about the meaning it had for him. When we did talk about meaning, Harold was certainly clear that there were other things that would help make his life more meaningful in the future, and that they would not be possible unless he changed his drinking. (1997, p. 155)

Many clients are disappointed to find that their existential therapist does not subscribe to the concept of addiction just as they are often disappointed not to be labelled with the term schizophrenic or some other mental illness category since such a label is thought to explain their dis-ease with life and to bring in its wake a specific treatment which the expert therapist can conduct on the passive client. The client, in short, is rescued from considering his own responsibility for his situation.

Consequently, then, I do not 'treat' my clients for any form of addiction – and this includes 'shopping addiction', but rather am concerned to explore with them the behaviour they describe to me.

Whether therapists seek to elucidate the meaning which the behaviour has for the client, or explore their value system, probably makes little difference: the aim is to increase the client's awareness of their way of being in the world. As Cohn, in his critique of the notion of an unconscious, expresses it

> It is the quality of our engagement with what appears to us in the world that determines the degree of our awareness. If we are no longer aware of what appears to us, it has not gone away to some intra-psychic place from where it might return. *Our* awareness has moved away from it, *we* have disengaged ourselves. (1996, p. 81)

If, though, we return to the notion of addiction as it is currently utilised in the *Diagnostic and Statistical Manual*, Edition Four, which underpins the work of medically trained mental health workers, and which provides a challenge to all those of us who seek to find meaning in the behaviour of those who experience psychological dis-ease, we find that the function of the category 'addiction', as a condition 'out there in the world' to which the addict falls prey tends to remove responsibility from both client and therapist.

I would like to suggest that the job of the existential therapist is precisely to reintroduce the concept of responsibility in those experiences which are so often considered either as illnesses which are visited upon helpless victims or as emanating in some manner from unconscious desires which the client cannot make sense of without the expert assistance of an analyst or psychodynamically trained therapist. Psychoanalysis operates on the basis that the client needs the insights of an expert. The Twelve Step Programme, that other refuge of the 'addict', starts from the premiss that the client must put his faith in the counsellor. The existential approach, in contrast, may appear somewhat harsh – after all the client is burdened enough with his distressing behaviour without the added problem of admitting his responsibility for it. In answer to this we may cite research which demonstrates that suicidal clients experience great relief when therapists acknowledge that they can, indeed, exercise the freedom and choice to kill themselves. It seems that an acknowledgement of responsibility can bring with it an awareness of power and capability. Essentially, acknowledging the possibility that clients can end their lives can lead them on to consider how they are living their lives and how they might want to live them in the future.

All of these doubts and provisos, though, spurred me on rather than discouraged me since they suggested that an existential perspective on this subject – which has become increasingly the subject of public speculation and interest over the last few years – might offer some new insights. Practitioners of the existential-phenomenological approach have been keen to make it intelligible to other therapists and to the general public. Since the American psychiatrist Irvin Yalom began to popularise the approach via his *Love's Executioner and Other Tales of Psychotherapy* (1989), writers based in the UK have followed this lead. The case study – the story of the collaborative venture of a therapist and client to explore the clients' lived world – lends itself to such an exploration.

As regards identifying a client who had presented for therapy as a shopping addict I still have difficulties. I had, however, worked intensively with a client, Paul, in weekly sessions over a two-year period and one of the areas of his life which he was concerned to look at had as its focus his need to bestow gifts to his immediate family and the compulsion to shop for these gifts. This behaviour, and his wish to understand it, formed one of the main reasons why Paul entered therapy. The theme of gift-giving ran through the first year of our work and it is this aspect of the therapy which I present in this chapter.

THE EXISTENTIAL-PHENOMENOLOGICAL APPROACH

Since I shall be considering the concept of shopping addiction from the perspective of existential-phenomenological psychotherapy, I shall outline, however briefly, the core characteristics of this approach. Numerous texts have been written devoted to a more comprehensive account of both its philosophy and practice, and the interested reader is referred to van Deurzen (1988, 1997), Cohn (1996), du Plock (1997), Spinelli (1989, 1997) and Yalom (1980), each of whom will provide further leads into this complex but rewarding orientation. For my present purpose I will limit myself to six assumptions which together provide the foundation of existential-phenomenological client work:

1. Human beings are 'thrown' into the world, in the sense that they find themselves in a situation which is given rather than chosen. A baby cannot choose to be born into one family, with a different set of circumstances, rather than another, or to be born with particular physical attributes and genetic profile. Similarly, as we are all born so shall we all die. While we cannot choose these 'existential givens' we can choose our response to them and it is in doing so that we create our own values and our own life. As Sartre expresses it, 'Man is condemned to be free.' While this may seem quite clear, given some reflection many clients (indeed all of us at certain times) resist such an active

view of their place in the world, preferring to attribute the shape of their life to fate, chance, economics, upbringing, or a hundred other 'external' factors which can be pressed into service.

2. Since human beings are thrown into the world it makes no sense to attempt to understand them without also coming to grips with their context. This is necessarily true of human beings in the therapeutic relationship; neither client nor therapist is present in the consulting room as simply client or therapist. As Cohn (1994) expresses it: 'When we see a client his/her family, partner, social nexus etc. are also present in the room. For the existential therapist, there is in fact no "individual" therapy.' This must also be the case for the therapist, though their personal world should not be permitted to impinge inappropriately on the client's work. In existential therapy, as distinct from psychoanalytic or psychodynamic therapy, it is understood that the therapist should not, indeed cannot, be a blank screen.

3. Since it is the 'phenomena' – those things which appear – that are of concern in existential therapy, the therapist should take care to be open to this and to engage with it as fully as possible. The therapist generally stays in the here and now of the client's experience rather than importing normative theories or gathering evidence from previous sessions to support the hypotheses which such theories entail.

4. Just as clients invariably bring their context into therapy, so they bring their past and their hopes and fears for the future as well as their experience of the present moment. Existential therapy is often misunderstood as discounting the past, but this is not so. However, it does reject the reductionistic notion so often encountered in therapy that the past 'causes' the present since such a deterministic approach denies the ability of humans to be creative and to make choices about their lives. Many clients restrict themselves to living only in the past, or the present or future, and in such cases much of the work in therapy is concerned with enabling the client to experience himself or herself in relation to all three.

5. The existential approach is concerned with the whole being of the client and rejects dichotomies such as mind and body, or psyche and soma. The way in which we relate to our body cannot be split off from any other of the dimensions on which we encounter the world.

6. If we can choose our response to those aspects of our lives which are given, it follows that we can also fail to choose or can make choices

which do not really reflect our needs. This necessitates the formulation of types of anxiety and guilt which are distinct from neurotic anxiety and guilt. The feelings we experience as a result of our attempts to evade authenticity are of a specifically existential nature and should be approached as such if they are to be worked with.

The account of my work with 'Paul' will, I hope, illustrate the way in which these characteristics impact on client work. In particular I intend to illustrate how Paul's response to the existential givens of loss and isolation, and extinction in death, placed stultifying limitations on his freedom to choose his own life. In working with him on clarifying this block to freedom we found that we were working with his immediate family too, insofar as he was able to describe these relationships in the context of therapy. I was concerned to stay as close as possible to Paul's account of his way of being in the world. It was tempting to introduce 'expert hunches' about, say, his sexuality or early life experiences but I generally refrained from doing so since they would have been more about my need to remind myself that I was the therapist in this encounter than anything deriving from Paul's account of himself in the here and now. In therapeutic communication, as so often in ordinary conversation, less is more. While I strove to 'bracket' – to set aside – my own phantasies about the cause of Paul's difficulties, perhaps precisely because I generally succeeded in doing so, there emerged in the here-and-now of the therapeutic encounter a fairly clear picture of his view of past, present and future and the fears which pertained to each. The existential rather than neurotic nature of the anxiety which Paul experienced as a direct result of the choices he had made indicated existential therapy and contraindicated approaches which would have failed to engage fully with this existential material.

THE CLIENT

Spinelli has written of existential-phenomenological theory that it

> ... presents us with a view of human existence that places *anxiety* at its centre. It suggests that our experience of living is never certain, never fully predictable, never secure. Instead, our very embracing of life presents us with all manner of 'challenges': challenges to the meanings we have built up and live by, challenges to the aims and purposes with which we imbue our lives, challenges, indeed, to the very continuation of our existence. Our responses to any or all of these challenges can range from an attempt to create a protected environment that will repel any perceived threats to our sense of physical or psychic security, to the undertaking to foster a chaotic lifestyle

which, paradoxically, fixes its meaning and purpose upon the unwavering belief that 'all is meaningless'. (1997, p. 6)

Paul's story, as it unfolded, represented perhaps the most extreme of the former of these responses that I have met with in my own work as a therapist. His attitude towards gift-giving and shopping provides an example of his strategies for keeping his world safe. By the time he came to see me this strategy had failed and was now a further source of the insecurity it was intended to counter. In appearance he was dapper, very neatly dressed in a well-cut grey suit. I recall noticing that though it was a dry day in early summer he clutched a tightly furled umbrella. His shoes shone with polish. Having first noticed his clothes, I turned my attention to his face – the reverse of the order in which I usually find myself responding to prospective clients. What I saw was a pleasant, if harassed, expression, framed by a schoolboyish severe haircut, his dark hair almost scraped back from an old-fashioned side parting. He was, all-in-all, a youngish, almost boyish man encased in rather too-old clothes. I estimated his age at no more than thirty, an impression which was subsequently confirmed when Paul told me that he was twenty-eight, but on writing up my usual very brief notes on this interview later the same day I found myself jotting down Virginia Woolf's description of the young T. S. Eliot as wearing a 'four-piece suit', and I wondered whether Paul would be able to bear to unbutton himself in therapy and allow himself to breathe more easily. My overall impression of Paul at this first meeting was one of immense, barely contained distress and a desperate need to talk. Over the next few weeks I found myself listening to the story of his life. I rarely prompt clients in our early meetings, or give pointers about the direction I feel they should take in their accounts of themselves. The way in which they appear, the business of telling me about themselves, their hesitancy, the assumptions of shared understandings they take for granted, their reluctance to grasp some parts of their story directly, all tell me as much about their way of being in the world as do the words themselves.

Paul was no exception to this: he was meticulous in his presentation of himself; he, as it were, began at the beginning and went on until he had reached the present. For the next two months he told me about himself in great detail; more important he told himself about himself. He had had, he said, an idyllic childhood. It could not, simply could not, have been better. It did indeed sound idyllic. He painted a picture of a childhood which seemed to belong in the 1930s or 1950s rather than the late 1960s and early 1970s. It was a world in which the sun always shone, a world of endless warmth and unconditional love. Paul had been brought up in the genteel suburbs of a big city, the first child of doting parents. It was a close, loving family, with perhaps a tendency to be rather insular and self-sufficient. Both parents, though, were ambitious for their son and saved hard and coached him into a prestigious public school as a day boy. Any suggestion by his teachers that he might board was instantly dismissed by Paul's mother, much to his own relief. Such a separation, on either side, was unthinkable. Paul was a clever child who flourished intellectually and quickly showed a talent for Latin and Greek which he would pursue later at university.

This idyll was to continue for some years: Paul proudly carried home glowing reports of his latest academic achievements at the end of every term and his parents felt that he was in every way the ideal son – obedient, hard-working, kind and considerate to a fault. Even the birth of a sister when he was eight years old added to, rather than diminished, the feeling of love and security in which Paul basked. He did not perceive her as a rival since she was so much younger and in time he began to coach her (as his parents had coached him) in order to get her into a prestigious school.

Asked if in this account of an invariably happy childhood he had any recollection of the usual ups and downs, rows and disagreements of family life, Paul could think of none: the only possible cloud in this blue sky was the death of his maternal grandfather who had lived nearby when he was eleven. He did not dwell on this though, but quickly returned to his account of happy days. I wondered what it must be like, given that he had come to see me and was clearly distressed about some aspects of his life, to recall such a wonderful childhood; it seemed to me the contrast must be a painful one. Many of my clients come to see me, I told Paul, because they feel that things had gone wrong in their childhood, yet he had spent several sessions impressing upon me just how perfect his own had been. He responded to this observation somewhat heatedly, saying

> But that's exactly the problem. I'm in a far worse position than your clients who come to you moaning about their terrible childhood experiences. For them there must be some hope that things can improve. But I've had the best of my life. Nothing in the future can compare with the times I had as a child. I have nothing left to look forward to, everything good is in the past.

I reflected back to Paul that it sounded as though, unlike my other clients, he could have no hope of improvement. Yet the fact that he had come to see me suggested that he did hope for something. After I had spoken he was silent for several minutes before looking up from the floor and saying, in a very low voice,

'I've come now because I'm frightened.'
'Of what, of the future?'
'Yes of the future ... of growing up and growing older. Not just that, though. There is something else now, something new: I'm scared of what I might do, I'm scared that I'm having violent thoughts and fantasies. I even wonder if I could lose control and actually be violent ... something has to break.'

In this first session, and for several months to come, it seemed that Paul's distress lay in anxiety about his ability to grow up and to go out into the world to forge his own identity. The idyllic childhood which he described functioned to trap him in his early experiences of being loved and nurtured. In contrast, the project of constructing his own life which, necessarily, would involve developing relationships, perhaps of a caring, intimate nature with others outside his immediate family circle, seemed initially irrelevant. When I raised this as a possibility in subsequent sessions, pointing out that I had noticed how rarely he mentioned anyone beyond his family, he was at first dismissive and, when challenged, angry that I should introduce 'irrelevancies'. It did, indeed, seem that everything good was in his past and that nothing in the future could match the quality of these relationships or, worse, compensate for their inevitable loss.

In some respects this was, quite literally, a hopeless situation for both client and therapist: it was certainly not the case that I could stop the march of time, let alone magically transport Paul back to his childhood. It is important in successful therapeutic work to validate to an appropriate degree the story of the client; the therapist who denies the client's emotions, who refuses to empathise with the client's experience of life, cannot hope to build a therapeutic alliance capable of weathering the turbulence which therapy generally entails. At the same time, merely to validate the clients' version of events is to deny them an alternative perspective on their problems – the challenge of the other which, withheld, makes authentic engagement impossible but which employed judiciously can free clients to see themselves in a different light. In working with Paul, I felt that his wish was that I should join him in grieving over the loss of the past. At the same time, the fact that he was coming regularly suggested that he had an urgent need to disentangle himself from this way of thinking. While finitude is an existential given, our response to it is a choice. Paul's decision to see the absurdity of life, its essential meaninglessness, as an insurmountable tragedy was seductive because it let him off the hook of needing to make his own meaning in life. I felt the seductive power of it myself, and had to bracket (set aside) my own tendency to dwell on the ultimate futility of life.

Curiosity, initially the therapist's, and as therapy progresses curiosity on the part of the client too, can provide a way of moving beyond this tendency to sink beneath the weight of the realisation of the absurdity of human aspiration and toil. Such an awareness is vital, of course, if we wish to strive to live authentically, but in the early stages of therapy it may be more helpful to take the stance, 'given all of this, clients nevertheless strive to make a life', and to wonder how it is they do this. In Paul's case I was curious about this insistence on the past and fear of the future. It seemed to me that to take it at face value was to miss something: there was something about the way Paul had learned to attune himself to the world which, far from reflecting a secure and happy childhood, spoke more of a demand for perfection and isolation. He often referred to this time as idyllic, but I began to wonder whether there was something stultifying in the idea. We often use the term 'idyllic' when we speak of a short period of time such as a holiday, but how many people would be able to imagine living always in an idyllic world where everything is invariably perfect and everyone is content? Far from being a positive experience it seemed to me it would, especially for a developing child, be a very demanding and difficult place to find oneself. Real life, with its successes and reverses, its arguments and misadventures, offers a far more trustworthy and balanced experience.

Paul recounted to me that, finally, his parents' encouragement of his education led him to obtain very high grades at 'A' level and the offer of a place to study at a prestigious university some distance from the family home. Not surprisingly it was difficult for him to make the transition from schoolboy to student; far from being a celebration of his achievements the approach of the first term was viewed by the whole family as the end of innocence and an erosion of the family unit.

In fact, cut adrift from his familiar life, Paul was totally lost and didn't survive the term before leaving. As he put it to me,

> My first term was a very unhappy one. I had a false start ... it was all so over-whelming and I couldn't find my feet. The academic work went fine but I was terribly lonely and collapsed in on myself. I had some counselling – it was a lifesaver really – and managed to hold out until the end of term. The university were very understanding and I started again the following year, by which time I felt quite a lot stronger and more confident in myself. It's funny really, my grades were the highest, but I couldn't believe in myself and I couldn't believe in the encouragement my tutors were giving me.

In this short first term he described himself as 'homeless', as 'cut adrift from life'. His one connection with the family he had left behind was the gifts he bought and stored up to give them when he returned home at Christmas.

SHOPPING FOR COMPANY

Paul described to me how he began going out to shops in order to be with people but he found this was a double-edged sword since when he saw family groups he found he became more and more anxious and homesick and aware of the fact that he hadn't broken free from a family mould:

> I was still very much a part of a close-knit family unit, and I was still a rather childish unit within that ... and the shopping that I did was initially window shopping ... just looking into shops, and waiting around shops, and watching other people shop ... a shopping voyeurism almost and constructing little stories around the shopping that other people were doing and composing little family lives as a result of that but then it became more desperate.

The end of the first term was Christmas, and for Paul Christmas was associated with family, reunion with safety. He began in late October, after no more than four or five weeks of vicarious shopping, to shop quite furiously. As he described it, it became almost addictive because of the hidden motives that he had not consciously acknowledged at that stage:

> I was buying Christmas presents ... going into gift shops, toy shops and card shops and by buying these presents I was somehow vouchsafing the future, I was somehow ensuring that my family and I would survive the term, see the end of the tunnel. I was using money that was meant for books etc. ... because somehow presents meant survival ... If I bought someone a present they would be there at Christmas because they would have to receive it. Illogical and irrational as that may seem. And the presents were amassed ... I put them away in my room at university and having them there was somehow comforting, a solace.

Unfortunately this strategy didn't work: as time went on he felt more and more desperate and he described to me how one day he found himself stumbling around the streets with tears in his eyes, not even able to look in shop windows, just walking aimlessly.

At that stage his parents were visiting him on quite a regular basis. He decided not to go home because, as he said,

I needed to see this through. They visited me on a Sunday when, at that period, the shops were shut. It was the only time I didn't shop for gifts, or think about shopping. So the presents hadn't worked as magic charms, they hadn't worked as totemistic objects, but I don't think I really accepted that at the time because when I returned shopping was still important to me. It changed insofar as instead of my parents visiting me, I would go home once a fortnight and as soon as I returned after each visit I would go straight into a shop and buy something and I would have to buy something for my parents and my sister and that would keep them safe for another fortnight.

It seemed to me that Paul's shopping and gift-buying were symptomatic of a more fundamental problem: if he was unable to move away from his parents, and in particular from his mother, he would always remain a child, would never have to leave his idyllic childhood. If he never grew up he would never have to steer his own course through life, and he would never have to die. As Yalom expresses it:

... an individual may guard himself from the death anxiety inherent in indi-viduation by maintaining a symbolic tie with mother. This defensive strategy may succeed temporarily but, as time passes, it will become a source of secondary anxiety; for example, the reluctance to separate from mother may interfere with attendance at school or the development of social skills; and these tendencies are likely to beget social anxiety and self-contempt which, in turn, may give birth to new defences which temper dysphoria but retard growth and accordingly generate additional layers of anxiety and defence. (1980, p. 111)

Spinelli describes this idea of death anxiety as an anxiety not so much about death *per se*, as about 'the fragility of human existence'. This death anxiety, which he suggests might more properly be called 'temporal life anxiety'

seeks to point us to our diffuse experience of the fundamental uncertainty of being, such that every step we take, every act we initiate, expresses, at its heart, our inevitable movement towards non-being through unknown and unpredictable life-circumstances. How each of us deals with death anxiety is likely to be as varied and unique as our experience of being alive. We might, for instance, seek out ways to avoid risk and uncertainty as much as possible and, thereby, cocoon ourselves into a lifestyle bounded by regime and habit, as bereft of novelty and surprise as humanly possible. Equally, we might throw ourselves into a life which seems to require doubt and risk, whose very uncertainty revels in its defiance of security and predictability. (1997, p. 10)

It seemed to me, listening to Paul's story, that he had chosen the strategy of closing down his life, of refusing, effectively, to live his life at all, save in those aspects of it where he was able to create the illusion that he was still a child. The message appeared quite simple: if I refuse to become an adult I will maintain myself as a child, and I will never die. Moreover, if my life is arrested, so too are the lives of the family members who are closest to me. Of all the clients I have worked with, Paul's dilemma was the clearest example of the problems which attend on the denial of death. As Yalom has written '... a life dedicated to the concealment of reality, to the denial of death, restricts experience and will ultimately cave in upon itself' (1980, p. 210).

At the point where Paul came to see me his life had indeed begun to cave in on itself and in the first few months of therapy I found myself accompanying him into the deepest despair. Part of this disintegration was the realisation that he did not have the power to make his parents, and particularly his mother, safe from the encroachment of time. Just as important, though, he began, as he recounted his story, to doubt whether his childhood had, indeed, been the idyll which he had presented in our first few sessions.

I encouraged him to tell me more and more about this time, confident that he would come to a clearer understanding of his childhood if I was an open and attentive listener. As he talked, a very different version of his childhood began to emerge. Far from a careful innocent time, it seemed that Paul, as the elder child, was the focus of major difficulties within the family, and in particular of his mother's insecurities about life.

Living, it emerged, was anxious work, and the world a dangerous place. The family, and especially his mother, invested Paul with the power and responsibility at an early age to keep them all together and safe. Most importantly, this was a role Paul chose to take on and he did so with a vengeance. As he described it, he became 'the sin eater' for the family unit and in doing so he placed himself at the centre of the family, alongside his mother, and increasingly pushed his father to the periphery.

Paul was as a very young child caught up in what the existential psychiatrist R. D. Laing has called a 'double-bind': his parents instilled in him the importance, above all else, of a stable, loving family, yet they rowed frequently and bitterly. His parents recounted to him that when only six or seven years old he had the power to bring such incidents to a close by doing little more than walking into the room. Since the perfect family did not row, it followed that where he was there could be no disagreement to witness. As he grew older he found that both his parents, but particularly his mother, bestowed almost miraculous peace-making powers on him: he was her 'knight in shining armour', always riding up in the nick of time to bring both parents back from the brink of an irreconcilable parting.

Pretty soon, as he recalled, this peace-maker role became central to his sense of himself. Without this function in the family he would, he felt, have almost ceased to have a separate existence at all. Paradoxically, if the original situation was that the family unit would dissolve without him, he now found that he was in danger of disintegrating without it. He must, then, constantly keep the family as the focus of his attention through the act of buying gifts for each of them, and, in presenting them with these gifts, keep himself constantly in their consciousness.

I stated, as the first assumption of existential-phenomenological work, that human beings are 'thrown' into the world, but are able to create their own values and their own lives. Yet the picture Paul drew appeared to be one in which he was the passive victim of the wishes of others. There need be no contradiction here if we bear in mind the theory of human development implicit in the work of Sartre. As Barnes expresses it:

> My consciousness at first is purely non-reflective-consciousness: at this stage I am not aware that I am aware of the world. I merely project myself out into the world, relating to it: I am pure intentionality. During this time my original project is shaped, the fundamental choice of my being is made: I choose myself through an attitude and action: I vote for my destiny with my feet and without making rational conscious choices. I become who I am by doing what I do. (1990, p. 42)

If it is this pure intentionality – the manner in which we are always and invariably stretching out to the world of objects in order to interpret them – which accounts for our original choice of being, by which we regulate ourselves in the world, we can see that, at least theoretically, this choice could have been other, and could, in consequence, have given rise to a quite different personality structure. As Cannon puts it:

> These prereflective choices, which include such things as my taste in food and clothing as well as *my way of relating to other people*, may never have been reflectively conceived ... Yet ... all of my concrete choices, all of my various ways of being, doing, and having are clues to my fundamental project of being – the meaning of my being in the world. (1991, p. 39; emphasis added)

This account of the original 'choice of being' by which we regulate ourselves in the world suggests – because of its focus on motivation rather than causality – that a radical modification of our fundamental project is always possible. We should not, though, underestimate the cost to the individual of such radical change. Sartre gives the example of a man who is hiking with friends and, on becoming exhausted after some hours, throws himself down at the roadside, and refuses to go on. Sartre, taking the role of the hiker, says that

> Someone will reproach me for my act and will mean thereby that I was free – that is, not only was my act not determined by any thing or person, but also I could have succeeded in resisting my fatigue longer ... I shall defend myself by saying that I was *too tired*. Who is right? Or rather is the debate not based on incorrect premises? There is no doubt that I could have done otherwise, but that is not the problem. It ought to be formulated like this: could I have done otherwise without perceptibly modifying the organic totality of the projects which I am; or is the fact of resisting my fatigue such that instead of remaining a purely local and accidental modification of my behaviour, it could be effected only by means of a radical transformation of my being-in-the-world – a transformation, moreover, which is possible? In other words: I could have done otherwise. Agreed. But *at what price?* (1956, pp. 453–4)

The price for Paul would be a particularly high one: not only would moving away from the role within the family which he had adopted at so young an age leave him without a sense of identity, it would also bring him face to face with the passing of time and with his own mortality and that of all his family members. His attempt to evade death anxiety, to strike a bargain with this existential given, had not worked of course: Paul thought constantly of his own death and of the death of his parents. In seeking to banish death he had only increased its hold over his life. I struggled to find a way of communicating my thoughts to Paul in a way that he would not find intolerable. Fortunately, in the process of clarifying his own thoughts and feelings, Paul made the connection himself; and he did so in a way which also illuminated the meaning of shopping and gift-giving further.

He had told me about the past, about how he had tried to maintain his sense of self as a student by gift-buying. Now he told me about the period between his eventual graduation and the present. During these six years he had returned to the parental home to take up, effectively, where he had left off, sleeping in the same single bed, but now going out each day not to school but to work as a civil servant in government offices within easy walking distance. Shopping remained important to him, indeed he used up much of his salary at weekends when he would scour the larger department stores. His parents, now retired, and his sister, married and with her own home (though still living nearby), were both surprised and concerned to be the recipients of increasingly expensive gifts such as televisions, food processors and microwave ovens.

When he was away at university he described the function of shopping as

> somehow shopping was keeping people alive, it was keeping people I wasn't with, couldn't watch over safe ... This was highly self-congratulatory ... it implied I had the power of life and death over other people and it was keeping me alive too because if you shop you survive.

Far from reducing in its importance for him as might have been expected now that he was living at home again, shopping began to take on a whole new significance. He began to make connections between his ability to shop and the shopping habits of his family, and in particular his grandmother who had lived a few streets away.

> My grandmother, who was very elderly and was widowed (my grandfather died very tragically when I was a child), had been a strong and self-sufficient person and had coped but the day that she went downhill was the day she stopped shopping. She had stumbled trying to get on a bus to go to the local shopping centre, developed a fear of travelling on public transport and had then restricted herself to shopping at the top of her road and that was *her* shopping for company. I started to see awful parallels between myself and my grandmother in her twilight years. So again survival and death became associated with shopping. And of course it became more and more restricted and in the end she was having things delivered to her, had meals on wheels. That is I think the serious decline for her – she lost touch, she lost contact and lost a certain will to continue and senility was setting in.

He described how when his mother was coming to terms with his grandmother's death one of the things he felt himself thinking or feeling was that it was very important that his mother should continue to shop. It was a sign of robustness, it was a sign of not going gently into that dark night.

> And in fact my mother still shops quite regularly two to three times a week and takes the same bus and route as my grandmother, an unnerving parallel, but a sign of longevity for me. So I encourage my mother to shop as much as possible. Now the trouble is that my mother's physical ailments tend to be connected with arthritis – mobility is vital for shopping. So any indication she is reluctant to shop is an indication of physical renunciation and so the encouragement from me becomes almost frenetic – Surely you can ... , Here's

a little errand ... And I find myself on a Saturday going into town in the same spirit ... its very important to shop ... I'm glad that we can now shop on Sundays because it takes away the awful dread of Sundays that I've always had ... probably always will have.

CONCLUSION

In some respects, as a standard case study, my work with Paul was a failure, by which I mean that there was no 'Aha' moment, no point at which the skill or wisdom of the therapist enabled the client to make the connection which he had missed before, and which would speed him from hysterical misery to ordinary human unhappiness. If this work does not contain any conjuring tricks, if no rabbits are made to appear from hats, it is typical of much of my work as a therapist. Clients, I find, generally have an inherent wisdom about the ways in which they are living their lives. They know when they are falling short of their desire to live fully and they often need only an opportunity to clarify what they are doing to get back on track. I say 'only' but of course it is the ability to be truly present with another, attending to their story (in the sense that 'to attend to the soul' is the etymological root of the word psychotherapy) in a manner which enables the therapist to enter into the client's lived world, to see it through their eyes, while also standing apart to offer the challenge of a different perspective where the client is in difficulties, which makes the difference between existential psychotherapy and a discussion with a friend or acquaintance.

So it was in my work with Paul: he knew, only too well, the difficulties he was in. The patterns, rules, and structures which he had constructed over the years in ever more frantic attempts to keep himself safe and out of the adult world were intimately known to him, had become part of himself. Now, finally, the dam which he had built up was about to burst and the consequences terrified him. In therapy he was able, at first tentatively and then with greater and greater confidence, to explore the unknown which had been damned up for so many years.

I have related only an aspect, albeit a crucial one, of the first six months of the therapy. Paul and I were to work for a further eighteen months, gradually unravelling his old, sedimented, way of living and clarifying the possibilities for the new. If there was no moment of sudden revelation followed swiftly by cure it is because such a view of the therapeutic process is alien to the existential approach. While it is true that clients are frequently able to make significant changes in their lives during existential therapy the therapist does not set out to cure them of anything. What the client presents in therapy is not a certain set of symptoms indicative of underlying illness, but rather their own unique attunement to the human condition. Clients may feel dis-ease with the way they are living their lives but they cannot be 'cured' of this dis-ease any more than they can be 'cured' of life. Paradoxically, Paul's dis-ease, his compulsive shopping, was an important indicator of his wider malaise, his frantic attempts to stop the clock and return to a largely mythical, carefree childhood.

Paul and I reviewed our work together after three months, and again at the end of six months. Perhaps the most important thing to come out of our first two reviews was Paul's struggle to express what he was feeling, to relax and unbutton that 'four-piece suit' even a little and his relief (particularly at the six-month point) to have been able to do so. I would not underestimate the tension between wishing to remain the same and feeling compelled to change which is so often experienced by clients, nor the fear which accompanies it. Paul reported that he felt torn between two equally strong impulses in our early sessions and that he also felt a sense of shame that he was in therapy at all. He stated that my willingness to listen and give him space to discover what he needed to do in therapy, and the clarifications I sought when his story was confused, gave him a sense of safety and also of challenge which enabled him to name and face up to his difficulties in living.

In some respects this suggests that I did relatively little in sessions, and this is true up to a point. Certainly I was more concerned to 'be' with Paul than I was to 'do' anything either to him or for him. He remarked on this himself on more than one occasion when he felt a session was particularly hard work. I am mindful, though, of the distinction which the German philosopher Heidegger made between 'leaping in' and 'leaping ahead' in our relationships with others. There is a world of difference between these two different ways of attending to the client: 'that which leaps in and dominates, and that which leaps forth and liberates' (1962, p. 159). The first, 'leaping in', takes responsibility away from the client and places it with the therapist who rescues him or her. In the second the therapist encourages them to make their own, authentic, choices. It was this authenticity, this possibility of becoming his own person, which I felt was crucial for Paul if he was to go out into the world.

From the perspective of shopping addiction, Paul presents an interesting departure from the stereotype 'victim' of this 'condition'. The shopping addict is usually presented as a young woman who has been beguiled and ensnared by the expectations of her peer group and our consumer culture, or else she is a woman of middle age, with an empty nest and a sudden need to find some meaning in her life. Paul, in contrast, was an articulate and highly intellectual man who used shopping and gift-giving over a number of years in an attempt to quell his existential anxieties about loss, separation and death. Looking back at my notes I do not believe either of us ever employed the term 'addiction' at any time during the therapy: I have already stated my position on the effect such a label can have. As regards Paul's view I can only speculate on his reasons for avoiding the term. I suspect that he realised his difficulties in living were very grave and that to call himself an addict would have been to distance himself from them, rather than make the painful journey towards a genuine engagement with them. He was neither conscious nor unconscious of the meaning of his behaviour: rather its meaning was clear to him, or partially hidden and unclear to varying degrees at different times. In the final analysis we might say, with Yalom, that the meanings he gave to shopping represented a highly creative defence against death anxiety. I would hazard that the account Paul gave me of his shopping behaviour differs from that of the everyday shopper in intensity but not in type.

POSTSCRIPT

I saw Paul once more, about a year after our last session, when he rang to make an appointment to 'talk over some plans I have, and my worries about whether they are realistic or not'. Paul seemed considerably more at ease with himself, and far more self-assured than when we had first met. He was obviously excited by an imminent career change: he was about to leave the civil service to take up a position in a specialist publishing company, where he would be able to make use of his long-ignored expertise in classical languages.

He mentioned in passing that he was still living in his parent's house, but this seemed to be more a matter of choice and even a pleasurable experience, rather than a neurotic defence against death anxiety. He did not mention his previous difficulties with regard to gift-giving and I felt that there was no reason why I should introduce this subject. The Paul I met that day was very different from the old Paul and the very fact that he had decided to come and talk to me about his plans for the future encouraged me to hope that he was now actively engaging with life, and in the swim of things, with all the pleasures and problems this brings, rather than frantically splashing about in the shallows.

REFERENCES

American Psychiatric Association (1994) *Diagnostic and Statistical Manual of Mental Disorders*, 4th edn. Washington, APA.

Barnes, H. (1990) Sartre's Concept of the Self. In *Sartre and Psychology: Review of Existential Psychology and Psychiatry*. Seattle, WA.

Bergmark, A. and Oscarsson, L. (1987) The concept of control and alcoholism. *British Journal of Addiction*, 82, 1203–12.

Cannon, B. (1991) *Sartre and Psychoanalysis: An Existentialist challenge to clinical metatheory*. Kansas, University of Kansas Press.

Cohn, H. W. (1994) What is Existential Psychotherapy? *British Journal of Psychiatry*, 165, 699–701.

Cohn, H. W. (1996) *Existential Thought and Therapeutic Practice*. London, Sage.

Drew, L. R. H. (1990) Facts We Don't Want to Face. *Drug and Alcohol Review*, 9, 207–10.

du Plock, S. (ed.) (1997) *Case Studies in Existential Psychotherapy and Counselling*. Chichester, John Wiley and Sons.

Heidegger, M. (1962) *Being and Time*. Tr. J. Macquarrie and E. Robinson. Oxford, Blackwell.

Joyce, J. (1992) *A Portrait of the Artist as a Young Man*. Harmondsworth, Penguin.

Sartre, J-P. (1943) *Being and Nothingness: An Essay on Phenomenological Ontology*. Tr. Hazel E. Barnes. New York, Philosophical Library, 1956.

Spinelli, E. (1989) *The Interpreted World. An Introduction to Phenomenological Psychology*. London, Sage.

Spinelli, E. (1997) *Tales of Unknowing. Therapeutic Encounters from an Existential Perspective*. London, Duckworth.

van Deurzen, E. (1988) *Existential Counselling in Practice*. London, Sage.

van Deurzen, E. (1997) *Everyday Mysteries*. London, Routledge.

Warnock, M. (1970) *Existentialism*. Oxford, Oxford University Press.

Wurm, C. (1997) Deciding about Drinking – an Existential Approach to Alcohol Dependence. In S. du Plock (ed.), *Case Studies in Existential Psychotherapy and Counselling*. Chichester, John Wiley and Sons.

Yalom, I. (1980) *Existential Psychotherapy*. New York, Basic Books.

Yalom, I. (1989) *Love's Executioner and Other Tales of Psychotherapy*. London, Bloomsbury.

5

The Incandescent Shopper: An Existential-Phenomenological Perspective

David Horne

Today you're unhappy?
Can't figure it out?
What is the Salvation?
Go Shopping.
(Arthur Miller 1985)

As we start this millennium Britain has opened the doors to the Trafford Centre in Manchester, the most extravagantly built shopping and leisure centre in this country. Three miles of polished granite-and-marble boulevards front 280 shops. Expectations suggest that more than 30 million customers – spending £13 billion a year – will pass through those doors.

Has its creator anticipated the shopping shape of things to come? The basic principle on which it exists is quite simple. Modern consumers want to shop and want shopping to be fun. Its designers expect it to change the way we shop, think and live. But is this really an advance in our civilisation? And just whom will it please?

The greater importance of shopping in the consciousness of humans today runs through the whole fabric of millennial society. It affects the meaningful experiences of shopping and sets goals and shapes dreams. Today the selections of celebrities for popular biography appearing in national magazines are those successful in entertainment, leisure and most importantly, consumption. It focuses on them in terms of their having money and time to spend. The displayed characteristics of popular idols can all be integrated around the concept of the consumer. And the faculties of reflection, imagination, dream and desire so far as they exist, move in the sphere of concrete, shopping experience.

The eternal curiosity of human beings concerning their very own nature, existence, and relationship to life, has given rise to the creation of a myriad of therapeutic approaches. Existential philosophy, which attempts to explain the nature of life and humans, is centred on humans.

My assumption in this chapter is that death is one of the most inexorable givens of the human condition. The awareness of our finitude and the denial of the physicality of our death in relation to our existence may create a pervasive restriction of awareness and experience and lead to ontological insecurity and intense anxiety. An existential perspective would suggest that death and life are interdependent and that the integration of the acceptance of our temporality and eventual non-existence may enhance the authenticity of our mode of 'being-in-the-world' (Heidegger 1962, p. 78).

In this chapter I propose to address the existential-phenomenological experience of shopping. With the knowledge that the subject is pervasive I would like to consider the following. Is shopping a weapon against existential crisis in relation to death/anxiety, guilt, meaninglessness and the nothingness of being? Does shopping provide an identity and a way of constructing a Self, thereby avoiding the existential void or the lack of self? I will also try to explore shopping as a primary, significant and novel relationship to the world, whereby it creates a contrived, contained and predictable world in opposition to the chaos and uncertainty of the world.

Existentialists use the word 'facticity' to designate the limiting boundary or factor in existence. We have not chosen to be in the world or be alive. Our sense of the human existence of our life is a factical given. Our existence in time embraces a need to create a past, present and future in which we are the existent being in focus. We may have a sense of the possibilities of our future but, if we see our life as a line or continuum, we know that somewhere along this line we shall cease to exist and play no more part in the events of the world.

No adequate history of the multiple meanings of shopping has been written. People have no articulate philosophy of shopping. Their feelings about it and their experiences of it influence their satisfactions and frustrations, the tone of their lives. The effects of shopping as an activity (known to people or not) are hard to define. Yet the intrinsic meaning of shopping as purposive human activity has become an issue in early twenty-first-century enquiries.

Most views of shopping have ascribed to it an extrinsic meaning. Medieval thinking insists that riches exist for man, not man for riches.

A Renaissance view of shopping may have seen it as intrinsically meaningful, focusing on the physical and mental process of shopping itself. It would see the reasons for shopping in the shopping itself and not in any ulterior realm or consequence.

I will argue that as well as salvation, status or power over other people and prestige, it is the process of shopping itself that is satisfying. Natural opiates, dopamine and seratonin are stimulated by the excitement of the experience.

In the world today technological development and material progress sometimes seem to create for some at least, greater alienation from life, rather than a better quality of life. For those lonely in a city, the mere fact of meeting people at the place of shopping may be a positive thing. Even anonymous shopping contacts in large centres may be highly esteemed by those who feel too closely bound by family and neighbourhood. Satisfaction in shopping often rests upon status satisfactions from shopping associations. As a social role played in relation to other people, shopping may become a source of self-esteem, whilst shopping among friends or family. The fact of shopping with skill and despatch may also be a source of self-esteem.

Heidegger has used the expression 'thrownness' (*Geworfenheit*) as a metaphor for man's factical condition (Macquarrie 1972, p. 191). We are thrown into existence at the moment of our birth and we are thrown out of life at some point in our life. Our existence never escapes from the tension between possibility and the facticity of our existence and finitude. Our sense of temporality is linear, stretching to our death and non-being. 'As Austin Farrer once expressed it: "The loneliness of personality in the universe weighs heavily upon us." To put it somewhat quaintly, it seems terribly improbable that we should exist' (p. 190).

Death anxiety may be a unique and personal anxiety relating to our basic sense of finitude, but may embrace the fear of the 'event' of dying, the sense of ceasing to be and the events of happening or non-happening after the 'event of dying'. Existential writers and philosophers refer to the 'fragility of being' (Jaspers), of dread of 'non-being' (Kierkegaard), of 'ontological anxiety' (Tillich) or of 'the impossibility of further possibility' (Heidegger, cited in Macquarrie 1972, p. 201).

To become aware of death as the ultimate possibility in our life is to experience the tensions among the dimensions of temporality. If we accept that death haunts us and leads to a sense of unease in our being-in-the-world, and a primordial sense of anxiety, we can appreciate the strategies such as shopping that we employ to deny aspects of death and the human condition.

The existential theory of human beings does not constitute a scientific explanation of life or being human. Each individual is unique. Humans are not a static entity. They are continually in the process of changing; because they are not 'fixed beings' they are more than they know and more than they can know. The whole being of a person (body, emotions, and thoughts) is dynamic. From this stance, one of a perpetual changing personality and impermanence, the question of Self is raised. Can there be one?

Heidegger preferred the term '*Dasein*' rather than Self. He viewed self as essentially a relational construct as an a priori of existence. Heidegger's concept of Dasein may help us to understand our relationship to shopping and the role it plays in shaping the people we perceive ourselves to be. The concept suggests that it is 'being-with' which is primary and not 'I'. 'Being-with' is not just about relating to others but proposes a way of relatedness to the world and others even if others are not present.

I would contend that the self is a fundamental unit of human experience in so much that it cannot be removed from our thought/experience. Self-consciousness is a mental construction whereby interaction of impersonal mental and physical phenomena composes an attribute of the self and thus creates the sensuous perception of self-consciousness, a transparent tulle. It therefore does not exist on its own.

It comes about as a consequence of our 'being-with' in a particular context. As a result our thoughts, perceptions, beliefs and values are generally not just ours but representative of the society in which we live and are therefore shared. This constructed sense of self, because it is not something self-existing, comes to reveal another aspect, a sense of lack or void when it tries to express itself in some concrete form in the world.

Conditional consciousness cannot however objectify itself, rather like the tip of an iceberg, which is reliant on hidden depths that it is unable to realise because it is a manifestation of it. Being unable to do this causes the self continually to try and escape from the nothingness of being. To reconcile this void we need to project it onto something. The act of shopping tries to provide this, by suppressing the sense of lack or existential void. The oft quoted phrase 'I shop therefore I am' has become synonymous with 'being'. Death, meaninglessness and groundlessness can be kept at bay, yet intrinsic to the sense of self is the suppressed sense of lack.

This void in its unadulterated form appears as an existential guilt and anxiety, different symptoms revealing the same problem which can become unbearable because it consumes one's very being. Oniomania or shopaholism can provide an alternative for some. Rampant consumerism, like comfort eating, may be a cry for help, a contemporary bid to cope with life in the face of withered spirituality.

THE CASE OF JAKE

Jake, a client, came to see me after the sudden death of his father. In the two-year interim between his bereavement and the commencement of our sessions Jake felt he was in trouble as he was spending at least five hours a day in shops with only a modest income and he craved the atmosphere.

When I started seeing him he was full of anger and resentment and blamed the hospital for his father's death. He would arrive, each session, hands full of the ever-present shopping bags. Initially, I had an image of these bags being 'bags of anger' that he was carrying about with him.

His father's death had knocked him off course. It was the 'first hiccup' in his life. Now his confidence had been knocked too. Jake's worldview was life as a continuum. One grew up, got a job, married, bought a home, had children; a world in which there was no pain or anything that stopped one from pursuing these goals. Jake had been able to maintain this view by surrounding himself with purchases that fitted in with his scheme of life and image of self. Difficulties arose for him when he had to deal with increasing shopping bills and questioning from his employers about the amount of time he had been taking off (in order to go shopping). He needed and created tremendous order in his life. Yet now his experience was disorder in life.

Jake's view of life did not encompass that we die. He had brought to therapy the assumption that the process of therapy was to translate intentionality into actuality so that he could have the life he believed he needed or wanted. Jake's actualisation gave life and reality to possibility and hope for the capability of him to change and integrate his experience of bereavement. However, the price for such was a demanding and literally expensive undertaking for him. The emotional energy it released led him to question his views on life. It provoked intense anxiety. He asked me how was he to cope without the 'stockade' he had created by shopping? Without that he expressed his fear about what he would find on the other side. It might be 'nothing' and he may be confronted with his own mortality.

EXISTENTIAL ANXIETY

Heidegger in his early writing finds anxiety as the basic way in which humans find themselves in the world and revelatory of being human. An awareness of this anxiety reveals humans' existence as possibility (Macquarrie 1975, p. 66). Yet possibility is finite; at any time, upon death, existence and its possibilities stop. He also suggests that anxiety may cause humans to be confronted with their responsibility and the notion to embrace authentic being. Experiencing ontological anxiety, humans are called upon to face their anxiety with courage and abandon hope of finding external meaning. 'Along with the sober anxiety which brings us face to face with our individualized potentiality-for-Being, there goes an unshakeable joy in this possibility' (Heidegger 1962, p. 358).

Becker suggests that facing the truth of the human condition without psychological defences leads to neurotic or psychotic behaviour and perhaps even mental paralysis. Yet to hide from this fact is to seek security in a world of projections and transferences. The irony of man's condition:

> ... is that the person seeks to avoid death, but he does it by killing off so much of himself and so large a spectrum of his action-world that he is actually isolating and diminishing himself and becomes as though dead. (Becker 1973, p. 181)

Increasingly the shopper is living for the external world rather than for him- or herself. If there is no intrinsic connection between shopping and the rest of a person's life, then he or she must accept the shopping as meaningless in itself, and seek meanings elsewhere.

Shopping may be a necessity in terms of provisions or it may be the most significant part of some beings' inner lives. It may be experienced as exuberant expression of self, as bounden obligation or as the development of human nature. Neither love nor hatred of shopping is inherent in human beings, or inherent in any given type of shopping, for shopping has no intrinsic meaning.

Heidegger (1962, p. 96) suggests that materiality is a characteristic of Being. 'Things' or entities have an ontological character and can be 'invested with value'. For him one way of being in the world is whereby humans are at the centre of the world and the world is there for their purpose. The world is 'ready-to-hand' (p. 117) and characterised by its consumption.

Shopping gratification is such that human beings may live in a kind of quiet passion for their shopping alone. What is necessary for the shopper, however, is that the tie between the thing and the purchaser is psychologically possible; if the shopper does not own an item, it can be owned psychologically in the sense that the consumer knows what goes into its procurance. The consumatory satisfaction that humans have in the product is meaningful to them.

I believe a supreme concern, the whole attention, is with the commodity and the process of its purchasing. There is an inner relation between the shopper and the thing he or she desires, from the first image formed of it through to its completion, a purchasing dependency which makes the shopper's will-to-shop spontaneous and even exuberant.

Heidegger proposes that these entities only become accessible if we encounter them with significant concern; they then become 'equipment'. However, equipment cannot stand alone. Each is relational to other equipment. Shopping for clothing is invariably part of an image, furniture part of an interior. Therefore things or equipment are manipulatable and at our disposal. The details of shopping are meaningful because they are not detached in the consumer's mind from the commodity or product to purchase. Consumption is twofold. Shoppers consume both the things as well as significant meanings of those things.

Heidegger claims that we may become inauthentic, thus taking us away from ourselves. It is an inevitable condition of being-with-others or over-concerned with materiality. He would see this in terms of 'fallenness'. In falling humans are trying to escape from themselves. Groundlessness and meaninglessness of Dasein's being-in-the-world reveals itself as anxiety. 'Only because Dasein is anxious in the very depths of its Being, does it become possible for anxiety to be elicited physiologically' (Heidegger 1962, p. 234). This anxiety does not have an object. Anxiety consists of a conflict between being and non-being (Yalom 1980) between the potential for emergence of being and the loss of present comfort and security. It is an unavoidable concomitant of freedom. Developing such objectless anxiety is a straight route to realising the nothingness in our being. There is an essential connection between anxiety and the formation of the self.

> The self comes to control awareness, to restrict one's consciousness of what is going on in one's situation very largely by the instrumentality of anxiety, with, as a result, a dissociation from personal awareness of those tendencies of the personality which are not included or incorporated in the approved structure of the self. (Sullivan, cited in May 1977, p. 169)

It is not just that we deny something. The denial is the very thing that constitutes the self. The sense of self is reduced from its rational position to a model of evasions. This might explain why it is so difficult to understand who or what we are because such a consciousness can have no being, only a function. So the sense-of-self is not only a lack in so much that it appears as an ungrounded awareness, but also its function is to repress anxiety too (Loy 1992).

As anxiety is eager to objectify into fear of something, some humans use shopping as a way to defend themselves against a sense of ontological lack. There are few legitimating symbols for shopping, yet gratifications and discontents are associated with it. Widespread disposable income or credit and the routinisation of shopping have reduced it to a commodity, of which money has become the only common denominator. The sharp focus upon money is part and parcel of the lack of intrinsic meaning that shopping has come to have.

Rollo May shares Heidegger's recognition that inherent in anxiety there is a positive potential. He writes: 'anxiety is the basic, underlying reaction – the generic term; and fear is the expression of the same capacity in its specific, objectivated form' (May 1977, p. 224). Anxiety 'is objectless because it strikes at that basis of the psychological structure on which the perception of one's self as distinct from the world of objects occurs' (p. 207). Moreover, it is not possible to escape anxiety by conceiving ourselves to be unable to experience anxiety. We cannot even conceive of an ideal self free from anxiety, as our existential lived experience is often at odds with this ideal self. As anxiety is in our very 'make up' there is no possible statement of experience that we can make that does not contain anxiety. Even saying 'I can imagine myself free of anxiety' is an anxiety-derived statement.

So is shopping an activity that brings inner calm? Can the essence of a human being rest upon his or her shopping and their choices? Sartre (1956) suggests that because human existence precedes essence, one exists before one's purpose is achieved. This question can put humans in continuous conflict. We unwittingly face anxiety and anguish by shopping because we are forever free to make choices and with every choice we stake our self-identity.

In using the term 'shopping' I am also referring to 'Unshopping', a phenomenon whereby some consumers shop with the intention that their purchases will be returned or exchanged. (This is quite different from unshopping as currently used to address the problems of over-consumption in the developed world.)

THE CASE OF BETH

Beth was a woman referred for therapy by her doctor since she was suffering from lung cancer. At the time of beginning her therapy with me, she was in remission. She had also become compelled to shop.

For Beth, a single, unemployed mother with four children under the age of eight, shopping was a form of escapism. She would spend days shopping, having released herself from her children with the aid of her mother. She would work her way down a shopping street, not missing a shop and felt she had to purchase something in each one. Beth spoke of a sense of control that she had in this activity. She knew she would return 90 per cent of her purchases. After all, her small maisonette could not accommodate the effects of her sprees. And once purchased, the item had little satisfaction for her. 'I just love new things', she admitted.

When we began to work together she only alluded briefly to her diagnosis of cancer which she referred to as her 'death sentence'. Instead, she presented her problem in terms of being 'trapped' by her children. Beth also felt she had 'wasted her life' and I felt this was clinical leverage to bring her into the present and to reflect her lack of living in time. The shopping had become a very powerful metaphor in our work; the compulsion to shop reflected her hope that her illness could be countered and appeased by goods. Beth wanted to believe that shopping had the power to mutate her inner experience of emptiness and powerlessness.

Gradually, whilst reflecting her assumptions about the waste of her life and her lack of reference to the cancer, she began to gain courage to look at her fears. Although she was in remission the chances of a reoccurrence of the cancer were high. Beth moved to living in time and to accepting her death by engaging with her problems, rather than transposing them in a shopping environment.

Beth had felt free to begin her shopping according to her own plan, and plan and performance were one. She was the mistress of the activity and of her being in the process. It suggests that her sphere of independent action was large and rational. She could be responsible for its outcome and free to assume that responsibility. Sartre states '... absolute responsibility is not resignation; it is simply the logical requirement of the consequences of our freedom' (Sartre 1956, p. 708).

The shopper's activity is, perhaps, thus a means of developing a sense of self. It is not that the development of self is an ulterior goal, but that such development is the cumulative result obtained by devotion to and practice of the activity. As humans give it the quality of their own minds and skill, they are also further developing their own nature; in this simple sense, humans can live in and through their shopping, which confesses and reveals them to the world.

Yet there is a continual undermining of our wish for an ideal self because what we actually experience is a sense of insolidity or groundlessness, between being and non-being. We cannot assume that the shopper makes comparisons between the ideal of shopping dexterity and one's own shopping experience. We cannot fruitfully compare the self of one shopper to another.

What we can say is that the self has no substance in Being but that anxiety is found when one looks for the self. The central ground, which the self occupies, is anxiety. By trying to deny anxiety we are also implicating an end to the sense of self as something autonomous and self-grounding. May also says that in anxiety:

> the security base of the individual is threatened, and since it is in terms of this security base that the individual has been able to experience himself as a self in relation to objects, the distinction between subject and object also breaks down. (May 1977, p. 208).

For some shoppers there is no split between shopping and recreation or between shopping and culture. If recreation is supposed to be an activity, exercised for its own sake, having no aim other than gratification and shopping is carried out to keep one happily occupied, then it is also recreation. Humans shop and play in the same act, thus expressing themselves and at the same time in that act they create meaning. Their shopping is a poem in action. Those who find free expression of self in their shopping are those who securely instrumentalise and externalise intimate features of their person and disposition (Dittmar 1992).

In almost every act of shopping the shopper does not have to sell a degree of his or her independence, unlike other areas of life such as work where often humans are within the domain of others and independent decisions are often subject to management by others.

Free to plan their shopping and to modify that plan, humans are able to manage and manipulate their shopping. Shoppers are free to control their shopping actions. If there is no split between their shopping and play, and their shopping and culture, then this is a common-sense fact of existence. The shoppers' purchasing determines and infuses their entire way of being. Shopping provides power and power provides freedom, in the sense that one has the power to shop when one wants and for what one wants.

If humans are driven by an unacknowledged intuition of their groundlessness, they can try to compensate for it by aspects of shopping – skill, power, disposable income/credit and status. These aspects must be taken into account to understand the meaning of shopping and the sources of its gratification. Any one of them may become the foremost aspect of the activity, and in various combinations each is usually in the awareness of the shopper.

In *Being and Time*, Heidegger tries to understand who Dasein actually is. He suggests that this can be found within the nature of our being-with:

> In that with which we concern ourselves environmentally the Others are encountered as what they are; they are what they do. In one's concern with what one has taken hold of, whether with, for, or against the Others, there is constant care as to the way one differs from them, whether that difference is merely one that is to be evened out, whether one's own Dasein has lagged behind the Others and wants to catch up in relationship to them, or whether one's Dasein already has some priority over them and sets out to keep them suppressed. (Heidegger 1962, pp. 163–4)

Today our problem with anxiety and how we experience it has changed with society. Shopping has become socially acceptable behaviour. Traditionally, religion would have consoled humans by putting anxiety to rest; the lack would be filled in or groundlessness grounded in God. I would agree with Sartre that God is not an external being but rather a name given to the fulfilment that each individual seeks. Every shopper wants to find/be God. He suggests that existentialists believe 'that every man, without any support or help whatever, is condemned at every instant to invent man' (Sartre, cited in Kaufmann 1956, p. 295).

Moreover, existentially we cannot eliminate anxiety, only reduce it. Kierkegaard suggests that if we can eliminate anxiety, it can be only be found by facing anxiety (Kierkegaard 1980, pp. 155–62). Through anxiety we can find freedom.

Only this century has shopping been more and more widely available. One of the most ostensible features of social life today and one of the most frenzied is mass shopping activities. Self-alienation is characteristic of urban life. Tillich refers to Kierkegaard in *The Courage To Be*.

> He realised that the knowledge of that which concerns us infinitely is possible only in an attitude of infinite concern, in an existential attitude. At the same time he developed a doctrine of man which describes the estrangement of man from his essential nature in terms of anxiety and despair. (Tillich 1952, pp. 125–6)

Humans are estranged from one another and manipulation is inherent in human contact. Each tries to make an instrument of the other, and in time a full circle is made: one makes an instrument of oneself, and is estranged from It also. Frankl calls this self-stupefaction:

> ... it is a means to an end, that of self-stupefaction. What the old scholars used to call 'horror vacui' exists not only in the realm of physics but also in that of psychology; man is afraid of his inner void, of the existential vacuum, and runs away into work or into pleasure. (Frankl 1967, p. 120)

To achieve and exercise the power and status derived from consumption may be the very definition of satisfaction in shopping, and this satisfaction may have nothing whatsoever to do with the actual experience as the inherent need and full development of human activity. It may offer hope to become real by being acknowledged by others. On the other hand consumers may try to resolve their sense of lack by fusing with others. Therefore humans compensate by striving to become more real than others, or they seek reassurance by becoming no less real than others appear to be.

Time spent shopping can lift men and women out of the grey, level tone of everyday life and forms a standard with which that life is contrasted. With the decline of the home as the centre of psychological life and the rise in leisure hours per week, the sphere of shopping takes over the home's functions. Humans find a new anchorage in shopping. The terms by which it is now organised have become the centre of character-forming influences, of identification models: it is what one human has in common with another; it is a continuous interest.

Prestige in the realm of shopping involves at least two humans: one to claim it and another to honour the claim. Gustave Le Bon wrote:

> Whatever has been a ruling power in the world, whether it be ideas or men, has in the main enforced its authority by means of that irresistible force expressed by the word 'prestige' ... Prestige in reality is a sort of domination exercised on our mind by an individual, a work, or an idea ... This domination 'paralyses our critical faculty' and fills us with 'astonishment and respect' ... . (Gustave Le Bon 1952, pp. 129, 130, 131)

The bases on which people raise prestige claims, and the reasons others honour these claims, include disposable income/credit and power as these invidiously distinguish one human from another. In the status system of society these claims are organised as rules and expectations. They regulate who successfully claims prestige, from whom, in which way and on what basis. The level of self-esteem enjoyed by people is more or less set by this status system. Status phenomena are conceived as the realities of social and personal life. However, the extent to which claims for prestige are honoured may vary widely. Some deferences that are given may express genuine feelings of esteem. If we lived in a society in which everyone's prestige was absolutely set and unambivalent then those who claim prestige on the specific bases of material wealth would be honoured because of their material wealth. So the exact volume and type of deference expected between any two people would always be known, expected and given and each person's level and type of self-esteem would be steady features of their inner lives.

Yet, in society, prestige is highly unstable and ambivalent. Claims expressed are not necessarily understood or acknowledged by those from whom deference is expected, and when others bestow prestige, they do so unclearly. People may claim prestige on the bases of their material wealth or appearance but, even if it is given, it may not be because of their appearance but rather, for example, their education. So the prestige system is more like a maze of misunderstanding, of sudden frustration and sudden indulgence, and so people's self-esteem fluctuates, is under strain and full of anxiety.

This not only applies to the shopper, but to the shop employee as well. Salespeople frequently attempt, although unsuccessfully, to borrow prestige from their contact with customers, and to cash it in among work colleagues as well as friends away from the shop. The person working in a suburban corner shop cannot successfully claim as much prestige as someone working in a city designer store. Prestige may be borrowed directly from the commodities they handle; graded according to the 'expensiveness' of them, although this is not as likely as borrowing from the type of customer.

Both the shopper and the salesperson vicariously play the roles they think they would like to play, cashing in their claims for esteem. Salespeople may also consider they have the power to change others, an attitude that may be considered the opposite to borrowing prestige from the customer and also gives satisfaction. Prestige is the shadow of shopping and not merely social nonsense that gratifies the individual ego.

The most important characteristic of all these activities is that they astonish, excite and distract but they do not enlarge reason or feeling. What is psychologically important is that this mass shopping has created in a society of shoppers a shopping ethic. Now shopping itself is judged in terms of shopping values. The sphere of shopping provides the standards by which other areas of life, such as work, are judged; it lends to work such meanings as work has. Much of one's life is sacrificed to the making of money with which to shop. It does not create a community in which humans are able to take more personal responsibility for coping with increased anxiety and resolving their own ontological lack.

EXISTENTIAL GUILT

Existential guilt is also inevitable in human existence. It could be seen as another symptom manifesting the same problem as existential anxiety, a suppressed sense of lack that is intrinsic to the sense of self. Ontological guilt wants to become guilt for something, because then humans can believe they know how to reconcile it. Anguish and despair are not the result of one's symptoms but their source. They are necessary to shield one from death, meaninglessness and groundlessness.

Yet there is another problem. When ontological guilt is experienced more purely as an unobjectified feeling that 'something' is not quite right with me we become aware of it as a neurotic guilt. By feeling not worthy in some way we are seeking a way to cope with this ontological guilt. Ontological guilt arises from an inconsistent feeling of believing in oneself and not believing in oneself. Their conflict is a sense of lack, which causes one to question one's being. The self feels bad about its own sense of self.

Do we need to feel guilty and what role does guilt play in determining the meaning of our lives? Nietzsche proposed '"guilt", as the sole cause of suffering' (Nietzsche 1996, p. 118). In *On the Genealogy of Morals* he was suggesting that:

> only in the hands of the priest, this real artist in guilty feelings, did it take form – oh what a form! 'Sin', for such is the priestly name given to the re-interpretation of animal 'bad conscience' (cruelty turned inwards against itself) – has been the greatest event so far in the history of the sick soul: it represents the most dangerous and fateful trick of religious interpretation. (Nietzsche 1996, p. 118)

He observed that humans would suffer willingly if they were given a reason for their suffering. If nothing is more painful to endure than pure lack, we need to project it onto something, because only then can we get a handle on it.

I would not agree with Nietzsche that 'original sin' is the ultimate cause of our suffering. As with shopping it attempts but does not succeed with ending our sense of lack, and maintains that religion could absolve this guilt.

The 'gods' humans worship determine how they live. Gods have always changed, but today they are widely organised and their worship is universal. In organising the fetishism of goods, shops have made gods out of flux itself. For example fashion used to be something only for the rich, but shops have democratised fashion for all consumers. It activates the imagination and has cultivated a great faith in the Religion of Appearance.

The psychological effect of a division of disposable income depends upon whether or not shoppers and their associates are in the same position (Featherstone 1991). Pride and skill are relative to the skills one has exercised in the past and to the skills others exercise, and thus to the evaluation of one's shopping activity by other people whose opinions count.

Many humans' claims to esteem are expressed, as their label implies, by their style of appearance. Claims for esteem are raised on the basis of consumption. Frankl suggests:

> A vehicle is frequently bought in order to compensate for a feeling of inferiority: The sociologists call that prestige consumption. I know of a patient ... although he possessed a sports plane, he was not satisfied, but wished for a jet plane. Apparently his existential vacuum was so great that it could only be overcome by supersonic speed. (Frankl 1967, p. 122)

This 'class' consciousness, as a psychological fact, means that the individual shopper in a particular position accepts only those who are significant to their own image of self. The amount of money spent shopping may be seen by the shopper and by others as the best gauge of their worth. This may be all the more true when relations are increasingly 'objectified' and do not require intimate knowledge.

THE CASE OF JASMIN

A client, Jasmin, came to therapy. Her belief was that people were pigeonholed because of the way they look. She described her world where bigotry was rife, a world where not only were there racism and sexism, but clothes-ism. Jasmin felt dismissed for the cut of her cloth and that others had a short-sighted inability to look at the personality beneath. She revealed how clothes and glamour were everything to her. Her style of dress was that of a 'Hollywood Star'.

Yet there was a paradox. Jasmin felt that clothing was her mask, which released her from herself and enabled her to escape from the limitations of this world. Much of our work concerned her need to be freed from the mask of her own body. She viewed her body as something external rather than internal.

During our work she reached a point where she could not differentiate between the real Jasmin and the image. Her cycle of life and shopping gave rise to different images of self: there was the everyday image often based upon work and there was the image based on shopping. The shopping image was heavily tinged with aspired-to and dreamed-of features and was fed by mass-media personalities and happenings. There was also the glamour of being attracted to certain shops and haute couture.

Her withdrawal from her sense of identity and ownership of her body led her to an existential despair consisting of aloneness and anxiety. In her existence there was a lack of the *Uberwelt* of spirituality, belief and aspiration, and rejection of the *Eigenwelt* of intimate and personal experience. There was also the pressure of maintaining her image and continually purchasing new outfits. Jasmin began to doubt her sense of 'personal specialness', which was based on her appearance.

Our work together tried to clarify and reconsider the missing elements in her existence as a human being. Shopping had anchored her to the world.

Judgements are rarely made about the world of shopping as presently organised compared with some other way of organising it. We do not know what proportions of human strata are 'satisfied' by their shopping and we do not know what being satisfied means to them. We can only speculate on such issues, as we do not know what such questions mean to people who answer them, or whether they mean the same thing to different strata of society. If society is a structure of shared guilt, then one solution to one's sense of lack is to project it onto a scapegoat.

We structure the world by the ways we secure ourselves within it, but how does this allow us to project our guilt and anxiety into the objective world? Paradoxically, attempting to ground oneself in the world is exactly what separates one from it. Freud's use of 'projection' and 'transference' are phenomena that challenge our assumptions about the division between subject and object. We assume that that which I am unaware of is hidden within me and that the objective world is what it appears to be, external to me.

Shopping can provide a world of self-existing dependable things, fixable in objective time and space and interacting in ways we can learn to manipulate. A predictable world can be automatised within which we can achieve our ends. We constitute the world in a way which hides the fact that we have constituted it. Therefore the sense of self can defend against anxiety and guilt, which is in that world, as it is itself, constituted at the same time. Repressing the fact that my objective world is made up is also to repress the fact that I am constituted (Loy 1992).

For projection and transference this could suggest that we might be able to find that which I am unaware of within me, not in some undiscovered mental place within, but actually embodied in my world. So to find my 'unconscious' I should look to the structures of my world.

> What really happens is not that the neurotic patient 'transfers' feelings he had toward mother or father to wife or therapist. Rather, the neurotic is one in certain areas never developed beyond the limited and restricted forms of experience characteristic of the infant. Hence in later years he perceives wife or therapist through the same restricted, distorted 'spectacles' as he perceived father or mother. The problem is to be understood in terms of perception and relatedness to the world. This makes unnecessary the concept of transference in the sense of a displacement of detachable feelings from one object to another. (May 1983, p. 154)

Furthermore, this is not to suggest that it is a satisfactory solution for humans characteristically to develop into the less restricted forms of experience. Humans need security. This becomes invested in social structures, which emphasise competing for socially agreed security and status symbols. Shopping satisfaction is related to income, and we might assume that it is related to status as well as to power. What such symbols probably measure are invidious judgements of the individuals standing with reference to other individuals together with the aspects of shopping; the terms of such comparisons must be made clear.

Today, features of shopping, disposable income, including credit, power, and status, have come to the fore in meaning for people. Disposable income, the amount and security of it, have become parts of the shopper's meaning. Shopping can also be for some a means of gaining status in society, whereby shopping carries various sorts of power, especially over other people.

Power is given to the shopper by the development of the market, which determines greater choice and time to shop, and by the shopping sphere, which leaves shopping operations free from discipline. There is a positive gratification achieved through the exercise of power whilst shopping. Power over consumer goods is important to the shopper. Status and power, as features of shopping gratification, are often blended. Self-esteem may be based on the social power exercised in the course of shopping.

So, in shopping, the world to be explored increasingly includes the social setting, the human affairs and the personality of shoppers.

Shopping enthusiasm reflects the happy willingness of shoppers to shop spontaneously and also indicates that it is easy for shoppers to climb social hierarchies. These hierarchies of class are characteristic of society. There is much confusion and blurring of the lines of demarcation, of the status value for example of clothing or houses, of the ways of spending money.

Present-day concern with shoppers' morale and shopping enthusiasm has other sources than the meaningful character of much shopping today. Whatever satisfaction alienated humans gain from life occurs within the framework of alienation; whatever satisfaction they gain from shopping occurs outside the boundaries of life. Shopping and life are often largely split. I use the term alienation as a lament and a form of collapse into self-indulgence.

However, can shopping really help us to defend against anxiety and guilt? The shopper may feel like a winner in a society in which shopping and shopping values are high profile. Yet in order to experience pure ontological guilt and anxiety it has to be relieved of any projection of its external cause. The association between emotion and its supposedly external cause has to be broken.

CONCLUSION

In life an increasing number of humans feel that pieces of themselves are broken off or fractured and these can be put back or repaired with the fixative of shopping. Shopping can offer a form of escape for some. It hides the fact of groundlessness and meaninglessness whilst at the same time attempting to make the fact more palatable. It can sustain the illusionary world in which many people now live and seems to serve whatever may be experienced as 'divine' within them.

Dissatisfaction with life may derive from a belief that 'I' do not really exist in the present. This is immediate and terrifying like death, yet death, invariably feared, can be projected into the future. The sense of self is a mental construction and therefore not self-existing, and this sense of lack is consistent with what existential philosophers and writers have revealed about ontological guilt and anxiety.

Such analysts of personal tragedy as Kierkegaard have done little to reinstate the emphasis on the power of man's intelligence to control his destiny. I would agree with Freud's discovery of the irrationality of humans. Those who are painfully aware of their conditions may obscure their knowledge by irrational shopping and other forms of self-deception. It is beyond rationality.

From birth to death, the Lord of shopping watches over us. It supplies necessities and at the same time creates unmet needs. People who did not know what they were creating have created shopping centres, and may have created an illusory balm, whereby people who are searching for meaning may feel that they can find it. With this view the self is a vessel, like an empty shopping bag, an inner void that has to be filled by concepts and possessions. Shopping attempts to cope with this void but it cannot succeed because it does not address the fundamental issue. Paradoxically, the shopper remains incandescent; masking a contemporary bid to cope with life.

REFERENCES

Becker, E. (1973) *The Denial of Death*. New York, The Free Press.
Dittmar, H. (1992) *The Social Psychology of Material Possessions: To have is to be*. Hemel Hempstead, Harvester Wheatsheaf and New York, St Martin's Press.
Featherstone, M. (1991) *Consumer Culture and Postmodernism*. London, Sage.
Frankl, V. E. (1967) *Psychotherapy and Existentialism*. London, Penguin Books.
Friedman, M. (1993) *The Worlds of Existentialism*. New Jersey and London, Humanities Press International.
Heidegger, M. (1962) *Being and Time*. Oxford, Blackwell.
Kaufmann, W. (1956) *Existentialism from Dostoevsky to Sartre*. New York, Meridian Books.
Kierkegaard, S. (1980) *The Concept of Anxiety*. Princeton, Princeton University Press.
Le Bon, G. (1952) *The Crowd*, 1896. London, Ernest Benn.
Loy, D. (1992) Avoiding the Void: The lack of self in psychotherapy and Buddhism. *The Journal of Transpersonal Psychology*, vol. 24, no. 2, 151–79.
Lunt, P. K. and Livingstone, S. M. (1992). *Mass Consumption and Personal Identity*. Milton Keynes, Open University Press.
Macquarrie, J. (1972) *Existentialism*. Harmondsworth, Penguin Books.
Macquarrie, J. (1975) *An Existentialist Theology*. Harmondsworth, Penguin Books.
May, R. (1977) *The Meaning of Anxiety*. New York, W. W. Norton & Company Inc.
May, R. (1983) *The Discovery of Being*. New York, W. W. Norton & Company Inc.
Miller, A. (1985) *The Price*. USA, Penguin.
Nietzsche, F. (1996) *On the Genealogy of Morals*. trans. D. Smith. Oxford, Oxford University Press.
Parsons, T. and Bales, R. F. (1956) *Family, Socialization and Interaction Process*. London, Routledge and Kegan Paul.
Sartre, J.-P. (1947) *Existentialism*. New York, Philosophical Library.
Sartre, J.-P. (1956) *Being and Nothingness*. New York, Washington Square Press.
Tillich, P. (1952) *The Courage To Be*. New Haven and London, Yale University Press.
Yalom, I. D. (1980) *Existential Psychotherapy*. New York, Basic Books.

6

Women, Body Image and Shopping for Clothes

Gemma Corbett

This paper will be devoted to that most fascinating subject for women – shopping. What should we do without that occupation, that solemn business of our days, that gives us such joy and such headaches, mental confusion, dizziness and causes our respective men ... such veiled amusement when we cite a day's shopping as infinitely more fatiguing than a day in the City or law-courts. (*Woman's Life* 1895. Quoted in Beetham, M. 1966, p. 190)

INTRODUCTION

Clothes and clothes shopping are regarded as two of women's greatest obsessions. A casual glance at women's magazines or the women's page of any daily newspaper reveals the inordinate amount of space devoted to what a woman should wear and what she must add to her wardrobe if she is to be regarded as stylish. Looking good by dressing well seems to be an imperative for women and as the quotation above implies, this demands work – work which is both painful and pleasurable. The female's pursuit of beauty is a topical issue (Baker 1984; Chapkis 1986; Freedman 1988; Wolf 1990; Johnston 1994; Friday 1996), and it has been argued that while this can be an enjoyable activity serving to enhance her power, attractiveness and ability to achieve her goals, nevertheless it can also become 'an obsession ... a trap' (Baker 1984, p. 9), which may seduce her into focusing attention exclusively on her body and perhaps neglecting other forms of self-enhancement. When a woman uses fashion to modify moods of sadness, she may be judged to be in the grip of behaviours which have been deemed dysfunctional – 'dressing disorder' (Frankenburg and Yurgelun-Todd 1984) or 'appearance obsession' (Johnston 1994). She may also become addicted to clothes shopping (Elliott 1994) which can cause serious problems, psychological as well as financial. It could be argued that the fashion enthusiast may be attempting to alleviate negative feelings about her body. Research has consistently shown that women in general have a much poorer body image than men. Jackson (1992), in a comprehensive study of the literature, concludes that: 'females consider their body attractiveness to be more important than do males ... [and] are more dissatisfied with their body appearance than are males' (p. 182). This chapter studies the experience of the 'ordinary' female shopper and asks if women use clothes shopping to deal with feelings of dissatisfaction about their bodies. The chapter begins with an examination of the development of body dissatisfaction among women. Then follows a consideration of clothes shopping. Third, there is a brief note about the research method. Sections four and five present and discuss the research findings and finally implications for therapy are considered.

THE DEVELOPMENT OF BODY DISSATISFACTION

'Women begin early in life with this sense that we aren't quite right' (Chapkis 1986, p. 6). Body image, which in this study is understood as 'a self-evaluation of body appearance, body parts and body functions' (Jackson 1992, p. 180) is developed in human beings from birth onwards and is strongly influenced by the cultural expectation that girls must be beautiful – 'made of sugar and spice and all things nice', as the childhood chant goes. However, alongside the niceness there is also a lack (Freud 1933/1991, p. 160) and the sense that the female is 'beautiful but unclean, alluring but dangerous ... a source of pleasure and nurturance, but also of destruction and evil' (Suleiman 1986, p. 1). It can be suggested that a woman internalises such ambivalent messages and this has significant consequences for her image of herself and her self-esteem. Gender stereotyping, which research has shown begins within twenty-four hours of birth, rates 'female children as significantly smaller, finer-featured and less alert' than males who are judged to be 'more alert, stronger, firmer, hardier and more coordinated than girls' (in Kaschak 1992, p. 45) and this, despite the fact that there is normally very little difference between newborn baby boys and girls in terms of length, weight and activity level. The traits parents perceive in their babies are the ones they expect to see and already, girls are often considered to be more decorative and charming but less active and alert than boys. Clothing styles may at times support this perception. Even in the seemingly more enlightened 1990s where there is greater awareness of the risks of stereotyping, mothers often dress their baby daughters in soft pastel shades, frills and ribbons while their baby sons are attired in stronger colours and action clothes, thus – one might suggest – scripting the infants for future roles – the girl as a beautiful passive charmer; the boy as an active purposeful achiever. As a little girl grows up, the affirmation she receives very often centres around something over which she has little or no control – the appearance of her body. She may learn very quickly that her female body must conform to certain standards set by others and this may lead in later life to problems with eating and chronic dissatisfaction with her appearance. She may receive the message that her value lies, not so much in what she accomplishes, but in how she looks. Mother exerts the greatest influence on her baby daughter. Her own experience of herself as a woman is communicated in countless ways. 'Most women', says Orbach (1993), 'live with feelings of self-disgust and dislike ... because of the process of psychological and social femininity they have lived through' and so, in bringing up a baby girl, 'a mother is inevitably transmitting some negative feelings about being female' (p. 59). These may be conveyed by mother's excessive preoccupation with her appearance, thus demonstrating to her daughter that the female body, while being admired as a beautiful object, is nevertheless essentially lacking and in need of constant improvement. Play activities for little girls – dressing up, toy make-up kits, Barbie dolls with outfits for every occasion – may drive home the message that our female bodies, even young slender ones, are not acceptable in their natural form. Fathers can also play a significant role in this idealising/devaluing of the female body. They too may be conditioned by the cultural image of woman as beautiful doll, made to delight the male eye. Maccoby and Jacklin (1974) cite a study in which fathers were requested to describe their little daughters' behaviour. Ten out of twenty fathers did so in the following terms: 'a bit of a flirt; arch and playful with people; a pretended coyness; soft and cuddly and loving. She cuddles and flatters in subtle ways. She's going to be sexy' (Quoted in Baker 1984, p. 73). As Kaschak (1992, p. 92) points out, even a renowned analyst like Harold Searles seemed to view his baby daughter in terms of her body and sexuality.

> Towards my daughter, now eight years of age, I have experienced innumerable fantasies and feelings of a romantic love kind, thoroughly complementary to the romantically adoring seductive behaviour which she has shown towards her father often times ever since she was about two or three years of age ... she would play the supremely confident coquette with me and I would feel enthralled by her charms. (Searles 1979, p. 296)

Such reactions from fathers may teach girls very early on to devalue their abilities and regard themselves as sexual objects whose function is to flatter and stimulate male sexual interest by using their bodies seductively. Little girls may conclude that although they do not have easy access to the power enjoyed by the possessor of the penis, never-theless they have the power to attract and control the other sex through the use of their bodies. As Greenspan (1983) remarks: 'The more beautiful a woman's body, the more power she has – either to win fame and fortune on her own, or to lure a man into marriage and win his fame and fortune vicariously' (p. 163). Hence, woman's eternal preoccupation with appearance. 'Women', she continues 'are fashion crazy, not because we are frivolous but because we know that our bodies are our only power and we take them as seriously as men take their work' (pp. 163–4). Little girls who are affirmed only in their bodily appearance and not in other ways, often grow up with a profound lack of self-esteem and a preoccupation with body and appearance.

Adolescence is the time when body image becomes an even more pressing problem for the young girl who may experience her body as suddenly out of control. Her body becomes rounded; pubic hair appears and she experiences her first menstrual period. She becomes extremely self-conscious. She is rarely satisfied with her body – either her breasts are too small or too large, her hips too wide; her hair too straight or too curly; she is too tall, too short – in other words, she does not, cannot, measure up to the current standards of beauty reflected in the faces and bodies she sees in the glossy magazines and on the cinema and television screens. She may see her body as 'other', as an enemy to be controlled. Orbach (1993) says: 'The adolescent girl is learning to develop a split between her body and her self' (p. 28), seeing her body as a thing apart from her real self – an object to be scrutinised anxiously in the mirror every day, to be judged and invariably found wanting, to be starved, restrained, manipulated, worked on in order to make it more pleasing to the gaze of others, more 'in conformity with the designated ideal of the day' (p. 10), and that ideal changes almost yearly. 'Since the 1960s, women's bodies have been getting slimmer and slimmer ... no woman today has the right body for more than a season or two' (Orbach 1993, p. 53). Her relationship to her body then, is one of perpetual warfare and a young girl's energy may repeatedly be diverted from more worthwhile pursuits into this unceasing effort to improve what society tells her is her greatest asset but which, in her experience, seems to be her biggest problem. Her interest in clothes grows and often she needs to spend inordinate amounts of time, money and energy in dressing in what is believed to be the contem-porary mode. However, all her efforts are frequently experienced as futile since the right look is well-nigh impossible to achieve. Freedman (1988) quotes studies which show that 'nearly half the girls in a survey of twenty thousand teenagers reported that they frequently felt ugly' and she continues: 'adolescent girls are tormented by poor body image partly because they have learned during childhood to overvalue, display and mistrust their appearance' (p. 130).

Body-image problems can continue to plague women into adulthood when the importance of attracting a sexual partner becomes a priority. It has been suggested that the male in search of a female partner places great value on female beauty. 'A survey of twenty-eight thousand readers of *Psychology Today* found that almost twice as many males as females considered physical attractiveness as "very important" or "essential" in an ideal member of the opposite sex' (Jackson 1992, p. 64). Small wonder then that women feel compelled to constantly work on their appearance through dieting, make-up, clothes buying, and, more recently, submitting themselves to the knives of cosmetic surgeons who 'depend for their considerable livelihood on selling women a feeling of terminal ugliness' (Wolf 1990, p. 234). Moreover, constant comparison of herself with the beauties in the media results in a persistent nagging insecurity about her physical appearance and indeed her basic self-worth since there is some evidence to suggest that body image and self-esteem are closely linked (Jackson 1992, p. 185; Sanford and Donovan 1984, p. 138). Worrying about one's looks is worrying about one's worth, one's lovability. Horney (1970) claims that 'a woman's self-berating on the score of looks ... is fed from a deep source. The question: "Am I attractive?" is inseparable from another one: "Am I lovable?"' (p. 138). And the answer to the second question invariably depends on the answer to the first. Hence the importance of enhancing her appearance to mask the imperfections which she believes 'are grounds for self-contempt and proof of her worthlessness' (Westkott 1986, p. 156). She needs the constant reassurance from those around her that she is indeed attractive and therefore lovable. And so she is acutely sensitive to the judgements and evaluations of others, conscious of herself and of the impressions she may be making on others, especially men. 'A woman must continually watch herself', says Berger (1972). 'She is almost continually accompanied by her own image of herself ... From earliest childhood, she has been taught and persuaded to survey herself continually' (p. 46). She is always on show, highly visible yet culturally invisible. By concentrating on fashion, a woman wishes to be really seen as opposed to being merely visible. She dresses well in order to feel good about her embodied self, to feel competent in her chosen role and equal to the demands of social surveillance. The downside of this may be that by too great an emphasis on the external image, a woman may substitute the cultivation of appearance for the deeper and more difficult task of cultivating the self. The second half of life has traditionally been seen as an opportunity to engage in this task of cultivating the self – a coming to a deeper awareness of oneself and integrating one's shadow (Erikson 1950; Jung 1961; Levinson 1978; O'Collins 1978). It is also a time of crisis, especially for a woman since, as the youth and beauty which she has taken such pains to cultivate fades, so too does her power as an erotic object in the eyes of men. As a woman ages, she may note a dramatic shift in the kind of attention she receives from others. Instead of being the recipient of interested, sometimes admiring glances from men, she may now be overlooked, visually dismissed as sexually undesirable. 'Ageing for women', says Sontag, 'means a humiliating process of gradual sexual disqualification' (Sontag 1972, p. 3) This may lead to deep doubts about her identity and value as a woman. 'When a woman believes that her identity depends on her beauty, ageing means that she loses portions of her identity – and her value – with each successive birthday' (Baker 1984, p. 151). Being viewed solely in terms of a beautiful object in the eyes of others is, of course, diminishing. It is true that in the process of becoming a self, we need to have the reflexive capacity to become objects to ourselves, to view ourselves from the standpoint of others (Tseelon 1995, p. 75). This self-objecti-fication is the same for men and women alike. However, when a woman internalises object status to such a degree that she has little or no sense of agency; that she feels that she has no self at all but is rather a collection of other peoples's (especially men's) desires and expecta-tions (Greenspan 1983, p. 187); that all there is to her is the external beautiful mask, so sought-after and lauded by society, then a real problem exists for a woman, especially as she ages. On the whole there seems to be a paucity of research on the effects on older women of the loss of physical attractiveness. The literature that does exist on the subject seems to take it for granted that women have the same concerns about body image throughout the whole of the life cycle. Beauty equals youth and so with gradual ageing the pursuit of beauty becomes a more urgent concern. However, a study carried out by Berkun (1983) contradicts the common assumption that women, as they age, are excessively preoccupied with their changing appearance and unhappy about looking older. Fisher (1973) also concluded that 'the extremely negative picture of body ageing that is current in our culture is largely in the eye of the young beholder who is confronted with an image of what he or she could become' (pp. 250–1). Having said that, there is evidence to suggest that our society does devalue older women (Greer 1991) and in grappling with the belief that being older and not so attractive is being less, some older women's preoccupation with their bodies may give the impression that they see them as problems to be solved, as enemies against which relentless war must be waged in order to recover something of the youthful, unblemished look of former years. The older woman's power as an erotic object has gone; so too her power to give birth and nurture the next generation. The knowledge and power which come through experience and which can equip her to fulfil a valuable role as model and mentor for the younger generations are often not acknowledged or valued. If they were, then perhaps she could allow herself to age naturally, taking pride in the signs of a long and well-lived life which are etched on her face and body. She could reject society's demand that she remain forever the child-woman and assume the power and status that she has earned as a woman who has lived, loved and worked well for many years.

Shopping For a New Improved Skin

It has been claimed that in modern society women are classified 'as consumers or as consumed rather than as producers/creators' (Williamson 1992, p. 97). Advertisers frequently portray the beautifully attired and perfectly formed female body as merchandise to be acquired and consumed by the purchaser (usually male) along with his rare wine, expensive aftershave or luxurious car. But women are also defined as 'natural' shoppers. 'Shopping is both women's work and identity' (Williamson 1992, p. 106) and they generally spend much more on clothes and have a more extensive wardrobe than men. Why do women shop? Researchers have discovered that shopping serves a variety of purposes other than the procurement of the needed object. It can be a leisure activity, sensory stimulation, a means of gratifying and rewarding oneself, an escape from boredom and feelings of depression, a way of spending time in the company of others, an opportunity to command attention and respect from sales assistants and to enjoy the feeling of status and power which that brings (Tauber 1972, pp. 47–8). It can provide temporary relief from stress, from feeling alone and depressed; it can enable the shopper 'to feel real and alive inside rather than emotionally dead or empty' (Krueger 1988, pp. 580–1). The experience of shopping, then, is just as important to the shopper as the actual purchase of a commodity. In fact research has shown that some consumers show great indifference to their purchases which 'remain wrapped and hidden in cupboards' (Elliott et al. 1996, p. 355). Addictive shopping has received not a little attention in recent reviews (Glatt and Cook 1987; O'Guinn and Faber 1988; 1989; d'Astous

1990; Elliott et al. 1996) and it has been suggested that such consumers are 'predominantly female' (Elliott et al. 1996, p. 355). The difference between the addictive and ordinary consumer is that the former uses shopping predominantly 'to remedy depression and emptiness and [it] is a chronic pattern' (Krueger 1988, p. 574). There is also present a limited ability to control the behaviour despite the fact that it has deleterious consequences for the individual. A negative body image can also trigger uncontrolled spending, especially on clothes. Johnston (1994) says that 'shopping for clothes can be a way of coping with appearance obsession' and that women may 'use fashion to compensate for a negative body image' (pp. 118–19). Krueger (1988), in his study of four female shoppers, concluded that compulsive clothes shopping occurs 'in individuals who are very conscious of how they look and appear to others'. Such people, he claims, have suffered a narcissistic injury – usually the breaking of an emotional bond with some significant person and so they have a compelling need to accumulate clothes 'in a desperate need to appear attractive and desirable' hoping that 'new clothes will fulfil [their] need for affirmation' (p. 575). They buy clothes, therefore, to fill an inner void, hoping that with the new outfit, they will feel emotionally satisfied, but, as in the case of Brittany, one of Krueger's patients, 'the good hopeful feeling would last until she wore the clothes for the first time. As soon as the tags were gone, the feeling was gone' (p. 577). Although not all women fall into the category of addictive consumers, nevertheless, many women do buy more clothes than they need and very often buy to repair mood and boost self-esteem. Many women's self-esteem depends on others' responses to them and since physical attractiveness invariably receives a positive response (Jackson 1992), clothes shopping seems to be a sure way of effecting a transformation which will elicit that admiration and acceptance which is proof that they are lovable and acceptable. The clothes are an attempt to provide a defence against the dreaded feeling that basically their bodies and their genitals are ugly or unacceptable. 'Feminine clothes constitute improved skin, minus the frightening genitals' (Bergler 1953, p. 99). Clothing is more than decoration; clothes shopping is more than a leisure activity or a means of replenishing one's wardrobe; it can be a plea for recognition, for significance. It can signify a desire to be looked at and to be really seen. As Chapkis (1986) says, 'men, having greater access to economic and political power have not the same need to parade their masculinity – wealth and social position being proof enough of their manhood' (p. 128). A woman's access to power is through her female body and so her need to improve the body through clothes-buying is in order to gain control and power, to be desired, because if she is desired, she is worth something. In buying the latest fashion, she is purchasing not only bodily perfection but a whole series of attributes which will make her desirable. She is buying an identity, a way of life, goodness, truth, love, knowledge, competence, success, whatever she needs most. With the right clothes she hopes to get the job, money, recognition, love and of course the man she desires. Unfortunately, as experience may demonstrate, this does not always happen. In fact, as Hatfield and Sprecher (1986) suggest, she may 'end up with friends and associates who care overmuch about the superficial – and these are usually not especially appealing people' (p. 375). So while the cultivation of one's appearance can be fun, helpful to the growth of body satisfaction and self-esteem, nevertheless 'one may do better in the long run if one concentrates primarily on developing personality/skills/character' (p. 370).

METHODOLOGY

This research was conducted in two stages. First a 'Clothes Shopping Dependency Scale' was distributed to women's groups and staffs of hospitals and schools. This instrument was adapted from Johnston (1994) and was used to assess women's motives for shopping. The instrument measured emotions surrounding shopping; if clothes shopping was used to improve body image; as an antidote for negative feelings or a response to conflicts in relationships. All items were assessed via a five-point scale asking respondents to indicate the frequency (never, rarely, sometimes, often, almost, always) that they engaged in various behaviours, experienced different feelings or found themselves in different situations. Of the 300 questionnaires sent out, 236 were returned – a return of 78.6 per cent.

The second stage of the research process consisted of fifteen in-depth interviews with 'ordinary' female shoppers. These indicated their willingness to be interviewed by ticking a box at the bottom of the Clothes Shopping Dependency Scale and supplying their name, address and phone number. They were then contacted and dates and times for interviews were fixed. Each interview, which was fairly unstructured and which aimed at exploring their sense of themselves and their bodies before, during and after a clothes shopping expedition, lasted between 45 and 60 minutes. All were tape recorded and transcribed verbatim and later analysed using a procedure based on Colaizzi's (1978) phenomenological method. Each protocol was read and significant statements were listed and clustered into themes. Meanings were then formulated and a final exhaustive description was drawn up incorporating all the material provided by the co-researchers who were later contacted for validation.

FINDINGS

The results of the mail survey seem to suggest that clothes-buying may be one of the ways some women use to improve their body image. By decorating the body in the latest creations, women believe that they look better and so they tend to feel better about themselves. Of the respondants, 51 per cent stated that buying new clothes makes them feel better about the way they look (20 per cent almost always; 31 per cent often); 14 per cent acknowledged that they use fashionable clothes to compensate for the negative view they have of their bodies (2 per cent almost always; 12 per cent often); 10 per cent believe that it is 'very important' to wear the latest fashion (5 per cent almost always; 5 per cent often); 15 per cent avoid social occasions because they have 'nothing to wear' (2 per cent almost always; 13 per cent often). The survey also suggests that clothes shopping provides an emotionally satisfying experience for a significant number of women (12 per cent almost always; 21 per cent often), although an almost equally significant number find that the opposite is true (9 per cent never; 22 per cent rarely). A number (17 per cent) shop to relieve feelings of boredom, loneliness or depression; 10 per cent of those surveyed feel guilt about spending money on themselves and this feeling was expressed by some of those who were later interviewed.

The interviews, conducted as they were in an unhurried fashion, facilitated the leisurely exploration of the participants' reflections and feelings before, during and after the shopping expedition. The following is a comprehensive statement of the findings.

There is general agreement that society seems to place much more pressure on women than on men to look attractive. Women feel they are judged initially by their external appearance. An attractive exterior opens doors. Lack of style, on the other hand, may at times be equated with lack of worth, intelligence, competence and other qualities. This emphasis on looks puts pressure on some women to spend inordinate amounts of money and time on body maintenance and can distract them from the pursuit of other, more satisfying goals. Others find that preoccupation with looks prevents them from being fully open and spontaneous in their relationships with men and women alike. When relationships fail, the conclusion is sometimes reached that they have not been careful enough to cultivate a sufficiently pleasing appearance. An excessive concern for appearance prevents women from being relaxed and at home in their bodies and above all it can lead to a chronic dissatisfaction with the body itself because no matter how much effort is expended, the peerless beauties on the TV screens or in the glossy magazines can never be matched. There is a certain fragmentation of the body – some parts being dissociated from the self and disowned because they are not pleasing and can spoil the overall look. 'I'm happy enough with my body except for ... my legs, stomach, sloping shoulders, feet, nose.' There is an expression of sadness that women find it difficult to say to themselves with any conviction that they look good. Comparison with other women, especially women in the media, reinforces feelings of lack of attractiveness. The battle against weight-gain and loss of looks due to ageing is on-going. The sense that the female body is ugly is so deeply internalised that some women, despite being complimented on their looks, find it difficult to believe and accept the praise. There is a sense of shame of one's body which can give rise in some to the desire to pass unnoticed, to merge with the crowd and to become invisible. Clothes are sometimes used to camouflage defects and to draw attention away from the 'ugly parts'. In some instances there is a need to downplay sexuality and to lessen its power by wearing loose-fitting clothes. Simultaneously there is a profound need to be noticed, to stand out from the crowd, to be special, above all in the eyes of a significant other. There is, in some cases, the desire to be seen as a sexual being and the power to attract the gaze of the other sex is regarded as confirmation of one's femininity, fundamental identity and lovability. Clothes draw attention to sexuality but the 'wrong' choice of apparel may render the woman invisible and undesirable with negative consequences for her feelings of self-worth and even her ability to function. Yet even with the 'right' clothes, there is no guarantee that the feelings within will change. Clothes transform the exterior but do not change the person within. Clothes can enhace the body, making the person feel attractive, more desired and more loved. This can boost self-confidence and raise self-esteem and women can at times be tempted to believe that more is better and become drawn into excessive shopping.

The shopping expedition is generally experienced as pleasurable, at least initially and is engaged in for a variety of reasons. For some, buying new clothes is experienced as a way of giving to oneself emotionally. Shopping is a means of feeding the self, of compensating for past and current deprivation – material or emotional. It can be a kind of material reward for a job well done; a form of leisure in the pleasing company of friends; an escape from boredom by introducing novelty into one's life although it is the experience of some that as soon as the novelty of the purchase wears off, there can be as much, if not more, dissatisfaction than before. It can be a conscious attempt to improve body image by buying clothes which flatter and draw attention to oneself.

The pre-shopping mood is generally one of anticipation and hope that one's desires will be fulfilled. To begin with, the experience is pleasurable, especially if no specific purchase is being contemplated. During the shopping experience itself, seeing, touching, smelling can be seductive, inducing the shopper to spend money on garments which look good in the shop but which, on arriving home, seem to lose their magic and give rise to feelings of disappointment and disillusionment. There is the wish to enter into solitary communion with the self, imagining how one will look in a certain garment or how others will react. Not all shoppers, however, experience positive feelings. For those who have a specific purchase to make, there can be feelings of anxiety and frustration, especially as time goes by and the desired object cannot be found. Comparing oneself to glamorous sales personnel and other women shoppers can lead to feelings of envy of those who have a better body shape or more financial resources than oneself. Hence shopping can often reinforce feelings of dissatisfaction with the body – its size, shape and weight. There is an awareness among some that in shopping, we are being sold more than clothes – the hope of beauty, status, love, acceptance, the esteem of others; in short, an image which promises that with the dress, life might be better, that one will be transformed into an object of desire and envy in others' eyes. This, of course, is an illusion perpetuated by the consumer society which seems to equate having with being. Some, aware of the big lie, feel resentment at a society where there is such a wide gulf between the 'haves' and the 'have-nots' and they endeavour to resist what they call the 'obscenity' of the fashion world. Guilt is another strong emotion experienced during the shopping trip. There is in some women a feeling of lack of entitlement to spend money on themselves. Some assuage guilt by shopping in charity shops, hunting obsessively for bargains or buying outfits for partners or children. If they do succumb to temptation, there is the tendency to hide the purchase from others.

The post-shopping experience is a mixture of emotions – elation at having made a good purchase, relief at having acquired a desired object or escaped the misfortune of having spent money foolishly. Sometimes the euphoria of having obtained something new disappears and guilt appears – guilt at having spent money on oneself. In some cases there is a reluctance to don the new garment. It is considered too good to wear and the wearer somehow unworthy of it. There is the sense also that the garment might be spoiled by putting it on as if contact with the body detracts from the newness and uniqueness of the garment, contaminating it in some way. There is a certain fear too that the garment may not fulfil its promise to correct bodily defects and effect transformation into a perfect being, so the wearing of it is deferred so as to avoid the feared disappointment. When the purchase is linked to a failed relationship, it loses its appeal and becomes a hated object reminding one of the hurt associated with the breaking-up of the relationship. For some the wrong purchase can ruin a whole day, affect performance and there can be no peace until the mistake is rectified. Shopping as a 'feed' is rarely satisfying and consuming more and more in the form of multiple buying can only lead to more serious problems.

DISCUSSION

A close analysis of the interviews seems to support the findings in the research literature: namely that there are some women who continue to be very much affected by the beauty imperative and that in spite of constant body maintenance practices they tend to see themselves more negatively than positively (Jackson 1992). Clothes are used to improve one's body image; either by drawing attention to good points or by camouflaging bad points. Shopping for clothes, while being pleasurable, can often reinforce feelings of dissatisfaction, especially when clothes do not fit or when one compares oneself to young, glamorous sales assistants or other more attractive female shoppers. This discussion will touch on three themes which emerge from the research. First, the equation of woman with body and appearance and its effects on her sense of self and her feelings of self-worth. Second, the simultaneous desire for visibility and invisibility and its relation to power and finally, the presence of guilt in many of the cases.

One's sense of self is very much formed on 'the basis of the appraisals of others using the reaction of others as mirror' (Mollon 1993, p. 21). From the cradle humans rely on the empathic responsiveness of their caretakers – usually mother – to confirm their existence, their lovability. Kohut (1971) speaks of 'the gleam in mother's eye' which supports the child's sense of self. This need for mirroring is enduring and as Friday (1996) suggests, women, who as children may not have felt seen or valued by mother on whose gaze they depended for a sense of themselves, may now feel the overwhelming need to capture the gaze, the attention of men, of sales assistants, in an attempt to compensate for the felt invisibility in the eyes of mother. In the never-ending filling up of their wardrobes, they may be seeking 'a look, an image arresting enough to make people [mother] change focus, abandon whatever, whomever they were taking in, leave them. Take *me* in' (p. 24). They are saying in their hunger for the gaze: 'Look at me. See me or I will die' (Friday 1996, p. 186). One of the participants in this study revealed that her principal aim in dressing fashionably was to attract the gaze of male colleagues. 'I like to be the centre of attention in that way ... I actively crave it and think about it all the time especially if I'm buying clothes for work.' Her preparation for work consists not so much in preparing her brief, but in choosing very carefully the outfit which will highlight her assets and hide her defects and so win the attention and admiration she craves. 'I enhance the part of me which I think is attractive and hope to draw attention away from my face which isn't attractive.' Wearing the wrong thing would mean that she would not be looked at or admired and when that happens the whole day is spoiled and her ability to function impaired. She seems to feel that a pleasing appearance, more than competence in her career, will win love and acceptance – a message which she now recognises has its roots in her relationship with her father. 'My father was always going on about how pretty I am ... he was a painter and very visually in tune ... he was the one who loved me a lot ... yet I've never really believed it.' One might suggest that this woman's sense of self is 'externally rather than internally defined' (Kaschak 1992, p. 97). It is an unstable sense of self since 'it is subject to redefinition based on changes in her appearance or evaluations thereof' (ibid.). Who one really is is often obscured by external appearance and another participant mourned the fact that 'people may get the wrong impression of me by my clothes – until they get to know me'. Some recognise that they sometimes feel as if they have a multiplicity of selves depending on the roles they are required to assume and the way they feel obliged to tailor, not only their appearance but also their reactions and conversations to suit others. Another woman speaks of her abandonment of the 'light, fluffy, feminine look' which seemed to be the expectation in her teens and twenties and now she feels more comfortable about expressing her feeling 'of substance'. At times, shopping for clothes feels like an assault on one's self-esteem. In not finding the right clothes and clothes that fit, some women tend to blame their bodies and themselves rather than a fashion industry which demands a standardised body for all women which must fit the clothes supplied by the shops. As Corrigan (1997) neatly puts it: 'Ready-made clothing demands ready-made bodies' (p. 64). One of the women in the study decried this subordination of the body to the fashion industry. 'I resent a sales woman telling me I'm not the right size ... it's the garment that isn't the right size.'

Being looked at and judged favourably can feel life-giving but there are looks which may objectify giving rise to feelings of self-hatred and shame. 'Shame results in the wish not to be seen' (Mollon 1993, p. 48), to become invisible. At the same time, there is also a desire and need to be seen. 'I don't want to draw attention to myself but at the same time I want to look attractive and be noticed.' 'Sometimes I feel dull and not wanting to be noticed and I dress like that but other times I feel sexy and definitely want to be noticed and dress accordingly.'

Visibility and invisibility and its relation to power is an issue which is always problematic for women. Power for a number of women in the study still seems to mean sexual power, the power to attract the other sex through body display. One woman rejoices in the power of her body to command attention. 'When I'm in a room with a lot of men and I'm the centre of attention – it feels good, very right.' At the same time she asks herself: 'Am I being taken seriously enough though? I do hope so.' And this is the dilemma women can find themselves in. If a woman is too attractively and strikingly dressed, too visible, she may be understood to be sending out sexual signals which may be at odds with her wish to be respected as a professional woman. On the other hand, if she dresses 'down' she risks being overlooked, even ridiculed and again her competence may be called in question. 'When I'm not well turned out, I tend to skulk in a corner, not socialise. I feel invisible, powerless.' As well as professional ability, it seems that women must also possess what Wolf (1990) calls the 'professional beauty qualification', a necessary 'condition for women's hiring and promotion' (p. 27). In shopping for clothes, one of the questions to be answered is: 'How will this garment convey my charm and femininity as well as my competence and professionalism?' Small wonder then that shopping can be a stressful business. Other women in the study spoke of their rejection of the myth that the only source of woman's power is her body. 'I don't need to display myself in beautiful clothes as much as I used to ... I don't feel I need to get that recognition.' 'I'm beginning to feel more comfortable about saying that I have got more substance now and I want to convey that.'

One noteworthy finding of this study is the pervasive presence of guilt. Most of the women feel guilty about spending money on themselves; nearly all hunt for bargains and a significant number shop in charity shops. 'I place a lot of importance on bargains.' 'I feel guilty about giving to myself and I usually end up spending on my husband and the children.' 'My husband has no qualms about spending money on his hobbies and on his car but I feel guilty when I spend money on clothes.' Guilt seems to be an emotion that women are 'at home with'. As Chaplin (1988) points out, women, having been traditionally blamed for society's ills, tend to respond automatically to failures in relationships by: 'it was all my fault ... I wasn't attractive enough ...

there must be something wrong with me' (p. 57). A woman's guilt may come from her sense of inferiority – that she 'is not worth that much [and] does not deserve a dress/bag/shoes ...' (Orbach 1993, p. 136), or from the feeling that in giving to herself, she is depriving the family of nurturance which it is her duty to provide. Some of the interviewees seem to be experiencing 'existential guilt'. They are struck by the 'perception of the difference between what a thing is and what it ought to be' (May 1989, p. 36). One woman puts this point very forcefully:

> I often think it's not right pampering myself by buying expensive clothes when so many people are without the necessities – that feeling gets stronger when I see people begging in the streets and fashionable women are hurrying by with their Harrods' bags and I think of the inequalities and feel guilty.

Such guilt, far from being 'neurotic' is surely a positive force, a call to the living out of deeper and more humane values and a rejection of uncontrolled consumption which causes deep divisions and suffering in our society.

IMPLICATIONS FOR THERAPY

Women who present themselves for therapy for whatever reason run the risk of being judged yet again on the basis of their looks. Hatfield and Sprecher (1986) claim that therapists 'are not immune to the glow cast by beauty [and] respond very differently to good-looking versus ugly people' (pp. 69–70). Not only is greater psychological disturbance more easily attributed to less attractive people, but also 'a client's appeal ... has a profound impact on therapists' first impressions, their diagnoses, and even on the eventual outcome of the therapy' (p. 71). Yalom's (1989) comments about his female patients are an example. Expressing his revulsion of what he terms 'fat women', he says: 'I find them disgusting ... breasts, laps, buttocks, shoulders, ... everything I like to see in a woman obscured in an avalanche of flesh ... How dare they impose that body on the rest of us?' (pp. 87–8). Clearly such attitudes betray a set of assumptions about women which can only be detrimental to the therapeutic process. The therapist who holds such views, instead of enabling women patients to rediscover, reclaim and rejoice in their bodies as an integral part of themselves, reinforces society's dictate that a woman's body should always be young, slim, attractive and pleasing to men. It further equates an attractive body with mental health. Even women therapists may conclude that if a woman succeeds in looking better her symptoms will cease. Kaschak

(1992) quotes 'therapy' carried out by one woman therapist which involved showing clients how to apply make-up more skilfully and dress more attractively (p. 105). Good therapy must surely include an analysis of the culture's myths about the female body and an examination of the multiplicity of meanings attached to a woman's looks. It involves an appraisal of the impact these myths may have on a woman's sense of self and on her self-esteem. It should aim at enabling women to 'de-emphasise androcentrically defined physical attractiveness' (Worell and Remer 1992, p. 99) so that they come to a greater acceptance and love of their own bodies and a sense of self which doesn't depend on appearance, body shape or the ability to attract a man (Ussher 1997, p. 456). It should enable women to take possession of the power that is theirs – the power to bring about change in their own lives and in society as a whole. There is a need certainly to change the internalised messages linking external looks with internal worth but as feminist therapists constantly emphasise, there must also be a commitment to the transformation of a society which delivers these messages and transmits values which have such a detrimental effect on women's development.

CONCLUSION

The results of this small study seem to suggest that women are still vulnerable to the beauty imperative and that in spite of the many advances brought about in women's lives by the feminist movement, they still seem affected by feelings of dissatisfaction about their bodies. Clothes and clothes shopping seem to be used to combat a negative body image. The experience of shopping gives rise to conflicting emotions – pleasurable anticipation, anxiety, anger, frustration, guilt, shame. It rarely, however, satisfies women's yearning for significance and meaning.

REFERENCES

Baker, N. (1984) *The Beauty Trap*. London, Piatkus Publications.
Beetham, M. (1966) *A Magazine of Her Own? Domesticity and Desire in the Woman's Magazine, 1800–1914*. London, Routledge.
Berger, J. (1972) *Ways of Seeing*. London, BBC and Penguin.
Bergler, E. (1953) *Fashion and the Unconscious*. New York, Brunner Pub.
Berkun, C. (1983) Changing Appearance for Women in the Middle Years of Life. Trauma? In E. Markson (ed.) *Older Women: Issues and prospects*. Toronto, Lexington Books.
Chaplin, J. (1988) *Feminist Counselling in Action*. London, Sage.

Chapkis, W. (1986) *Beauty Secrets: Women and the politics of appearance*. London, The Women's Press.

Colaizzi, P. (1978) Psychological Research as the Phenomenologist views it. In R. Valle and M. King (eds) *Existential Phenomenological Alternatives for Psychology*. New York, Open University Press.

Corrigan, P. (1997) *The Sociology of Consumption*. London, Sage.

d'Astous, A. (1990) An Inquiry into the Compulsive Side of 'Normal' Consumers. *Journal of Consumer Policy, 13*: 15–31.

Elliott, R. (1994) Addictive Consumption: Function and Fragmentation in Postmodernity. *Journal of Consumer Policy, 17*: 159–79.

Elliott, R., Eccles, S. and Gournay, K. (1996) Revenge, Existential Choice and Addictive Consumption. *Psychology and Marketing*, vol. 13 (8).

Erikson, E. (1950) *Childhood and Society*. London, Penguin Books.

Fisher, S. (1973) *Body Consciousness*. London, Calder and Boyars.

Frankenburg, F. and Yurgelun-Todd, D. (1984) Dressing Disorder. *American Journal of Psychiatry, 141*, 147.

Freedman, R. (1988) *Beauty Bound*. London, Columbas Books.

Freud, S. (1933) *New Introductory Lectures on Psychoanalysis*. London, Penguin Books.

Friday, N. (1996) *The Power of Beauty*. London, Hutchinson.

Glatt, M. and Cook, C.H. (1987) Pathological Spending as a Form of Psychological Dependence. *British Journal of Addiction, 82*, 1257–8.

Greenspan, M. (1983) *A New Approach to Women and Therapy*. Blue Ridge Summit PA, Tab Books.

Greer, G. (1991) *The Change: Women, ageing and the menopause*. London, Hamish Hamilton.

Hatfield, E. and Sprecher, S. (1986) *Mirror, Mirror ... The Importance of Looks in Everyday Life*. New York, State University of New York Press.

Horney, K. (1970) *Neurosis and Human Growth: The struggle towards self-realization*. New York, W.W. Norton and Co.

Jackson, L. (1992) *Physical Appearance and Gender: Sociobiological and sociocultural perspectives*. New York, State University of New York Press.

Johnston, J. (1994) *Appearance Obsession: Learning to love the way you look*. Deerfield Beach, Florida, Health Communications Inc.

Jung, C.G. (1961) *Memories, Dreams, Reflections*. New York, Random House.

Kaschak, E. (1992) *Engendered Lives: A new psychology of women's experience*. New York, Basic Books.

Kohut, H. (1971) *The Analysis of the Self*. New York, International Universities Press.

Krueger, D. (1988) On Compulsive Shopping and Spending: A psychodynamic inquiry. *American Journal of Psychotherapy*, vol. XLII, no. 4).

Levinson, D. (1978) *The Seasons of a Man's Life*. New York, Knopf.

Maccoby, E. and Jacklin, C. (1974) *The Psychology of Sex Differences*. Stanford, Ca., Stanford University Press.

May, R. (1989) *The Art of Counselling*. London, Souvenir Press.

Mollon, P. (1993) *The Fragile Self: The structure of narcissistic disturbances and its therapy*. London, Jason Aronson Inc.

O'Collins, G. (1978) *The Second Journey: Spiritual awareness and the mid-life crisis*. New York, Paulist Press.

O'Guinn, T. and Faber, R. (1988) Compulsive Consumption and Credit Abuse. *Journal of Consumer Policy 11*, 97–109.

O'Guinn, T. and Faber, R. (1989) Compulsive Buying: A phenomenological exploration. *Journal of Consumer Research*, vol. 16, 147–57.

Orbach, S. (1993) *Hunger Strike*. London, Penguin Books.

Sanford, L. and Donovan, M. (1984) *Women and Self-Esteem*. London, Penguin Books.

Searles, H. (1979) *Countertransference and Related Subjects: Selected Papers*. New York, International University Press.

Sontag, S. (1972) *The Double Standard of Ageing*. Toronto, The Women's Kit.

Suleiman, S. (ed.) (1986) *The Female Body in Western Culture: Contemporary perspectives.* New York, Harvard University Press.

Tauber, E. (1972) Why do People Shop? *Journal of Marketing,* vol. 36/4, 46–59.

Tseelon, E. (1995) *The Masque of Femininity: The presentation of woman in everyday life.* London, Sage Publications.

Ussher, J. M. (1997) *Fantasies of Femininity: Reframing the boundaries of sex.* London, Penguin Books.

Westkott, M. (1986) *The Feminist Legacy of Karen Horney.* New Haven and London, Yale University Press.

Williamson, J. (1992) I-less and Gaga in the West Edmonton Mall: Towards a Pedestrian Feminist Reading. In Currie and Raoul (eds) *Anatomy of Gender: Women's Struggle for the Body.* Ottawa, Carleton University Press.

Wolf, N. (1990) *The Beauty Myth.* London, Vintage Books.

Worell, J. and Remer, P. (1992) *Feminist Perspectives in Therapy: An empowerment model for women.* Chichester, John Wiley and Sons.

Yalom, I. (1989) *Love's Executioner and Other Tales of Psychotherapy.* London, Penguin.

7

The Ecology of Shopping:
A Transformational Experience

Rosalind Pearmain

We enter a new space ... has a kind of invisibility to those who have not entered it. (Daly 1973)

Space which is never separate from matter ... Space the shape of experience: the form of motion ... Space which she makes into lace ... Where she builds the house of her culture. Where her breast is a self-reflection. The place where she is recognised. And where she can see herself. Space where nothing is ever still and motion always changes shape. (Griffin 1978)

Irigaray claims that masculine modes of thought have performed a devastating sleight of hand: they have obliterated the debt they owe to the most primordial of spaces, the maternal space from which all subjects emerge, and which they ceaselessly attempt to usurp ... (Grosz 1995)

This exploration of shopping is based on the assumption that shops and shoppers cannot be considered separately as discrete entities within different fields of discourse. It involves challenging the abstract conception of a shop as a purely economic unit stimulating desire and consumption and of a customer as a precisely mapped individual within sociological or psychological matrices. People mostly talk about going shopping as a particular activity, as a verb, that involves a particular engagement with a particular environment in order to gain certain kinds of experiences. The goods acquired, while seemingly central, often lose their charge when transposed to the home. Those who identify themselves as shopping addicts will often simply accumulate at home the goods acquired still within their wrappings, unused. It is as if, once these goods are removed from their context, they lose the meaning that was constellated around their acquisition. Therefore, it might be more fruitful to consider the experience of shopping as a lived experience, in the same way that we talk about going for a drive, going for a walk, or for a swim. The environmental and perceptual aspects of shopping involve the subjective preoccupations of shoppers; the experience of form and texture, qualities, moods. Shops are another extension of personally inhabited spaces; they represent personal identities, preoccupations, fantasies and dreams. They involve a co-creation between the shopping environment and the shopper's own style of being-in-the-world.

Shopping takes up an increasing amount of people's time, energy and preoccupations. Yet, within the disciplines of interior design, of architecture, of environmental psychology, of psychology itself, there is an extraordinary void in accounts of the lived experience of shops and shopping. The main focus in material that appears in architectural journals and literature seems to be very much focused on the externals of shape and form against the background of space as an abstraction beyond human experiencing. In other words, the external visual perception of form is stressed without the accompanying other perceptual experience of spaces – the kinaesthetic experiences of space, the quality of air, temperature, of materials, of sound, of the orientation and maneouvring that we learn in negotiating the spaces that shops provide. For example, the only book of shop designs that could be found currently in print, consisted of highly expensive and beautiful designer shops in Italy. These were highly specialised and focused on the static, aesthetic spectacle. No person was visible within the photographs. The interiors, beautiful like temples, conveyed an abstracted notion of the shop as dedicated to aesthetics alone without the participation of living persons moving through. Some body had gone missing in all of this.

It is mainly within the feminist contribution to architecture that the internal experiences of lived spaces – as embodied space – are addressed. It is a compelling reminder of the famous or infamous study by Erickson (1951) on the ways in which young children of different genders played with bricks. Boys tended to build towers; girls tended to build enclosed spaces with openings. It is arguable that there are interesting gender differences in the experience of space (Kestenberg 1967). These have been observed in movement development patterns which focus on individuals' idiosyncratic relationship with space. These seem to indicate some gender disparities as to whether space is primarily experienced as an external or internal domain. Within the field of feminist studies, which has addressed the more internal emphasis on space for women, much attention has been paid to the lived experience of the home but not yet the shop. In a survey of a journal on environmental psychology, there was one article relating to a study on a shopping mall through sixteen years of its life. Similarly,

Mica Nava in her 'Modernity's Disavowal: Women, the City and the Department Store' (1997) also discovered an extraordinary absence of research into the role of women in urban development and public life in the nineteenth and twentieth centuries and in relation to the development of the department store, although she documents the increased recognition of the role of women as consumers.

This absence of person is a shock. The growth of shops and shopping landscapes marks one of the most evident areas of expansion and presence within our lives. New shopping domains are built within months, accompanied by new roads, more cars to reach them and longer opening hours to spend time in them. Shopping seems to be assumed to be obvious, the most self-explanatory of human behaviours which we can link with hunting and gathering, survival, the acquisition of wealth, the opportunity for self-expression and cultivation of lifestyle. Inevitably, perhaps, we have also identified a new problem that has developed in parallel, the notion of addiction to shopping.

The domain of shopping engages cross-disciplines – economics, design, architecture, urban planning, psychology, sociology, and now psychotherapy. Perhaps as a result of the sheer material base of a phenomenon so clearly identified with an object, the role of person, of subjectivity in this field has been missing. Furthermore, as noted, the presence of women in this world is missing. As David Uzzell points out, with some understatement, in the *Journal of Environmental Psychology*, that 'it seems to indicate a gender issue'. Most attention has been given to the study of the office, hardly any to shopping. 'Shopping has long had an image of being an unenjoyable chore undertaken by women ... Shopping has been seen as a very ordinary activity, part of the taken-for-granted world of everyday life' (Uzzell 1995, p. 300).

Shopping is mostly described within the sphere of economics. It is singularly an activity relating to the concrete and material aspects of existence; production, money, goods, transaction. Beyond functional analysis, there are ideas about the fetishism of commodities, of addiction to material possessions and acquisitiveness characteristic of the demands of late twentieth-century multinational capitalism driven by technological changes and the notion of continual economic growth and material wealth. Advertising is designed to evoke wishes and desires and to promise satisfaction. Possessing something conveys some kind of satisfaction.

Within this context, the notion of shopping addiction is also fairly concrete. People go on wanting goods because they are seeking satisfaction. But since goods cannot provide satisfaction, more and more are steadily accumulated. It is part of the mythology of contemporary western capitalism. Perhaps from a psychotherapeutic perspective, the acquisition may be viewed as associated with soothing, with calming, with stimulating, with enacting a manic kind of omnipotence, of revenge, of envy, of an attempt to fill inner emptiness. The difficulty with all of these conceptions is that they imply a kind of separateness of persons from environment, of objects from their context, of the internalised meanings of the individual from the domain of the shop. Fascinating in all of this abstract discussion and discourse concerning shopping, is the missing embodied human being living in a world of complex relationships, in which shopping is everyday and intertwined with a multidimensional system of meanings and perceptions. Each of us has a highly charged, lived relationship with shopping which is changing and developing daily throughout our lifespans. It is part of our ecology.

The Missing Person

The theme of the missing person, and of the feminine, re-evokes Simone de Beauvoir's discussion of the Second Sex (1997). But within the contemporary post-modern styles of discourse, the realm of the feminine has been further abstracted and relegated to the mystery of the 'other' or the 'different'. This kind of 'other' is evoked within trace references to the exotic, to the foreign, to the sexual, to the body, to the realm of sexual ambiguity, but increasingly in abstracted forms. Therefore, for example, the ways in which women's identity is constructed can be drawn on ironically or as an abstraction to evoke certain meanings and cultural forces. Surface idioms are used abstractly in the place of the substance of individual, idiosyncratic experience. Within images and styles of advertising, we may be reminded of a certain kind of femininity construed within the past communist regime in Russia for example, or of a Far Eastern kind of femininity, or of Hollywood glamour, but the actual person is not there. In discussion of shopping, the hierarchy of function and structure takes for granted the hidden presence of shoppers and their daily lives. This becomes subsumed and contained within the display and layouts designed to appeal psychologically or to stimulate quick buying. But then the person who is buying disappears – perhaps as a sociologically defined entity, a certain kind of consumer, a certain kind of participant within the economic system.

Where is anything of body or substance left after this abstract cul-de-sac? Macleod (1995) presents a paramount problem that is posed generally by post-structuralist theory which is the omission of any connection between an abstract notion of 'other' and women's actual social situation. The abstract notions of other, of absence and of lack that have been frequently used to convey the domain of women perpetuate their terms. 'While the rejection of masculine hierarchies has been rejected', argues MacLeod (ibid.), 'the feminine has become essentialised' – all that is dark, mysterious and otherworldly.

While feminisim has identified some historical factors that have distorted relations with the body and matter – (heard in such terms as 'the brute fact' and 'the dumb object'), Deborah Fausch (1996) emphasises the need to recognise that while the bodily may be feminine and the feminine may have body, it also has reason. A feminist approach to architecture may articulate and engender certain experiences that give validity to the bodily experience of self for both sexes and address contemporary culture's tendency to abstraction, distortion, mistreatment and banishment of the body from space. Architecture very often fails to include this. Henri Lefebvre (1992) questions how this process came about in our conceptualisation of space:

> The shift, which is so hard to grasp, from the space of the body to the body-in-space, from opacity (warm) to translucency (cold) somehow facilitates the spiriting away or scotomisation of the body. How did this magic ever become possible – and how does it continue to be possible? (Lefebvre 1992, p. 20)

Within the context of shopping, this disconnection of shopping spaces from the sphere of women is particularly charged when it is women who have been the predominant shoppers in contemporary life. It has been women who have primarily inhabited shops and who have given life to them. The ground of space, of our origins, of our primary experience of space through body, has become steadily abstracted and divorced and compartmentalised. In this way, the embodied life becomes a private, hidden domain of home, and the abstract, disembodied life is represented in the design of our urban spaces which are shaped as functional, processes for transport, productivity and consumption. In this mechanisation, we are again in danger of losing the ground, of relationship in how persons inhabit their environment; shopping is another kind of inhabitation and dwelling.

Within the field of psychology, shopping addiction again locates the focus externally onto the cold, opaque object of acquisition, the repetitive accumulation of goods which pile up within the subject's home. The stress on the object of acquisition as a visually separated external reality and the internal theory to account for addictive behaviour means that we have lost sense of the other elements of experience which are interwoven in inter-relationship with self and environment as a continuous whole.

THE REVIVAL AND WARMING OF BODY

In this chapter, I am interested in how the body, how the sphere of personally lived experiencing and meaning in shopping, can be revived and warmed into something of more substance and texture interwoven with daily living.

My enquiry into this area was shaped by the question: What do people experience when they go shopping? It seems insufficient merely to focus on the goods acquired. In pursuing this question, several sources of information were involved. The first was personal, 'going shopping' for me is inextricably linked with the means of travelling, the experience of shops – entering, exploring and leaving, the affective and sensory aspects of the whole. This personal view seemed to be supported by a study carried out in Guildford, England, whereby people were asked for their opinions about a shopping mall and High Street environment. Surprisingly, out of 270 people interviewed (one-third men, two-thirds women), the most important constructs were those centred on the sensory environment – the thermal, acoustic and luminary environment. The dominant evaluative perspective was of sensory-physical comfort. The second related to the proxemic environment – the degree to which people felt their personal space had been invaded or whether they felt a sense of space. They were key criteria for evaluating the environment. The third area, the retail environment – what shops are there – is third in importance; and the fourth, the managerial environment. Uzzell summarises:

> The sensory-physical environment is the most salient significance for the majority of users. Almost as important is the degree to which the environment provides sufficient personal space and social atmosphere. *Only after these two core criteria have been taken into account do users consider the extent to which it fulfils shopping criteria.* (1995, p. 304; emphasis added)

This was also true in relation to the High Street evaluations. It was primarily evaluated in terms of the level of comfort it provided and its ability to enable social and activity goals to be fulfilled. Only when these criteria had been met, was the quality of the shopping facilities considered. Here then, we are reminded that the primary experience of embodiment is in a kind of fit and comfort, an attunement or resonance with environmental cues. We are given natural materials, music, smells, colours, and innumerable surfaces and textures in which to orientate and find ourselves in new ways. We may seek soothing, energising traces of other environments, reminders of nature, of bliss, of shelter , community or home. Shopping experiences can provide us with an infinite array of such sensory/affective satisfactions contained within protective, bounded spaces. The ambience and quality of these may be more significant than the individual goods that are sold.

PERSONAL EXPERIENCES

I experience this particular department store as a kind of reassuring presence. It is always there, always trustworthy; when I go inside I feel safe and comfortable as if it is my place. It has become my place because it is usually where I go most often shopping. In contrast, I experience other department stores as slightly more hostile, more demanding, less caring of me, with harsher surfaces, brighter lighting, more impingement, more haphazard arrangements of goods; less consistency.

I approach then, this particular store with a kind of anticipation of ease when I push through the glass doors. Immediately, I feel a kind of ambience which is warm, has a quality of illumination that feels just right, and the arrangement and kind of goods that meet me provide a quality of texture of natural materials, of beauty, of some purer values that remind me distantly of fantasies of what a 'good life' should be like – with a solidity of ceramic or wood materials, or of enduring materials that have more substance than ersatz, imitation surfaces. I feel stimulation and pleasure at the combination of colour, texture, shape coherently organised yet with unknowns to discover. All this awareness is background to my purpose and intention for seeking particular goods, but it affects how I move, and how I relate to the environment. There is a sense of spaciousness, a kind of moral order and ethos; the place is far more than the limited number of actual goods I have in fact bought there. Whereas specifically the store may not have what I may wish to buy, its presence somehow supports the activity of shopping and provides me with a sense of being that is attuned and interesting; sufficiently complex and changing over time but remaining also the same. It is like the place of shopping that I carry within me as a good experience. I also have many other experiences of shopping environments where I feel estranged from myself, disturbed, alienated, lost and overwhelmed.

A recent article by journalist Judy Rumbold entitled 'Retail Therapy' (*Evening Standard*, 27 November 1998) was striking in depicting the quality of environmental elements as interwoven into the shopping experience. She recalled how as a child, in her first memories of shops, she was transfixed by the exquisite slicing of cheese and the catering meat-slicing machine's mesmeric action and rhythmic grinding.

Shops – I loved them, the chink of loose change in a till, the scrunch of a brown-paper bag, the clatter of wire baskets, the inane chat of the checkout girls. And then there were the trips to Woolworths ... a fledgling acquisitiveness that may well have had its origins at the pick-n-mix counter, but would later mushroom into something far less manageable.

Although she went on to discuss the objects she had acquired by starving herself as a student, she again returned to something more global and encompassing that drew her to shopping rather than objects *per se*:

Strictly speaking, mine was a habit that embraced all shops, not just those that sold clothes. Like an undiscriminating junkie who is as at home with a quart of Night Nurse as he is with an ounce of Class A crack, I was as enamoured of the haphazardly stacked shelves at the local Nisa store as I was of Harvey Nichols' exquisitely arranged aisles and immaculate floor-space ... I think my shop thing has always been about seeking out order, routine, exactitude and calm in a life that has always seemed chaotic, unmanageable and underpinned by feelings of barely suppressed panic. Stacking, folding, wrapping and packing: all – when performed by somebody else – deliver an almost sensual rush for me.

The stress on the tactile and sensory returned:

Where is the pleasure in electronic scanning and relentless credit-card swiping? What had happened to proper tills, brown-paper bags and a bit of amiable banter over the weighing scales?

After tracing her career in first acquiring expensive clothes and then expensive items for her home, she described her move to Dalston:

There, the prospects for retail blow-outs were limited ... My favourite shop sold only records and wool. Its neighbour was a florist with a sideline in hair-dressing. Dalston had great shops and I liked them all the more, because, mercifully, none of them ever had anything I wanted to buy.

An acquaintance of mine who is also a very enthusiastic shopper, was inspired to write some notes for me about her experience of shopping.

Markets are the first spaces which come to mind for their particularity, humanity and openness: Whitechapel, an old haunt, with characters, opportunities for bargains, bric a brac, cheap fruit and great quantities of vegetables; the locality is old, Huguenot refugees made their living from lace-making, refugees from Bangladesh [she mentions other environmental and

local features, and the surfaces and textures created by the Atlantis Art warehouse] – canvas, paint, pastels brushes, easels ...
The space of intimate surfaces, peeling paint, blackened stone, worn flagstones, freedom to wander at will, the sights of others and wondering at it all. Popularity because we are not alone here, people crowding round stalls buying all sorts of wares.
Why did I spend all those years returning to the market? Not bargain hunting ... pleasure in a way ... lingering the old walls, the walk ways to spend a Sunday morning, browsing in fascination at fabrics, memorabilia, antiques, snakeskins, – as though moving through time that mysterious element 'Woven in Air'. ... Texiles of incredible beauty: the thread running through it all, matters of the heart and the flotsam and jetsam of the market place brings to the surface of a dream like quality; ... the rich texture of things, the smell and look of oranges ... the wooden stalls covered with strange ironmongery or prayer rugs.
Now whatever did I buy? Not much of any lasting consequence – an old cotton slip, a pair of shoes, some lemons, a set of pans, a black velvet jacket a vegetable peeler. Certainly nothing in proportion to the time spent ... (Caley, personal communication 1998)

A Contrasting Environment:

Exposed. Just landed in the Lakeside shopping centre ... close to House of Fraser ... public amenities, coffee bar, large indoor water feature and armed with some plan. Sense of space..high ceilings ... light, escalators ... cleanliness and it's new. The best car park ever ... an art work, shining surface underfoot ... blue markings for signs ... no charges hence smoother operation. Even the cars have a sense of being looked after. Surfaces flat, glass, formica asphalt, concrete, metal. The package, all your favourite shops wrapped up together. Small trucks for kids ... beyond the shiny surface there is the landscape with an ironic sense of sea air from the nearby river and the everwatchful sky dazzling us as we make our way home. (Caley ibid.)

ENVIRONMENTAL PSYCHOLOGY

In the field of Environmental Psychology, considerable work has been focused on how people relate to different environments and the categories that are important in evaluation. In his study of urban nature, Herzog (1989) investigated participants' responses to aspects of nature within urban environments. The responses were based on criteria established by Kaplan's work on environmental preferences: spaciousness, refuge, coherence, legibility, complexity, mystery, typicality, nature and age. All of these seem significant in the above accounts. Refuge was defined as how much the setting provides the opportunity for being hidden. Spaciousness was defined as the feeling of depth conveyed by a setting, the feeling that one would have to go a long way to reach its furthest point. Coherence as 'how well the scene hangs together'; legibility was 'how easy it would be to find your way around in the environment depicted'; complexity was 'how much is going on in the scene, how much there is to look at; how much the scene contains a lot of elements of different kinds'; mystery was present when a setting promises more to be seen if you could walk deeper into it'; typicality referred to the 'extent the scene seems to be a representative sample of its class'. In their study, they found that coherence, mystery and nature were the most significant variables in predicting preferences for different urban environments. Tended nature was the most preferred category, concealed foreground second, and then contemporary buildings. Coherence and mystery have been consistently signficant as factors affecting preferences in relation to a number of environmental cues.

What can be discerned from this data so far? Firstly, that we cannot distinguish the act of shopping, of choosing and paying for a particular item in a shop, from the environmental field and individual perception of that field. Secondly, that what is important to people within an environment are elements such as sensory comfort and spaciousness, reported in one study relating to shopping, and the provision of coherence and mystery in another. What is conjured up from both subjective accounts and objective studies is the significance of sensory motor elements, diversity and texture, surprise and typicality. There is also a strong social aspect.

In his work *Getting Back into Place*, Edward Casey (1993) reviews the experience of the shopping mall by night and contrasts it to the natural world:

> To feel the ultimate desolation and the equally ultimate displacement that characterise this scene, imagine yourself locked in a mall overnight, empty of people and featuring only shadowy shops whose windows contain unmoving and unspeaking manikins. Nothing alive here ... nothing but the comedy – or the tragedy – of plastic and metallic objects and forms. Everything, including the site, is artificial ... One could not survive for long in such a hard-edged circumstance ... At best, real life and true place are represented in the mall, e.g. by photographs of wild places or by recorded sounds of animal or human voices. The three dimensionality of place and voice – their distinctive depth, their life – has been replaced by the two dimensionality of lifeless visual and auditory icons. Time and space come together in such a site and its attenuated images, but neither life nor place appear in this flattened-out homogenous scene. (Casey 1993, p. 269)

Contrast these images with those described by the author above. The sense of lifelessness, flatness, a cul-de-sac of immobility, no possibility is there. What is different is not the architecture nor the location but the social and psychological dimensions of the scene. This point emphasises the need to investigate our relation with outside, with environment, with objects in more helpful ways. In this example, the sense of the person in the shopping mall is of being outside, in the cold, out of touch with the natural world and with self. In the other examples, there is the precise opposite, the shopping environment gives a sense of inclusion, of warmth, shelter, stimulus and contact. So we have the contrast between spaces that are felt to be dwelt in, lived in and others in which we are perched precariously on the edge, concerned about our survival as if we had landed on another planet.

For Relph (1976), 'places are experiential fusions of human and natural order ... the significant centres of our immediate experiences of the world'. *Insideness* is then crucial to experience of place – the extent to which people belong to and identify themselves with place. In Relph's conception, there is a fundamental dialectical relationship in our environmental experience which centres on this polarity between insideness and outsideness. Whereas existential outsideness is associated with estrangement and alienation, existential insideness allows for an unselfconscious immersion in a place. This is a central component of place because there is no deliberate self-conscious reflection but it is full with significances (p. 55). In some shops we may experience 'inside' kinds of feelings; in others we may feel 'outside'.

THE MOVE FROM OUTSIDENESS TO INSIDENESS

How, then, can we understand how external constructions, how buildings can affect our experience of ourselves; how can they touch us and affect us? There are three examples outlined below which give some concrete examples of how buildings can be designed to create particular kinds of embodied experiences, interwoven with the visual experience. These examples may help to re-invoke the sense of internal space as a quality of relationship that unfolds as the person moves through the space or building. The crucial element is the kind of movement that is elaborated by the design of space vertical, narrow, closed in or open.

Deborah Fausch (1996) gives such an example in her discussion of Maya Lin's Vietnam Veterans' Memorial in Washington. It is described in bodily terms:

The first sight of it comes as a visceral shock – a sudden opening in the earth, a gash in the green turf which ruptures the infinite extension and perfect rationality of the ground plane. The visitor's slow movement becomes an imaginative descent into the tombs of the soldiers whose names are engraved on the reflective stone space.

Another example she cites is the stairway down to the UN Plaza in New York:

Here one descends a gentle curve past carved words from the Old Testament prophesying peace. Moving down along the beautiful marble panel inscribed with a hope so often disappointed induces an experience of poignant sadness that makes the actual etymological connection between motion and emotion.

The third example comes from the recent opening of the new museum for the Holocaust in Berlin. In press reports of its design we are told that this building does not have a conventional opening: part of the journey through its fractured and tormented design involves passing down stairs into darkness illuminated only by a narrow shard of light from a thin window so high up that it seems beyond reach or hope. In this way, the architect creates some of the inner experiences imagined for those who travelled in cattle trucks towards the camp in cramped darkness – with only that fissure of light.

Each of these examples captures profound and stirring aspects of human experience and honours these not by static monuments but by including present participants in a shared reverberation of mood, emotion and meaning. So buildings and architecture can play on us in the same way that music and other creative arts engage and touch us viscerally. In highlighting these possibilities of architecture in making foreground and explicit the background and implicit participation of body in experience and perception, a different approach to the domain of the personal and the environmental can be glimpsed. While our culture tends to emphasise the visual separation of buildings and the way that they penetrate space and make forms, these other architectural descriptions are giving an inside, more formless, sense of embodied perception of spaces that are moved through by the perceiver. In moving through these spaces, the perceiver's experience of self is transformed in relation to the space. It is a mutual relationship. It involves the in-betweens and the transitions between moments – the movement between inside and outside that mirrors our own self-reflectivity and conciousness.

If these ideas are gathered up in relation to the question of how we experience shopping and how meanings are constellated around

shopping, then we are compelled to recognise that such an interrela-
tion between person and environment is often denied or considered
unimportant. Spaces are not linked together as a coherent flow and
rhythm; they are often staccato and constitute discrete experiences like
thoughts rather than movements or feelings. *Going shopping* is a phrase
that is connoting such a connection between home and shop, in how
the transition is made, the in-betweens being integral to the experience
of shopping; how one goes, with whom one goes, the weather, the
transport, the food, how one day is different from another, how one
feels. The flow and the process are all part of one ecology.

THE ECOLOGICAL APPROACH TO PERCEPTION

James Gibson (1976) pursued this direction in his radical approach to
perception. He was concerned that models of perception had been
derived from static laboratory experiments, usually stressing visual
perception. He suggests that perception is shaped in an ecological
context. For human beings negotiating the environment, perception
is shaped by movement through spaces and surfaces that do not behave
like geometrical laws. In movement, surfaces are curved and distinguished by textural features, laminations which reflect light. His theory
of perception is of perceptual systems as achievements of the human
organism, not an appearance of the theatre of his consciousness. It
involves awareness *of*, not just awareness. Sensory modalities are
perceptual systems and perception is a psychosomatic act of a living
observer. The act of picking up information is a ceaseless and unbroken
activity. The sea of energy in which we live flows and changes without
sharp breaks. Even the tiny fraction of this energy that affects the
receptors is a flux, not a sequence. The continuous act of perceiving
involves the co-perceiving of the self. If we take the Gibson notions of
object perception a little further, into the context of shopping, then
objects possess a variety of *affordances* from the surfaces they offer. For
Gibson, all the notions of imagining, dreaming, rationalising and
wishful thinking, remembering, judging and so on, can be reconstrued
within his conception of ecological perception.

> To perceive is to be aware of the surfaces of the environment and of oneself
> in it. The interchange between hidden and unhidden surfaces is essential to
> this awareness. These are existing surfaces; they are specified at some points
> of observation. Perceiving gets wider and finer and longer and richer and fuller
> as the observer explores the environment processes in each case. (p. 255)

An important aspect of this model is the reminder that all perceptual systems are proprioceptive as well as exteroceptive because they all provide information about the perceiver's activities. This is often forgotten or unacknowledged within our cultural constructions of experience as being somehow *out there*. Information about the self is multiple, including sensations on skin, muscles, sights, sounds, and so on. From this perspective, the supposedly separate realms of subjective and objective are actually only *poles of attention*. 'The information for "in here" is of the same kind as the information for the perception of "there"' (p. 116).

Take these notions then, of a fluid ecological perceptual process, into the experience of entering and moving around a shop. We encounter the shop not as a geometrical unit, but as a series of curved surfaces from which we feel myriad qualities of texture, form, arrangement, of hidden things behind other things, of the way light is reflected from these surfaces and how we can move around densely arranged racks of clothes or goods and people, often at some speed, in the same way that animals can negotiate dense forests, or underground warrens.

For Gibson, place makes up the habitat and small places are nested within larger places. They do not have boundaries. They have both persistent and changeable features. For Gibson, the five perceptual systems correspond to five modes of overt and overlapping attention which are subordinated to an overall orienting system. Systems can orientate, explore, investigate and adjust, and so on. Perceptual systems can mature and learn. Sensations from one system can be associated with another; no new sensations are learned but the information that is picked up becomes more and more subtle, elaborate and precise with practice. So it is a lifelong process. So we become more skilled at picking up what shops can offer us faster. We translate from scanning the appearance of materials whether they are of certain qualities or others, how much they are made up of man-made materials, how much of natural ones, how well they are made, how well they are hung or put together. We detect from the kind of carpet and flooring, the ambience and feel of the shop, the lighting, the harmonious or jarring arrangement of signs; the sounds of tills, music, people, and how well the acoustic absorbs them. Quieter, more sound-absorbent environments will be felt as more relaxing and different music will have very different effects. Such cues are mostly cognised below the threshold of consciousness in a very fast pre-attentive awareness. It is interesting to consider what happens when we encounter different kinds of shops and try to find the messages from environmental cues to identify these codes. We are required to learn a new symbolic order within the syntax of the new shop and so we create a steadily increasing 'linguistic flair' to negotiate travelling through an expanding shopping environment. The environment offers *affordances* to the human organism; these *affordances* are not merely shaped by the subjective need of the perceiver. The affordances of the environment are what it offers to the animal. In the case of the participants observing urban nature, affordances such as spaciousness, refuge, coherence, and so on, were identified. Spaciousness gives us a sense of possibility, of choice, of freedom. Refuge gives us a sense of shelter, of containment, of safety. Coherence gives a sense of consistency, reliability, comprehensiveness, aesthetic unity. According to other sources of environmental enquiry, such affordances can be also in terms of mystery, personal space, legibility. In terms of those reporting about their shopping experiences, they convey a richness of perceptual systems, a stimulating array of textural variations, many disruptions of the continuity of surfaces. The notion of mystery is interesting. Perhaps it offers the possibility of the unknown, of new horizons. One of the valued preferences in subjects viewing urban landscapes was concealed foregrounds. For Gibson, this would be a description of hidden surfaces. When we hold a book in our hand, it contains worlds within worlds within it that convey the experience of moving through environments in many different surface laminations, places nested within other places. The possibilities within the book convey to us the sense of spaciousness and depth that is always greater before we read it than when we have read it. In the reading, we travel through its environment and, however spacious and unfolding, it has a finite ending when we close the cover.

Both these architectural examples and the style of Gibson's model of perception are emphasising the living, moving person within an environment, rather than a person who is perceiving only through thought or passively receiving visual stimuli from a desirable object beautifully arranged. The experience of shopping subsumes all sources of perception and meaning that are created as the person traverses different kinds of shopping environments. If we neglect this aspect of the lived relationship with shopping environments we are in danger of missing or distorting the meaning of shopping into a purely abstract and economic function.

MOTHER AS TRANSFORMATIONAL ENVIRONMENT

The way in which the experience of objects enables us simultaneously to perceive environment and our place in environment is also echoed in the work of Christopher Bollas. He draws on the Kleinian tradition of object relations which was modified by Winnicott's notions of transitional space and positions the mother as a kind of environment for the child. Bollas introduces the notion of the mother being a transformational object for the infant. In psychotherapy, the therapist is able to experience how this quality of transformational experience is mirrored in the transference and counter-transference – in the use that the patient makes of the therapist. Here we have a similar theme to Gibson: the way in which the infant/person makes use of the therapist as an environment.

Winnicott emphasised the invariant elements within the environment that the mother offers the child. Within this invariance there are enormous fluctuations of perception in holding, feeding, playing, cleaning, changing, dressing the child. For Bollas, it is important to stress that from these points of view the mother is 'less significant and identifiable as an object than as a process that is identified with cumulative internal and external transformations'. (1987, p. 14). 'The transformational object is experientially identified by the infant with processes that alter self experience.' The knowing of the object in symbiotic identification is one of an experience of being rather than representation. In adult life, Bollas maintains that adults continue the search for objects as transformational experiences. The quest 'is not to possess the object but rather to surrender to it as a medium that alters the self'. Such a transformation is associated with enviro-somatic caring which is connected with shifts in self-experiencing. Such an association, according to Bollas, is created by perception rather than desire. People will continue to seek things in adult life in order to recreate the particular quality of this early experience – whether it is a place, a thing, a belief system, a particular kind of event.

As an environment, the mother continually adjusts to meet the changing field of the infant's needs. This is a three-dimensional process – integrating many different perceptual systems – motor, sensory, and affective. The infant's world is transformed in feel, in the felt sense in this way. At the same time, the infant's development also changes the way in which the world is experienced and communicated. Daniel Stern (1985) discusses these changes in terms of a core and emergent self, an intersubjective self and a verbal self. These are different domains of relating. They would be made up of different organisations of perceptual systems. In adult life we often return to the quality of these transformational experiences every day. We can consider the meaning that people put on to having an aromatherapy bath when stressed and tired, having a drink, eating certain kinds of food, listening to certain kinds of music, being with certain people. Within these attempts at self-transformation, come moments of aesthetic meaning that perhaps capture the original quality of these infant/mother moments. What seems to be conveyed by Bollas, is a quality of attunement on the part of the mother environment yet which slightly alters and expands the experience of self. Something more is provided than was known about, yet which seems to feel good. For Bollas, the transformation is linked with a quality of symbiosis. Much of advertising promises this quality of aesthetic magic in its evocation of spaciousness, refuge, bliss, mystery, and so on. A tremendous amount of hope is invested in such ventures. What remains elusive in the quality of this search is the sense of being reminded of something known within but not accessible in thought or language, but which can inspire awe or reverence. Certain qualities of landscape may evoke it. Intense affective experience is linked with it.

Therefore as adults we could propose the idea that we are haunted by these transformational experiences and seek to symbolise them in innumerable ways. Shopping for particular kinds of goods may be part of this. More than this, we could speculate that the shopping environment itself represents something of the transformational presence of the mother in itself. For the shopping particicpants in the Guildford survey, it was sensory comfort that was the first important variable, second was the social element and only thirdly a particular retail outlet.

Before the mother is personalised, she has functioned as a region or source of transformation ... The ego experience of being transformed by the other remains as a memory that may be re-enacted in aesthetic experiences, in a wide range of culturally dreamed-of transformational objects such as new car, homes, jobs and holidays, that promise total change of internal and external environment.

> The aesthetic space allows for a creative enactment of the search for this trans-formational object relation and we might say that certain cultual objects afford memories of ego experiences that are now profoundly radical moments ... Intense memories of the process of self-transformation. (pp. 28–9)

Poetry, painting, music, then, can evoke a sense of profound rapport between self and other. In the relation with the mother, it is more than a transaction between objects. Feeding takes place within the mother's idiom, her rhythm of movements, the feel of her body, the sounds she makes. In development, the infant negotiates her environment through gesture and responses which are moulded into patterns; the true self is also combined with the adaptations to the other and the idiom of the person continues to negotiate the world in objects and experiences that express both the true and adapted self. In therapy, the therapist can become aware of how the patient relates to the object of self within and so reveals some of these early patterns in relation to carer.

SHOPS AS TRANSFORMATIONAL ENVIRONMENTS

As shoppers, then, we go on attempting to find transformational experiences and ways of expressing something of ourselves that resonates with our experiences of self.

Here is a concrete conception of what we may glimpse in the domain of the transformational space of the mother. I suggest that this description of a gigantic woman's body can also be imagined in an entertaining kind of way as providing some of the same kinds of environmental transitions that departmental stores also offer us. It is notable that this shift from sculpture to store is one that is not that difficult. Here we have surprising juxtapositions, different materials and forms, spaciousness, refuge, legibility, coherence, mystery. A Swedish artist (Niki de Saint Phalle) created a sculpture in 1966 that became architecture. It was called *Hon* – meaning She.

> The sculpture is about both space and desire. The metaphor for She was of women taking space for themselves. A gigantic construction of a woman lying on her back was made, which created a space which could be entered through a sacred vagina womb painted green. The spectacle was completed outside and in. The form created arches and hills, spaces to move in, under around and near. In some senses, She was the perfect incarnation of fantasy, a primordial experience of passage through a mysterious labyrinth from light to darkness and out to light again. Eventually one exited either from her side or from a door in her neck. Inside one leg, the artists designed a gallery cum slide replete with fake master paintings with fake signatures. A star-filled planetarium glowed under the dome of an oversized breast. There was a goldfish pond, a pink liquor bar with a neon halo on the ceiling, a sculpted man sitting on a chair, a public address system and a tiny cinema (Garbo's first film wherein she takes a risque swim was projected continuously). An elaborate spiral staircase leading from the belly to a small restaurant atop the abdomen was a central element. Finally in her head, Tinguely constructed one of his now famous revolving glass and light machines. It smashed bottles consumed in the tiny bar.(Hankwitz 1996, p. 172)

The department store could be seen as a kind of reverberation of the kinds of inhabited spaces that were created in this sculpture and could be still found in the shopping spaces we now dwell in. Perhaps this is what Lefebvre (1992) wished to remind us of in his recognition that space has lost this primary identity. What is important here, is not so much the filling of spaces with contents, but the kinds of sensory experiences we derive from a complex array of perceptual systems overlapping. In the descriptions provided by Judy Rumbold and my acquaintance, there are descriptions of sounds and textures, of rhythms of machines, of the experiences of metal slicing cheese and meat, of smells, of smooth and rough surfaces. There are also the surfaces of others, amongst whom we move and survey. The social aspects of shopping perhaps provide both a sense of insideness and outsideness. We can feel unselfconciously at home in the insideness of a large store yet safe within the distance of unknown persons; both space and refuge, coherence and mystery are combined. The first experiences of another's body and movement is full of activity and alterations in surfaces – surprises that are coherent and transforming.

There are also shops whose design creates more dissonance, broken-up surfaces, noise, lack of space and coherence. Such spaces create more sense of chaos, exclusion, marginality and a sense of being overwhelmed by stimuli. Perhaps such harsher, more deliberately metallic, industrial kinds of shopping environments are aimed at young people who seek to find a place separate from the connotation of homes, of parents; an interim space which provides louder and stronger, more functional environmental cues, with bass notes, darker colours; environments that translate rap, house, garage, techno music into spatial domains. Such domains are deliberately un-soothing, stimulating, harsh – moving away from maternal space towards a transitional space.

The objects that appeal to us in shopping may also provide in miniature, the same combination of a multititude of perceptual experiences as we glean from an environmental field. Beyond only function, when we buy things, we have to be in a certain kind of mood. Things acquired in unpleasant settings, when we were experiencing negative feelings, do not have the same value. They remain imbued with their context. The goods we buy tend then to possess the qualities of the environmental field and shops extend the appeal of goods by enhancing qualities within this.

SUMMARY

What do we get out of going shopping? What meanings are gathered around the environmental immersion of shopping places? Attention has been mainly focused on a view of person and object as separate and discrete events. The environmental and experiential ground which is central to shopping activity has been largely neglected. Feminist approaches to architecture and design can be illuminating in clarifying the missing dimension of embodiment and the inhabitation of space; Gibson's ecological approach to perception gives us a radically different perspective in which to understand the orientation of person and environment through the perception of surfaces, surface textures, laminations, persistences and changes as she moves through them. Christopher Bollas's work on the role of the transformational object in development adds a further dimension to understanding some of the psychological search for transformational meanings in *going shopping*. There is the opportunity here to consider in more depth the qualities and textures of environments and what they evoke within us. I put a plea for the sense of space as emerging from the experience of the mother's body. In reconnecting with the multidimensional topography of moving through spaces where inner and outer inter-penetrate, *some body* is found again. From a certain kind of abstract vacuity in contemporary discourse a sensory landscape of being may be restored.

REFERENCES

Bollas, C. (1987) *The Shadow of the Object: Psychoanalysis of the thought unknown*. London, Free Association Books.
Bollas, C. (1989) *Forces of Destiny: Psychoanalysis and human idiom*. London, Free Association Books.
Caley, B. (1998) 'Some Notes on Shopping' (personal communication to author).
Casey, E. (1993) *Getting Back into Place: Towards a renewed understanding of the place world*. Indiana, Indiana University Press.
Daly, M. (1973) *Beyond God the Father*. Boston, Beacon.
de Beauvoir, S. (1997) *The Second Sex*. London.
Erickson, E. (1951) Sex Differences in the Play Configurations of a Representative Group of Preadolescents. *American Journal of Orthopsychiatry* XXI, pp. 667, 692.
Fausch, D. (1996) *The Knowledge of the Body and the Presence of History – Towards a Feminist Architecture*. In D. Coleman, E. Danze and C. Henderson (eds), *Architecture and Feminism*. Princeton, Architectural Press.
Gibson J. J. (1996) *The Ecological Approach to Visual Perception*. Boston, Houghton Miflin.
Griffin, S. (1978) *Woman and Nature: The roaring inside her*. New York, Harper and Row.
Grosz, E. (1995) Women, Chora, Dwelling in Post-Modern Cities and Spaces. In K. Watson and K. Gibson (eds) *Postmodern Cities and Spaces*. Oxford, Blackwell, p. 47.
Hankwitz M. (1996) *The Story of Hon-Katedral: A fantastic female*. In D. Coleman, E. Danze and C. Henderson (eds), *Architecture and Feminism*. Princeton, Architectural Press.
Herzog, T. (1989) A Cognitive Analysis of Preference for Urban Nature. *Journal of Environmental Psychology* 9, 27–43.
Kestenberg, J. (1967) *The Role of Movement Patterns in Development 1*. New York, Dance Notation Press.
Lefebvre, H. (1992) *The Production of Space*. Trans. D. Nicholson Smith. Oxford, Blackwell.
Macleod, M. (1995) *Everyday and Other Spaces*. In D. Coleman, E. Danze and C. Henderson (eds), *Architecture and Feminism*. Princeton, Architectural Press.

Nava, M. (1997) Modernity's Disavowal: Women, the city and the department store. In P. Falk and C. Campbell (eds), *The Shopping Experience*. London, Sage.
Relph, R. (1976) *Place and Placelessness*. London, Pion.
Rumbold, J. (1998) Retail Therapy. *Evening Standard*, 27 November.
Stern, D. (1985) *The Interpersonal World of the Infant*. New York, Basic Books.
Uzzell, D. L. (1995) The Myth of the Indoor City, *Journal of Environmental Psychology* 152: 299–310.

8

Addictive Shopping as a Form of Family Communication

Paula Riddy

In their plurality, objects are the sole things in existence with which it is truly possible to co-exist, in so far as their differences do not set themselves at odds with one another, as is the case with living beings ... In short it is like a dog reduced to a single aspect of fidelity. I am able to gaze on it without it gazing back at me. This is why one invests in all objects all that one finds impossible to invest in human relationships. This is why man so quickly seeks out the company of objects when one needs to recuperate. We cannot but see this reflex of retreat as regression; this sort of passion is an escapist one. (Baudrillard 1994, p. 11)

INTRODUCTION

Shopping is usually described in the literature as a behaviour carried out by an individual with motivations that are based on personal identity or perception of personal need. The framework of current family and family background is not usually considered, but might be of considerable importance in understanding the context in which excessive shopping occurs for an individual. Elliott et al. (1996) write of power and control in the development and maintenance of a shopping addiction, sometimes partly influenced by the desire for revenge on the partner or on the whole family. Other studies have not been so specific, and Lunt (1992) calls for more research into the ways in which material objects can be involved in family dynamics. Baudrillard (1994) suggests that individuals invest in objects when they are unable to invest in a sexual relationship, as an alternative to becoming involved emotionally. Muensterberger (1994) conveyed a similar message about compulsive collectors; he in fact found in a study of compulsive collectors that this inability to invest in relationships was founded in an early pattern of maternal deprivation or abandonment. I shall attempt to address some of these issues in the following chapter.

Shopping is a subject that has been treated humorously, especially by programmes such as *Absolutely Fabulous*, with Edina and Patsy often weighted down by their purchases from Harvey Nichols. It has also been dismissed as a female pursuit and has received trivialisation by the media. Everyone shops, and the assumption is often made that it is a bit of harmless fun and that everyone can control their shopping. For some individuals, however, shopping can become out of control to varying degrees, and might be the demonstration of a deep feeling of lack as suggested above. In this chapter I would like to explore the idea of shopping as the communication of a need in the context of a shopper's family both in the present and in childhood.

SOME ISSUES THAT MIGHT BE RELEVANT IN SHOPPING ADDICTION RESEARCH

Addiction

'Addiction' is a term that has been readily associated with substance abuse, although there does not necessarily need to be an obvious chemical dependency for a behaviour to be labelled addictive. Orford (1985) in *Excessive Appetites* writes also of addiction to food, to sex and to gambling. The distinction between compulsion and addiction is not always clear in the literature. The American Psychiatric Association (1985, p. 234) define compulsions as: 'repetitive and seemingly purposeful behaviors that are performed according to certain rules or in a stereotyped fashion'. Some theorists use the term 'compulsion to apply to shopping behaviour that has become excessive or out of control' (Faber, O'Guinn and Krych 1987); O'Guinn and Faber (1989); others see elements of both compulsion and addiction (Nataraajan and Goff 1991); yet others prefer the term 'addictive shopping' (Scherhorn 1990). The last preference is justified on the grounds that although compulsions and addictions both involve a loss of control, compulsive behaviour, Scherhorn (1990) writes, tends to be against the will of the individual whereas addictive behaviour is an irresistible urge with some elements of control possible; more of a pathological habit. Addictions, he goes on to claim, are ultimately not enjoyed *per se*. One might hypothesise that excessive shopping behaviour contains many of the elements of compulsion and addiction, and probably lack of control on a continuum depending on the experience of the individual shopper. One element that renders the issue complex is the implication of shopping as a pathology, for under such a label there is a powerful judgement which I believe eradicates many of the more functional and even joyful aspects of shopping as a coping strategy or recreational activity for some people. There is also a large societal and cultural element in such categorisations. It becomes complicated to diagnose shopping addiction because of the component of wealth and poverty: a poor but infrequent shopper might appear to be very adversely affected by debt, whereas a well-off individual might overtly appear to be much less of a shopping addict, but their shopping might in fact represent a greater degree of psychological deficit. Perhaps the individual's own feelings that the behaviour is undesirably out of control might serve as a clearer indicator, but even such a self-judgement is likely to be based on personal access to financial funds as well as societal and familial induced guilt. Shopping for food is clearly a necessary activity; and in our culture shopping for clothes and luxury items is becoming more of a social norm and is also sometimes seen as a recreational activity. As an activity we all engage in on some level, shopping 'addiction' has much in common with over-eating, although the latter has a clearer point for diagnosis based on physical ill-health. Just as we all need to shop, we all need to eat, and a brief entry into the psychological literature into addictive eating might raise some hypotheses about shopping behaviour.

In spite of my attempt to remove pathologising from an examination of shopping behaviour, I am equally keen not to make the mistake of denying the existence of excessive shopping which is clearly a problem for some people. In his chapters on sexual appetites and over-eating, Orford (1985) claims that such disorders have been denied and have therefore received less attention in the literature than might be expected because it is unfashionable and unfeminist to suggest their existence. I am therefore also aware of the trap of denial – because shopping is a stereotypically female activity. A shopper's behaviour is pathologised much more readily than the equivalent stereotypically male activities such as sport and 'work' which I feel are slightly more likely to be seen as normal even when these activities are engaged in to excess. I would like to seek to understand rather than to pathologise.

A variety of explanations has been proferred to explain addictive behaviour in general, including the theory that addictive behaviour represents the wish to engage in an activity that is an avoidance of less desirable activities or personal issues:

> It is possible then, that one of the most significant functions of appetitive behaviour is to provide activity the exact form of which is unimportant compared with its ability temporarily to distract attention from unpleasant

emotion, in the same way that activity can temporarily reduce physical pain. (Orford 1985, p. 133)

Kaslow (1996) also discusses the ways in which addicts can use their addiction as a way of avoiding serious life issues.

Addiction and Narcissism

Narcissism is seen by psychoanalysts as a stage in infancy which leads to object-love, a stage in which the capacity to see good in others and bad in oneself develops. Some theorists see narcissistic pathology as resulting from a disruption in the mother/infant bond; others see it as stemming from 'envious and omnipotent attack' on the mother/infant bond (Good 1995). It can be seen as a defensive attack to protect the individual from the environment provoked by a hatred of dependency (in spite of the obvious irony that most addicts end up becoming dependent on their addiction and hence out of control) and drugs represent external objects that are needed. Such objects, at least initially, and unlike relationships with other people, are totally under individual control and might lead to a feeling of omnipotence. In addition, for the narcissistic individual, the addiction does not require emotional returns in the same way that another individual might. Shopping, too, could be seen as a search for an 'object', and one that is led by the shopper him- or herself.

A Jungian Perspective on Addiction

In *Addiction to Perfection*, Marion Woodman (1982) writes of anorexia as a frantic attempt at achieving the perfection of thinness in the absence of perfection in other areas of a person's life. Eating disorders may involve cycles of bingeing and vomiting, and can stem, Woodman (1982) believes, from a deep inner loneliness, an emptiness that can never be filled in spite of the compulsion to do so with food, drugs or alcohol. The addictive behaviour can be seen as an escape from inner fears. Woodman (1982, p. 13) writes: 'In their efforts to escape they say "it's better to be drunk than crazy, it's better to be vomiting than crazy, it's better to be fat than crazy".'

It would be interesting to explore whether addictive shoppers also have an inner emptiness and whether it is also, for some 'better to *shop* than be crazy'. Compulsive behaviour, including shopping, might be seen as an attempt to invoke a positive internal mother to fill a sense of emptiness and aloneness. In spite of the apparent contradiction, Woodman (1982) states that those who engage in compulsive behaviour perform their rituals alone: part of a withdrawal from a world they hate.

In Jungian terms, an addiction might be seen to demonstrate an archetypal pattern of mother and child dependence and perhaps the archetype of the orphan might be relevant. Individuals are seeking the comfort of a mother from other sources due to a lack of this in infancy and childhood or an inability to separate and to function in their own right. Indeed one could see shopping as a kind of search, and whether or not this is labelled as narcissistic, it seems important to at least investigate the family context of an addictive shopper's behaviour.

Addiction and the Family

The question of narcissism leads on to the question of addiction in the context of others. A narcissistic interpretation of shopping behaviour might suggest the hypothesis that shoppers have a lack of other sustaining relationships in their lives: for those in a family setting that there are indications of a complex family dynamic. Duck (1994) writes that disappointment and lack in relationships have not been studied in depth. Kaslow (1996) describes the potential frustrations associated with expressing a dissatisfaction within a relationship: if the attempt does not yield satisfactory results or is ignored altogether, then another problem is added to the existing one; that of imperviousness. The resulting effect can seem even worse to the dissatisfied partner. Thus a defence of not addressing problems may emerge, and it may be exacerbated by the tendency towards a narcissistic defence in either or both of the partners. The narcissistic personality of one partner, therefore, might lead to the withdrawal of the other partner, with one or both of them seeking relief or nurturance elsewhere. There are in fact a multitude of possible interractions of the factors of narcissism, addiction and withdrawal within a family. Nakken (1988) states that every time an addict 'acts out' he or she is saying one of the following:

- I don't need people
- I don't have to face anything I don't want to
- I'm afraid to face life's problems
- Objects and events are more important than people
- I can do what I want regardless of anyone else (Nakken 1988, p. 27)

Thus shopping might emerge as a defence against a partner's addiction to, say, drugs; and is a more socially acceptable addiction, allowing the blame to remain with the 'real' addict.[1] Kaslow (1996) states that 'addicts teach addiction', and that the families of addicts tend to deny the chaos of the family situation which leads to the use of dishonest coping skills and the denial of danger. Perhaps in families with just one addict member, the shopper, as well as the behaviour expressing his or her need for love, it might also express a need in the family for a 'fragile' member who can be seen by others as out of control. Scapegoat shoppers might in turn be willing to abdicate power, for example, allowing partners to cut up their credit cards.

The Family and Systemic Theory

I have already alluded to ways in which addiction may serve a purpose in family dynamics, and more specifically how it may cause huge swings in family dynamics. Minuchin (1974) discusses the use of mutual accommodation in couples. Entering a relationship requires some level of compromise and a new set of sub-systems. Such accommodation might lead to the need for alternative self-rewards – for example, shopping.

Family therapy can be seen as treating a social system rather than an individual. In general systems theory there exists the system itself, the systems environment (supra-system) and the systems components (sub-systems). The theory is concerned with the description and exploration of the inter-related systems. Each 'component' of the system is seen in terms of the function of the total system (Walrond-Skinner 1976). Homeostasis is the quality which enables a system to remain stable and steady through time; thus external events which impinge on its functioning will lead to an altering or re-balancing of the system's internal condition. Although such a process may be dysfunctional, it is not necessarily so. Walrond-Skinner (1976) expands the theory of homoeostasis to add the concept of morphogenesis or growth; thus, outside events do not necessarily lead to reappraisal within an existing framework, but might lead to development and change. There may be much circularity with such processes, so that there is not a definite cause and effect (and I believe that there is also likely to be multi-causality). A hypothetical example might be that a husband's drinking problem could lead him to distract from the problem by scapegoating his wife, who might be an enthusiastic shopper; she might in turn shop even more as an escape, thus distancing herself further from the family and prompting misbehaviour from the children; this in turn might prompt the husband to drink more and the wife to shop more. Thus complex feedback loops might be in operation within a family structure. Satir (1978) writes of four universal patterns of response within a family: placator; blamer;

computer and distractor (and combinations of these roles). From a psychoanalytic perspective, such roles in the family as scapegoat, victim and helper can be repetitions of familiar family patterns.

Summary

By examining theories of narcissism and systemic family therapy, it is possible to hypothesise that shopping behaviour could serve a variety of unconscious roles within the context of a family, of a relationship or of the lack of a relationship. It might express, for example, a wish for an object, for comfort, love, endorsement, specialness; a variety of needs that have not been met adequately in childhood and for whatever reason are not being adequately met in the present.

The limited range of research that relates similar theories to shopping addiction will be discussed in a later section. First, I would like to introduce the subject of shopping by discussing some of the historical background of consumerism.

SOME HISTORICAL PERSPECTIVES

Consumption might appear to be a modern phenomenon, and it has indeed changed over time. The historical antecedents of our acquisitive behaviour, however, can be seen as early as 212 BC when Marcellus plundered Syracuse and returned to Rome laden with Greek works of art. Rome itself, at the time of Cicero and Caesar, epitomised extravagance and overt consumption. The fourteenth century saw many *quelli del tresoro* or treasure hunters, such as Jean de Berry (1340–1416) who was a dedicated collector of fine objects. Seventeenth-century Holland was also rife with collectors, and also on the continent the Habsburgs. As early as 1696, it was possible to find comment on the apparent futility of such excessively acquisitive behaviour. Mary Astell, a diarist, wrote of the explorer/collector: 'he trafficks ... in every part of the world ... yet his merchandises serve not to promote our luxury nor increase our trade, and neither enrich the nation nor himself' (Mary Astell 1696, quoted in Muensterberger 1994, p. 202). Even Freud[2] was an avid collector of antiques, leading Peter Gay to conclude that: 'Freud's ... collecting of antiquities reveals residues in adult life of anal enjoyments' (Gay 1988).

Bocock (1993) writes of a British cultural heritage, dating back to Puritanism, which involves negative judgement on spending and on overt extravagance, and the endorsement of economical values. An element of this judgement, I believe, remains and can be seen in contrast with attitudes in America, where statements of wealth tend to be viewed more positively.

Industrial capitalism opened up in the eighteenth century, and advertising in newspapers began in the latter part of the century. There was a consumer revolution, theorised by Karl Marx in his analyses of industrial capitalism, which he believed to be founded on alienated labour. These workers were no longer producing their own goods and were therefore *forced* to become consumers. In a self-perpetuating spiral, alienation of labour has increased since Marx, as the consumer opportunities serve as a motivational force and people become trapped in a circle of wanting to buy, and justifying working by buying even more.

Later theorists at the turn of the century saw the emergence of department stores. Thorstein Veblen (1912) used the term 'conspicuous consumption' to describe the activities of wealthy members of American society who aimed to mimic the European upper classes. Georg Simmel (1903) examined German society and saw modern patterns of consumption as a reaction to the increase in city living, with spending as a defence against absorption into the anonymous mass. As Simmel writes: '... the deepest problems of modern life derive from the claim of the individual to preserve the autonomy and individuality of existence in the face of overwhelming social forces' (Simmel 1903). Thus the idea of consumerism as the articulation of a sense of identity emerged.

During early capitalism, people's sense of identity was founded largely on work roles and job title, providing a sense of who they were (Bocock 1993). Now people work not just to stay alive, but to provide self-rewards for working. Baudrillard (1988) writes that it is the *idea* of purchasing as much as the *act* of purchasing that is important. Marx stressed the importance of human creativity in non-alienated activity, and television has been a primary force in shifting leisure activity from the creative and active to the passive. Television has led to a greater need for identity expression; not only, I believe, by reducing the frequency of creative outlets as a source of self-definition, but by providing a set of images for emulation or contrast.

Consumer goods have become a central means of expression of identity (Kellner 1992). Veblen (1912) studied the use of status symbols, and found that not just single items, but whole 'packages' of goods could convey age, gender and ethnicity as well as social class. The last category is becoming increasingly difficult to express as goods which were previously restricted to the aristocracy such as champagne and smoked salmon, designer labels and skiing holidays, are filtering down the social scale. Members of other social groups linked by, say, geographical location, may seek to copy each other, leading to the formation of mini-cultures, membership of which is indicated by a certain kind of clothing or make of car. Bocock (1993) writes of the complex exchange of information between social groups, marketers and manufacturing industries (for example, through advertising).

Shopping and Gender

One example of an image created by a company is that created by Anita Roddick for the Body Shop. In a response to criticisms of female nakedness in advertising in the market in general, Ms Roddick has joined others in the use of male nudity in advertising. The message is: 'We are strong independent women and we can exploit and use men too.' In August 1996, Ms Roddick launched a campaign to increase women's self-esteem through advertising and her hope was that women identifying with her methods will endorse her products by buying them. It would be interesting to analyse the results of her campaign.

The example of the Body Shop also demonstrates an increasing trend towards the blurring of traditional gender roles as consumers. It has been noted that the traditional meanings attached to the masculine and feminine in art and the media are becoming diffused across the sexes (Tomlinson 1990). Firat (1994) notes that the increase in equality between the sexes has led to men being used as objects for harassment and oppression, not just women. Following the same line of thought, men are also being targeted as consumers of products that will make them more desirable to women, and advertising now presents sensual images of men as well as assertive images of women.

In spite of the increasing role of men as consumers, shopping is still often seen as a female activity. Firat (1994) also notes that in western culture the female was seen as staying at home and spending her husband's money while he worked, and that the associations with such consumption were, and still are, those of frivolity and as a topic for humour. As the 'female' role in the home has decreased with convenience food and modern technology, it is possible that shopping has become an important focus for the female identity. This might be especially relevant in a society where the expectation that women should stay at home is no longer as prevalent: those who do retain a largely domestic role might feel the need to express or reclaim their power through shopping.

Homosexual Male Identity and Shopping

Gay men are one group in our society whose image is ambivalent. The traditional taboos against homosexuality have been successfully challenged in western society in the 1960s and 1970s, with a small but more accepted sub-culture having emerged. There are gay bars and clubs and even the 'pink village' in Manchester. There are books, newspapers, magazines, holidays, dating agencies, telephone talk-lines and television programmes for gay consumers. Yet society provides clearer roles for heterosexual men than for homosexual men, and buying an identity might be especially important for the latter. Mort (1996) discusses the ways in which gay men use clothing as a means of expressing their sexual orientation:

> It involved declaring a commitment to homosexuality through visual presentation. Many of the resources which these young men drew on were clearly part of a shared knowledge of gay cultural history. (Mort 1996, p. 195)

In addition, the very act of consuming, as well as the goods that are bought, might be an important statement of sexual identity.

Heterosexual Male Identity and Shopping

Mort (1996) states that the 1990s have produced a culture in which there is a 'plurality of masculinities', such that it is also harder for heterosexual men to establish an image through clothes and visual presentation. Fischer and Gainer (1994) state that a major method for a man to assert his masculinity is through the consumption of sport, a more traditional method, just as perhaps women assert their femininity through shopping. It is certain, however, that men have become more active consumers of goods (Firat 1994), so it would be interesting to discover if shopping is able to hold a valuable place in the formation of male identity also, or if it is still 'hidden' – for example, behind such terminology as 'collecting', or with the justification of material need. It is in fact possible to discover many compulsive male shoppers throughout history by looking at male collectors: many are described in *Collecting: An unruly passion* (Muensterberger 1994). *All* of the collectors described by Muensterberger are men – for example, Honore de Balzac, Robert Sainsbury, and so on; whereas women who collect seem to be described in other sources as frivolous addicts rather than connoisseurs – for example, Imelda Marcos who collected shoes, Demi Moore who collects dolls. One might explain the differing terminology by *what* is being collected, that is, objects of antique value might be more likely to be collected, although many collectors cited by Muensterberger collect items at least as frivolous as dolls and shoes, such as teddy bears. Alexander III and Nicholas II of Russia each had a penchant for jewels and Fabergé *objets d'art*; so does Elizabeth Taylor. From this evidence it seems that there might be a subtle discrimination on the grounds of gender, especially as shopping is not seen as a stereotypically male activity; it is easier for many to categorise a compulsive male shopper as a collector. It is, in fact, easy to see the term 'collecting' as a kind of academic validation for a typically male activity, whereas the remarkably similar female equivalent is seen in more judgemental terms. Perhaps with the blurring of masculine and feminine roles in society, men will be able to own these obsessions in the future. The changing role of men as consumers is, I believe, an important development in the history of consumerism.

Shopping and Individual Identity

Following existentialism and then structuralism, in which the consumer was seen as an almost helpless pawn in his cultural environment, post-structuralism proposed that the consumer is an active individual in charge of carving out a sense of identity through his display of possessions. Baudrillard (1994) saw this active participation as an interaction between goods and individual, with the individual purchasing goods to express an identity and in turn the goods themselves influencing the individual's 'choice' of identity. He sees consumption as the consumption of ideas rather than of objects, and sees the process as doomed to fail at satisfaction:

> there are no limits to consumption. If it was that which it is naively taken to be, an absorption, a devouring, then we should achieve satisfaction. But we know that this is not the case: we want to consume more and more ... it is a total idealist practice which has no longer anything to do with the satisfaction of needs. (Baudrillard 1994)

He is saying that it is ideas that are being consumed, not objects, and that this leads to a sense of emptiness when the purchase has been made. I would be interested in investigating whether consumption can in fact be seen very much as a search for the satisfaction of needs, but perhaps of more emotional rather than of physical needs. This point will be discussed in greater depth later in the chapter.

The discussion of the formation of identity through social grouping is complicated in post-modernity. There is greater fluidity of movement between social and cultural groups and the traditional social status hierarchy has disintegrated (Bocock 1993). Rather than just aiming to belong to the next social class up, there are other concerns which affect the striving for identity through consumption, such as excitement, attractiveness and style.

The use of symbolism to express identity does not necessarily mean potential happiness and a sense of belonging. For Lacan (1977), who discussed language as a system of symbols, the symbol itself is linked to absence or non-identity. A word can be used to express an object that is not actually there. Similarly, one might hypothesise recreational shopping as the symbolisation through purchases of an emptiness or lack that may be rooted in the unconscious.[3] This point will be discussed more fully later, with reference to family dynamics.

Bocock discusses the ways in which advertising can tap into 'desires' in the unconscious, which, as he states, can be unpredictable:

> Desires appear as in a state of flux; they are fluid; they flow in unanticipated directions. They are related to sexual potentialities of the human body, and this has become articulated in images, symbols and representations in the decades since the invention of cinema, magazines and colour photography, and, above all, television. (Bocock 1993, p. 93)

Consumerism appears, therefore, as difficult to control, but also to explain and to research.

The emphasis on consumption as symbolism has advanced consumer research from theoretical models which view the consumer as an almost mechanised information processing unit (Holbrook 1987). To conceptualise individual identity as membership to ethnic, cultural and social groups misses many other messages that the consumption of objects, or even just consumption *per se*, might convey.

Csikszentmihalyi and Rochberg-Halton (1981) have written about the meanings of objects and possessions to the individual. They refer to the transient and superficial nature of an identity founded on consumerism. Objects, they claim, are used by individuals as 'role models' and as symbols of potentiality and striving. This representation can be a message to others, but also a message to the self, perhaps of personal specialness.

Rarity, cost, antiquity and designer labels can all enhance the feeling of or wish for such specialness. Individuality can then be expressed in the ways in which objects are handled in the home after purchase, for example, coordination of colour schemes in interior design; or in setting up a stereo system in a particular way. Objects might also have shared meaning for different members of the family, such as holiday souvenirs or gifts, and might therefore have a special place in consolidating happy memories and a sense of family unity.

Interestingly, there emerges almost a contradiction in the ways of forming a sense of self as described above. Self-differentiation appears to be in contrast to cultivating large group membership or shared identity within the family. The differentiated self, however, is vulnerable and impermanent, and by observing the pattern of a larger group membership one aims towards a self that extends beyond the fragility of the individual identity. It might be reasonable to hypothesise, from the above discussion, that for individuals without a clear sense of differentiated self, belonging to a group identity becomes crucial. The reverse might also be true. For individuals who have feelings of *not* belonging, of being left out, or of a lack in the smaller group, that of family, there might be an enhanced need to strive for a more differentiated self. The struggle might well involve the use of objects and the method for obtaining them is usually shopping.

Shopping could thus be seen as a search for a differentiated self where there is a lack of identity or of belonging elsewhere. The consumer literature has also referred to possessions as extensions of the self (Belk 1988) and as expressions of cultural heritage in a foreign country (Mehta and Belk 1991). Objects of a more durable nature, such as cars or clothing, have been found to be more likely to be used to define the self (Bloch and Bruce 1984).

Collecting might also lead to feelings of personal achievement and satisfaction (Belk 1995), but with the added risk of its leading to addictive behaviour, they claim. Werner Muensterberger (1994) gives a most extensive overview of the psychology of collecting in his book on the subject, and he places much emphasis on the unconscious value of objects with especial reference to events and experiences from childhood. There are many similarities between collecting and shopping, and in many cases they are likely to be the same phenomenon. In attempting to delineate the differences between the two activities I found two main differences. First, it is possible in some cases to collect waste products which are essentially free of charge (for example bottle tops). Second, and more noticeably, *all* of the collectors described by Muensterberger are men. Perhaps, as Mellon (1995) suggests, there are different categories of shopper, each with different and distinct features but with overlapping motivations and family factors. She defines the following categories: the 'money in love' spender, who shows affection to self by shopping; the 'blue light' spender, who hunts for bargains; the esteem spender, who buys symbols of status such as designer labels; the overboard spender, who has an insatiable desire to collect objects; the 'I'll show you' spender, who wishes to feel superior by spending excessively; the spin of the wheel spender, who enjoys the risks of spending. It is likely that any individual shopper might have elements from more than one, or even all, of these categories, but Mellon (1995) establishes collecting as a kind of shopping.

Collecting, Shopping and the Unconscious

I have already made reference to some of the more stereotypically psychoanalytic interpretations of the unconscious meaning of objects. Objects might have other hidden meanings. Lawrence (1990) concludes that addictive shoppers might be primarily motivated by an unconscious castration anxiety. Addictive shopping might also be related to anal retention. A child's early experience of excretory functions is referred to in the psychoanalytic literature as a precursor to adult ways of giving and taking, of holding back or letting go. Thus Muensterberger writes with reference to collecting:

> Building up heaps of things in a collection or piling up money or amassing rubbish such as old newspapers, empty beer cans or discarded umbrellas ... often clearly and quite understandably function as a bulwark against deep-rooted uncertainties and existential dread. (Muensterberger 1994, p. 21)

One might see the collector as an 'anal type' who gains satisfaction from the retention of objects. As well as an expression to others of self-worth, objects serve as a symbolic substitute for emotional support, a sort of illusory protection against danger. Such theorising leads to the subject of transitional objects, described by Winnicott (1951). The child seeks a transitional (that is, temporary) object as a substitute for mother's absence. He reaches out to an object to deny the separation from his mother. Shopping, one might hypothesise, could be for some people a search for the transitional object in the absence of a satisfactory internal mother. If shopping becomes compulsive, it might indicate that the individual is locked into a fruitless search which is doomed to failure.

The discussion so far has centred on the potential importance of the actual object or possession of the object to individual identity. The question of object relations leads on to the hypothesis that perhaps it is the *search* for an object; that is, the actual act of shopping that is important and not necessarily the meanings of the goods purchased. Certainly this would make more sense in the context of the compulsive shopper and it might be important to focus more on the actual experience of shopping. Orford (1985) in *Excessive Appetites* states that to be active in spending money, no matter what the acquisition,

indicates success, just as sexual conquests rank as successes to those who are addicted to sex.
Muensterberger (1994, p. 18):

> People tend to search in later life for the equivalents of love and tenderness they may have lacked during their early years. Some find relief in religious pursuits; others turn to supposedly magical aids such as alcohol or drugs, or indulge in a never-ending search for some kind of cause or some kind of goal to find an expression of their need to relate.

The search for objects can be a time and energy consuming pursuit and this involvement itself might be a distraction from a sense of emptiness or from dilemmas in daily life or in relationships. As Levine (1970) points out, the search for goods and maintenance of them as possessions can easily take over a person's whole life, until he or she no longer has the mental or physical energy for anything else.

Shopping and Narcissism

To refer back to the earlier discussion of narcissism, addiction has been related to narcissistic personality disorder (Good 1995); so, too, might excessive shopping behaviour. In support of the idea, Lawrence (1990) refers to shopping as an easier way of having a relationship, that is with an activity rather than with another person: 'The female shopper has something that need not return her love. She need not perform in order to elicit a desired response as nothing is asked of her' (Lawrence 1995, p. 69). Similarly, Baudrillard writes: 'For it is the subject, the epitome of narcissistic self-engrossment, who collects and eroticizes his own being, evading the amorous embrace to create a closed dialogue with himself' (Baudrillard 1994, p. 19). Such withdrawal might occur *instead* of an actual relationship, or instead of expressing or receiving certain emotion in a relationship. Purchased objects are something for the self, and carry the message of personal specialness not because of what is purchased but because of the act of self-giving, yet it rarely works and certainly not in the long term.

Shopping and Parental Shopping Behaviour in Childhood

There have been a few theorists who have specifically linked childhood experience with later adult shopping behaviour. Belk observed that parental material rewards to children (Belk 1988) and contemporary gifts bestowed supposedly by Father Christmas in return for good behaviour (Belk 1987) may prepare children to reward themselves with self-gifts when adults.

Muensterberger (1994) writes of emotional, and possibly material deprivation in childhood as potential precursors to compulsive collecting behaviour in adulthood. Mellon (1995) writes that the mother's attitude to money and spending can influence the child who might either adopt the same patterns or rebel and become like the opposite of their parents.

Profile of a Collector

Muensterberger's discussion of collecting is very applicable to shopping. He describes the compulsive nature of collecting, the unsuccessful attempts to give up and the often resultant situation of debt. His profile of a compulsive collector does not rely on a single personality trait but rather a combination of remarkably similar life events, social deprivations and subsequent difficulties in maintaining relationships or in achieving satisfaction from them. Given the similarities between collecting and shopping as behaviours, it would be interesting to observe whether interviews with shoppers reveal a parallel with that found by Muensterberger in his interviews with collectors (Muensterberger 1994). He observed that many collectors had suffered trauma in early life, and that their search for new objects for their collection represented an unconscious search for the reassurance that they are wanted and lovable. In the case of one collector of 'bells', the source of comfort could be immediately traced to the catholic orphanage where he had suffered emotional deprivation but had received comfort then from the sound of the church bells. Also, the collector of maps had overcome his sense of inferiority as a child when directing his father on the frequent long journeys in the car. Collecting involves a magical escape into a private world, like a child with his toys, and the objects, he claims, can act as a surrogate guarantee of emotional support to counteract feelings of loss and helplessness. Indeed, the shopper, certainly at the moment of purchase, is likely to feel some power over his environment, however temporary or artificial. The objects themselves might even be seen by collectors to have a magical value. As well as the objects themselves perhaps having magical value, it might be the very act of collecting that is a denial of death. Addicts feel the need to repeat their 'message', and Freud himself spoke of his own collection of antiquities as being dead when there is no new acquisition to be made. Baudrillard (1994) theorises that an object acquires its exceptional value by being absent from a collection; that the acquisition of the final item would in fact denote the death of the subject. Furthermore, he claims that the subject is able to defend from the possibility of his or her own death by envisaging it in a material object. This was true on an overt level of collectors of ancient relics and ritualistic symbols. On an unconscious level, objects such as masks or even everyday commonplace objects might have archetypal and symbolic significance (see Aniela Jaffe 1964) to the individual. The trauma or perception of loss in childhood leads to the yearning and hunger that can manifest itself in collecting. Muensterberger hypothesises out of a narcissistic need for a substitute for relationships with people, who have proved themselves to be unreliable sources of emotional gratification. Objects are indeed more controllable than humans and can lead to a sense of mastery. Muensterberger's use of case studies demonstrates his view of the 'typical' collector most clearly, and I would therefore like to outline briefly one of his examples.

Honore de Balzac: Renowned Collector and Expert Shopper

The famous French novelist de Balzac most certainly felt emotionally deprived as a child and lacked a 'good enough' mother. At birth, he was sent to live with a child nurse for four years at a house several miles from his parental home. His mother was aloof, and from age four to eight he was primarily cared for by a governess. He was then sent to a boarding school for the next six years, during which period he saw his mother only twice. He often lamented throughout his life that he did not have a mother. As an adult, he had a love of luxury, and spent years spending way beyond his budget on fine art and objects of all kinds. Like many collectors, he wanted to buy only the best, which represents, Muensterberger claims, a form of projection that relates to their self-image. Often said to have written novels with strongly autobiographical themes, de Balzac wrote *Le Cousin Pons* in 1947, about a fanatical collector whose habit sought to correct for his feelings of failure in life. De Balzac's own mania for collecting ran parallel to his assiduous eighteen-year courtship of the Countess Eveline de Hanska, the great-niece of the former queen of France. He sought to obtain her hand in marriage once he had furnished a house in a style that would befit such a noble aristocrat as she. Tragically, just four months after the wedding he died from peritonitis. Balzac's story is similar to that of most of the collectors reported in Muensterberger's (1994) book, and it would be interesting to observe if a similar profile emerges for shoppers, or indeed if a profile emerges at all.

Although Muensterberger makes no specific reference to Adlerian theory, connections can be drawn with the psychology of collecting.

Adler has written about the impact of ambivalent mothering, prolonged maternal illness and separation from parents which he believes can each lead to the development of a magnified sense of inferiority (see Dinkmeyer et al. 1987). The importance of warm and responsive mothering is central to the theory of interpersonal psychotherapy. One potential reaction of children to not receiving the nurturing that they need is withdrawal from the mother as an alternative to expressing anger, which might not be heeded (de Zulueta 1993). Such an effect can last into adulthood, with the learnt pattern of withdrawal from relationship contact being continued due to a belief, perhaps unconscious, that their needs will not be met by interaction with others. In fact for them reliance on another human being for emotional needs has become fraught with anxiety.

Shopping and the Family Culture

As I have already stated, there is a lack of research into the possible connections between family dynamics and shopping behaviour. Csikszentmihalyi and Rochberg-Halton (1981) write about the meanings of domestic symbols in families and suggest the existence of two different types of family; 'cold' families and 'warm' families. 'Warm' families were those in which they found household objects to be associated with symbolic meanings, perhaps emotional or sentimental associations. 'Cold' families, by contrast, tended to own objects for their practical use and were less likely to generate warm symbolic object representations of the transpersonal value of the individual. The researchers hypothesised (but did not test) that in 'cold' families, where the gratification of the individual's needs were paramount, there was more likely to be an interest in 'terminal materialism'; the consumption of goods for their short-term value. There is the implication, then, that a compulsive shopper might be trapped in a cycle of needing instant gratification from new objects, due to an inability to instil value into the objects that they have: a search for value and meaning.

Such hypotheses might lead to the question of what else might be represented in the seemingly insatiable search for new goods in terms of meaning for the individual. Various possibilities emerge, such as a lack of meaning in a person's life in general, in relationships or in life purpose.

Summary

It seems clear from the research to date that shopping behaviour, especially excessive shopping behaviour, is likely to be an expression of some conscious or unconscious message that is not necessarily overt. From this perspective my aim is to find out from shoppers: what are you saying by shopping, what does it express? Such information might be hard to elicit, but I wanted to aim towards an exploration of common features among shoppers; and of more idiosyncratic features of their behaviour and of their life in general. I was keen to engage in research that would raise issues rather than be limited to a set of pre-determined hypotheses as might occur with a questionnaire or very structured interview. I therefore conducted a series of semi-structured interviews with self-proclaimed addictive shoppers.

A SMALL STUDY OF ADDICTIVE SHOPPERS

The group of twenty-seven shoppers that I interviewed (three men, twenty-four women) had responded to a notice that explained the nature of the research as concerned with 'shopping, sadness and addictive shopping', and this wording presumes a connection. Also the interviews were being conducted in a psychotherapy department, and participants might have had fantasies of receiving therapy. In spite of these biases, however, the members of the group were all apparently consumed by the desire to shop, and the emotions surrounding their behaviour were expressed with great feeling.

Mood and general psychological well-being received much comment in the context of the desire to shop before a shopping trip, and in stories of during and after such a trip. Low mood was the commonest mentioned trigger to shop – for example, 'I shop if I'm gloomy or irritated by my husband' and 'If I'm fed up I reward myself with a purchase.' Shopping was often seen as a potential cure for a specific problem, such as compensation after an argument with one's husband, or after a bad day at work. This attempted cure did not seem to have any durable benefits, however. Most of the participants mentioned pleasurable emotions during a shopping trip, but the pleasure does not appear to last long beyond the purchase of the goods. Guilt was common, and some shoppers spoke of disgust and depression. Other respondents had some pleasure in the possession of the goods, but expressed more long-term anxieties about the value of their habit. The three respondents who reported no negative reaction after shopping were, interestingly, all single, and were the same three who reported no childhood trauma (although one was disowned by her parents as a teenager). Childhood trauma was in fact a commonly reported element in this sample. About half reported major trauma during childhood that involved the disruption of the mother–child bond, such as mother leaving home or being in hospital for extended periods. Of the remaining participants there were a variety of childhood disruptions, such as having a depressed mother, being disowned as a teenager or many family arguments. It is interesting that apart from the participant who was unwilling to comment on his childhood, *in all of the participants there had either been a family imbalance in childhood or the mother had been an obsessive shopper.*

One might wonder if this trend of family difficulties continued into adulthood, and indeed for most participants relationships appeared to be problematic. All of the participants except one reported fundamentally negative elements of their current primary relationship (or of not being in a relationship), and this was usually connected by the participant to shopping – for example, that shopping was a compensation or a distraction from their relationship. One woman reported: 'Shopping was a relief from my emotional life, something over which I had some control', and another: 'Unfortunately I married a man with no feelings ... shopping is something for *me* without the complication of a relationship.' Participants who were not in a long-term relationship also expressed a dissatisfaction with their marital status, for example: 'There's an element of looking around and seeing other people of my age with families and I still feel I'm struggling on my own ... I haven't got a relationship, it's partly my fault – a fear of commitment', and another participant said: 'I have always felt an outsider: alienated, lonely, alone.'

The interviews showed much evidence to support for a theory that connects addictive shopping behaviour with family, as childhood and current relationship difficulties were an issue for most, perhaps almost all of the participants. It is important to stress that the report of such findings does not prove any kind of causal structure: perhaps, for example, shoppers who have suffered from relationship problems are more likely than other compulsive shoppers to volunteer to be interviewed by a psychotherapist, due to possible hopes for 'treatment' or for sympathetic contact. Nonetheless the results are an interesting pointer to the sorts of issues that are relevant for these shoppers and might therefore be relevant for some others. The results of childhood problems and relationship difficulties are consistent, however, with a theory of shopping behaviour as a narcissistic search. The search appears to be fairly indiscriminate, and it did not seem to matter what was bought.

All of the interviewees mentioned buying clothes for themselves. Other items included cars, food with memories of childhood, paperweights, irons, jugs, clocks, pictures, and so on. Interestingly, only one interviewee described going on a shopping trip with a firm idea of what she was about to buy. The other participants would search for *something* but they knew not what for. One might argue that their search was of a more psychological than of a material nature. The circularity of shopping as a coping mechanism was highlighted by the reports of how participants felt *after* shopping: that most of them felt some negative emotion such as guilt or depression. It seems that shopping had worked as a coping strategy only in the short term: or perhaps it is better to feel depressed about spending too much money than it is about a less controllable factor such as a painful marital situation. For those with unhappy personal relationships, shopping might well be successful in diverting the negative emotional feeling onto a less difficult source. Shopping certainly seems to represent more than a pleasurable diversion. It was preceded, for the majority of participants, by low mood, and appears as a compulsion to buy something, *anything*. The items purchased might remain unworn, even still in their bags or in the boot of the car.

For those participants who discussed image and the hope invested in their purchases, there was inevitable disappointment. The search, for what they might not even be aware, had been a failure. How can it succeed when the searcher is not aware of his or her aim? There instead remains a kind of fathomless narcissistic black hole. One participant expressed a sentiment that many others were unable to express but may have shared: 'It is fulfilling a need somewhere. I'm not sure what. Its like there's something missing inside. I can't really put my finger on it.'

Other themes raised by participants were also of a psychological nature and included self-image, self-worth and potency. A few interviewees enjoyed the power that they felt at the moment of purchase, whilst a larger group commented on their hopes that the goods would in some way enhance their self-worth. Some participants wanted something 'for me', a few others mentioned shopping as an escape, which could be similar to seeing shopping as a compensation in the sense that it aims at achieving a certain kind of balance. The literature on gambling suggests that such activity is a search for omnipotence as a result of childhood problems (Bergler 1958). Shoppers mentioned childhood problems as well as current problems with self-esteem, self-worth and the issues of power and control. Perhaps the shoppers too were searching for an area in their lives where they felt they had real control, albeit temporarily.

In spite of the apparent level of shopping, only two participants had become bankrupt, and only three spoke of very large debts. The rest of the sample had kept their spending within barely manageable limits:

with the constant risk of financial disaster. Unlike with many addictions, the serious risks had been mostly contained, and the participants had not plunged into the pit of financial ruin, although there was real risk and perhaps excitement.

The profile of one shopper may bring these themes to life (the identifying features have been changed). It displays many of the elements and issues that were highlighted in the previous section.

Case Study of a Shopper

Sally met me to discuss what she describes as her shopping addiction. She appeared keen to talk openly.

Sally, forty-eight years old, is the youngest of four children. When she was two and a half her mother suffered a nervous breakdown and was admitted to a psychiatric hospital for several months. During this period Sally stayed at her grandmother's house and has vague memories of being molested by an uncle who lived in the same house. On returning to the family home her relationship with her mother appeared to involve a reversal of parenting: she found her mother was very emotionally needy but unable to give Sally the love that she felt she needed. This asymmetry continued until the children were adults, when their mother tried to prevent them from leaving home.

Sally feels that the experience of her childhood has left her feeling disconnected from relationships in general in her adult life, and she described an unhappy marriage, which apparently perpetuated the sense of feeling under-nurtured.

Another apparent element of Sally's childhood was the way that she experienced sexuality as overtly and inappropriately displayed in the family home. She recalled sleeping with her parents and 'saw things happening'. Sally connected her shopping activity with her professed disconnection from relationships and disgust of sex. She married a man who she claims, 'has no feelings', and she is revolted by the thought of sexual contact with him. Shopping, she sees, as perhaps a distraction from these extreme sexual and marital problems. In addition she buys mainly clothes for herself because she finds that they act as a kind of cover for her body and make her feel less disgusted with aspects of her sexuality. There was an apparent contradiction which Sally mentioned herself: she is extremely keen to look her best, but hates any reaction from men.

Sally longed for the attention of a caring mother or nurturing partnership that she never felt she had experienced. She was, however, revolted by the sexual aspect of relationships that had apparently been present in early childhood relationships. These sexual aspects were for her not consistent with a loving mutual relationship. Shopping itself, she felt, was something that she had control over and had none of the complications of an interpersonal relationship. It appeared to be a kind of self-nurturing in place of an internal mother role. Satisfaction was sought from an outside source; from interaction with 'goods' rather than with herself or others.

The short-term trigger to shopping is, for Sally, a low depressive mood, but shopping is a very short-term 'cure', if that, as she feels ashamed after a shopping trip. The compulsion to buy something overwhelms her, and she buys anything even if she can't find something that she likes. She becomes trapped in a self-propelling cycle of low mood, search for a solution, followed by low mood. Sally also feels disgust at her shopping behaviour, a word that she also applied to her feelings about sex. It is as if shopping is an alternative to sex, but is unconsciously realised as such and shopping therefore becomes disgusting, just as her uncle and her parents were felt to be disgusting.

When asked what shopping meant to her Sally replied that it was a lifeline because she felt so desperate, that she could perhaps buy clothes to look OK on the outside when she felt a mess on the inside.

The Case of Sally: Comparison with de Balzac

The similarities between Sally and the case studies described by Muensterberger (1994) were striking. In the case of de Balzac, an avid collector, he had also been separated from his mother for a lengthy period at a young age: he was sent away for the first four years of his life, and went to boarding school at the age of seven with the most minimal of contact with his mother during that period. Like Sally, he lacked the opportunity to feel loved and lovable, which might have led to greater feelings of inner stability and self-regard. He similarly had problems with personal attachments. His extensive appetite for books and for the acquisition of objects stemmed, Muensterberger (1994) believed, from an awareness of his own isolation. The fear of being alone was a drive towards his craving for possessions and his acquisitiveness. Perhaps it is not a coincidence that both de Balzac and Sally collected material objects; perhaps their unconscious beliefs that the search for human contact would result in disappointment led them to search for more reliable non-human 'objects'. De Balzac remained engaged to his love for almost twenty years, thus holding any intimate human contact at a distance that allowed safety. Sally, too, not only chose a man 'with no feelings' whom she could keep at a distance emotionally, but felt threatened by any sexual contact with him. Muensterberger (1994) describes de Balzac's eccentricities as 'a bulwark against his morbid fear of rejection and being left out and nearly forgotten'. Perhaps Sally's purchases of clothes were, as she alluded to, a barrier between herself and the human contact that she unconsciously feared would end in rejection.

For de Balzac and Sally, and for many other of the participants, the search for goods can be seen as a search for emotional replenishment. The reasons for this need for emotional replenishment may be rooted in childhood, and there is much evidence in the study of childhood disturbance. In Adlerian terms, ambivalent mothering, prolonged illness of the mother or separation from the parents can lead to a magnified sense of inferiority (see Dinkmeyer et al. 1987). Other interpersonal theorists discuss how a lack of sufficient nurturing in childhood can lead to an emotional withdrawal by the child, which might persist in adulthood and be characterised by an inability to invest in relationships (de Zulueta 1993). Muensterberger's (1994) results, and those of the present study, are both suitable for the application of the theory of narcissism.

Other Issues Raised by the Study

The question might arise at this point: Why shopping as an addiction? The respondents appeared to be conformist addicts: not only have they apparently escaped from conflict in their lives by shopping, they are also perhaps too 'well behaved' to rebel by the adoption of an addictive behaviour that is not socially acceptable. Several of the participants mentioned that shopping was an acceptable addiction: that everyone shops and that it is not taken seriously or judged too harshly. One interviewee felt that her parents, who were religious and morally rigid, had been able to accept her shopping addiction but would not have been so tolerant of another addiction. In the search for the object it might be important for this group that they do not jeopardise their chances of future successful nurturance from anyone around them: indeed shopping addictively might lead to those other adults being sympathetic and offering practical help, which is perhaps better than nothing.

Shoppers have a hidden obsession and can conduct it in the anonymous but isolating mass of other shoppers who shop for tangible material needs. Almost all of the interviewees described shopping alone, which highlights the anonymous nature of the task. Addiction as an attempt to fill an emptiness or void is a theme also discussed by Marilyn Woodman (1982) in her book *Addiction to Perfection*. She describes the way that those with compulsive syndromes carry out their rituals alone, and the present study found that all shoppers interviewed shopped alone. They found that their search was in fact impeded by the presence of others who served as an irritation and a distraction from the important task of shopping. Woodman also describes addiction, as her title suggests, as a search for perfection. The anorexic can diet better than anyone else and therefore feels good at something. Some shoppers in the present study felt that shopping was an expression of their creativity and that they were good shoppers. One might hypothesise that they do not feel good at anything else or, to return to narcissistic theory, that they wish for predictable positive feedback from a controllable object (although this aim is not apparently fulfilled). Rituals are predictable and give a sense of security. Shopping might therefore represent a comfortable ritual.

The Role of Shopping in Family Life

As shopping is a necessary part of daily life, it might be easy to be unaware of the intense and important role that it holds for many individuals. Also, shopping behaviour might be serving as a balance for other aspects of an individual's life and might aid the denial of other problems.

It seems that for many interviewees in a current relationship, shopping is a means of escape that excluded others. Several interviewees mentioned shopping to escape from relationship issues or contact within the relationship, and others spoke of shopping as a compensation for less pleasant aspects of their relationship or work situation. Thus shopping had become a method of communication, although possibly a silent one if it is acted out in secret. It is a way of building a wall around oneself and might be saying 'go away' or 'change' to the partner by this method of action (or inaction in other areas). This method of coping that excludes a partner could to be addressed in therapy. Also relationship issues might have been obscured because they have become secondary in the person's life to shopping and are perhaps not in the conscious mind. This might be a convenient state of affairs for both partners. In several cases in the study, a partner was in fact another kind of addict (usually an alcoholic). Shopping might therefore represent a collusion of interpersonal emotional withdrawal.

Hidden Meanings of Shopping

During the interviews I found myself asking about what communication was contained in their shopping behaviour, and what it might enable or prevent a person from doing. An example of how powerful such questions proved to be can be seen in the case of Barbara (all distinguishing features have been changed).

The possessions that Barbara acquired appeared to hold a particularly symbolic value for her. She had hoarded so many goods that it was very difficult for guests to the house even to enter and move around, whilst finding the kettle proved to be a challenge. Her bed was used to store further assorted items on, so that there was only a small space for her to sleep in, and even the toilet seat was piled high with an assortment of books and papers. She had toyed with thoughts of moving house, but knew that it would be impossible for an estate agent even to visit. I commented that at some level the idea of being firmly rooted in one place seemed to be very important to Barbara, and I asked if she had any associations with this idea. She responded with a painful memory of living in poverty with her mother as a child, and, following an argument between the landlady and her mother, of being evicted noisily into the snow-covered hills of Scotland at three o'clock in the morning with only a cardboard suitcase. She had certainly made sure that she could not be moved so hurriedly or against her will again.

As many of the interviews touched on deep issues, the potential uses of psychotherapy are highlighted. The potential importance of narcissism in the formation of shopping addiction has been discussed earlier, and has much relevance for psychotherapy. Implications for treatment include the need for awareness of the search for a primary object and the desire of such clients to have connectedness. This leads to the possibility of merger in the client's own life and in the consulting room (Cooper and Maxwell 1995), with the possibility of extreme distress on separation for holidays and other breaks. The aim of the therapy is to understand the client's deep need or 'lack'.

After an activity that so many described as the only outlet that was really for themselves alone, it is noteworthy that so many felt guilty, especially as most of the participants had contained their debt within manageable limits. Do they feel guilty about giving themselves a reward? Perhaps this is a marker for a deeply rooted family belief system, or for an inner sense of unworthiness. Is the guilt of a more existential nature, do they feel inner guilt that they are avoiding realising their own potential, that they are aware at some level that shopping is a trivial distraction from more central issues in their lives? Some of the participants spoke of an inner 'lack', some others felt the need to project an impressive outer image to mask an inner turmoil, yet others needed to be in control of some element of their lives. The issue of self-worth appears again to be of importance and worthy of investigation for those individuals.

Shopping was also described by many participants as a reward, a compensation or an escape. Such comments allude to other areas of the interviewees' lives that are unsatisfactory for them. The question arises of the nature of these dissatisfactions: in most cases the dissatisfaction was reported as being relationship-based.

Other questions that are raised by the research include the issue of why shopping had been 'chosen'. Future research could also usefully concentrate on the many questions raised in the previous section: on the apparent neediness, sense of lack and emptiness of compulsive shoppers. It certainly appears that it *is* extremely relevant to include exploration of the family context of an addictive shopper in any future research.

I shall conclude with the words of one interviewee who explained: 'Perhaps it [shopping] limits your self reflection ... it stops you examining yourself too closely. You might find something you don't like. I'm frightened to look.' One might ask, what *are* they searching for so desperately, as they rummage around car boot sales and shopping centres but not around the core of their own psyche?

NOTES

1. A feature of co-dependency is the issue of the partner of the addict needing to be needed.
2. Also see Forrester (1994) for a more in-depth discussion on Freud and collecting.
3. One example of which might be the purchase of newspapers in which massacres (e.g. Dunblane) are reported and avidly read as a substitute gratification of the death drive. Bocock (1993) reports that Dichter (1946) hypothesised that men buy convertibles as substitute mistresses and that the electric razor would not take over in popularity because of the unconscious death wish (in Bocock 1993).

REFERENCES

American Psychiatric Association (1985) *Diagnostic and Statistical Manual of Mental Disorders.* Washington DC, American Psychiatric Association.
Baudrillard, J. (1988) *Selected Writings.* Cambridge, Polity Press.
Baudrillard, J. (1994), The system of collecting (translated by R. Cardinal). In J. Elsner, and R. Cardinal (eds) *The Cultures of Collecting.* Harvard University Press.
Belk, R. W. (1987) A Child's Christmas in America: Santa Claus as deity, consumption as religion. *Journal of American Culture,* 10 (1), 87–100.
Belk, R. W. (1988) Possessions and the Extended Self. *Journal of Consumer Research,* 15: 139–68.
Belk, R. W. (1995) Studies in The New Consumer Behaviour. In D. Miller (ed.) *Acknowledging Consumption.* London, Routledge.
Bergler, E. (1958) *The Psychology of Gambling.* London, Harrison.
Bloch, P. H. and Bruce, G. D. (1984) Product Involvement as Leisure Behavior: The case of automobiles and clothing. In T. Kinnear (ed.) *Advances in Consumer Research,* vol. 7. Provo UT, Association for Consumer Research.

Bocock, R. (1993) *Consumption.* London, Routledge.
Cooper, J. and Maxwell, N. (1995) The Search for a Primary Object. In J. Cooper and N. Maxwell (eds) *Narcissistic Wounds: Clinical perspectives.* London, Whurr Publications.
Csikszentmihalyi, M. and Rochberg-Halton, E. (1981) *The Meaning of Things.* Cambridge, Cambridge University Press.
de Zulueta, F. (1993) *From Pain to Violence.* London, Whurr Publishers.
Dinkmeyer, D. C., Dinkmeyer, D. C. and Sperry, L. (1987) *Adlerian Counselling and Psychotherapy.* New York: Macmillan Publishing Company.
Duck, S. (1994) Strategems, Spoils and The Serpent's Tooth: On the delights and dilemmas of personal relationships. In W. R. Cupach and B. H. Spitzberg, *The Dark Side of Interpersonal Communication.* Hillsdale NJ, Lawrence Erlbaum.
Elliott, R., Eccles, S. and Gournay, K. (1996) Revenge, Existential Choice, and Addictive Consumption. *Psychology and Marketing,* vol. 13, no. 18.
Faber, R. J., O'Guinn, T. C. and Krych, R. (1987) Compulsive Consumption. *Advances in Consumer Research,* 14, 132–5.
Firat, A. F. (1994) *Gender and Consumption: Transcending the feminine?* In J. A. Costa (ed.), *Gender Issues and Consumer Behaviour.* London, Sage.
Fischer, E. and Gainer, B. (1994) Masculinity and the Consumption of Organised Sports. In J. A. Costa (ed.) *Gender Issues and Consumer Behaviour.* London, Sage.
Forrester, J. (1994) Mille etre: Freud and Collecting. In J. Elsner and R. Cardinal (eds), *The Cultures of Collecting.* Harvard University Press.
Gay, P. (1988) *Freud: A life for our time.* New York, Norton.
Good, L. (1995) Addiction as a Narcissistic Defence. In J. Cooper and N. Maxwell (eds) *Narcissistic Wounds: Clinical Perspectives.* London, Whurr Publications.
Holbrook, (1987) O, Consumer How You've Changed: some radical reflections on the roots of consumption. In B. P. Bagozzi N. Dholakia, and A. F. Firat (eds) *Philosophical and Radical Thought in Marketing.* Lexington MA, Lexington Books.
Jaffe, A. (1964) Symbolism and the Visual Arts. In C. G. Jung (ed.) *Man and His Symbols.* London, Penguin Arkana.
Kaslow, F. W. (ed.) (1996) *Handbook of Relational Diagnosis and Dysfunctional Family Patterns.* New York, John Wiley.
Kellner, D. (1992) Popular Culture and the Construction of Post-modern Identities. In S. Lash and J. Friedman (eds) *Modernity and Identity.* Oxford, Basil Blackwell.
Lacan, J. (1977) *Ecrits. A Selection,* London, Tavistock Publications.
Lawrence, L. (1990) The Psychodynamics of The Compulsive Female Shopper. *American Journal of Psychoanalysis,* vol. 50, no. 1, 67–71.
Levine, P. (1970) Eating Disorders and Their Impact on Family Systems. In S. B. Lindner (ed.) *The Harried Leisure Class.* New York, Columbia University Press.
Lunt, P. and Livingstone, S. (1992) *Mass Consumption and Personal Identity.* Buckingham, Open University Press.
Mehta, R. and Belk, R. W. (1991) Artifacts Identity and Transition: Favourite possessions of Indians and Indian immigrants to the United States. *Journal of Consumer Research,* 17, 398–411.
Mellon, O. (1995) *Overcoming Overspending.* New York, Walker & Co.
Minuchin, S. (1974) *Families and Family Therapy.* London, Tavistock.
Mort, F. (1996) *Cultures of Consumption: Masculinities and social space in late twentieth century Britain.* London, Routledge.
Muensterberger, W. (1994) *Collecting: An unruly passion.* Princeton, Princeton University Press.
Nakken, C. (1988) *The Addictive Personality: Understanding compulsion in our lives.* New York, Harper/Hazelden.
Nataraajan, R. and Goff, B. G. (1991) Compulsive Buying: Towards a reconceptualization. *Journal of Social Behaviour and Personality,* 6, 307–28.
O'Guinn, T. C. and Faber, R. J. (1989) Compulsive Buying: A phenomenological exploration. *Journal of Consumer Research,* 16, 147–57.
Orford, J. (1985) *Excessive Appetites: A psychological view of addictions.* Chichester, John Wiley & Sons.

Satir, V. (1978) *Conjoint Family Therapy*. London, Souvenir Press Ltd.

Scherhorn, G. (1990) The Addictive Trait in Buying Behaviour. *Journal of Consumer Policy*, 13, 33–51.

Simmel, G. (1903) The Metropolis and Mental Life. In D. Levine (1971) *On Individuality and Social Form*. Chicago, University of Chicago Press.

Tomlinson, A. (ed.) (1990) *Consumption, Identity and Style*. London, Routledge.

Veblen, T. (1912) *The Theory of the Leisure Class: An economic study of institutions*. New York, Mentor Books.

Walrond-Skinner, S. (1976) *Family Therapy: The treatment of natural systems*. London, Routledge.

Winnicott, D. W. (1951) *Transitional Objects and Transitional Phenomena*. London, Tavistock Publications.

Woodman, M. (1982) *Addiction to Perfection*. Toronto, Inner City Books.

9

Social Power, Self-Identity and Addictive Consumption

Richard Elliott

The study reported here explores the role played by consumption in the exercise of power within personal relationships and the opportunity it provides for the expression of creativity and control. It is assumed that addicted consumers are not qualitatively different from 'normal' consumers but merely lie further up a continuum of consumption behaviour (d'Astous 1990), so by focusing on addicted consumers it is intended that insights into more 'normal' consumption can be developed.

The existence of a small group of consumers, perhaps 1–2 per cent of the population, who maintain a pathological form of shopping behaviour has been identified by recent studies in the USA (O'Guinn and Faber 1989), Canada (Valence et al. 1988), Germany (Scherhorn et al. 1990) and the UK (Elliott 1994). These consumers (predominantly female) buy for motives which are not directly related to the actual possession of the goods – in fact, many of the purchases remain wrapped and hidden in cupboards. They persistently repeat the behaviour despite its leading to severe financial and social consequences, such as huge levels of personal debt and even marital break-down. The act of shopping itself is an important element, as many people seem to need to engage in a shopping process rather than obtain goods from a catalogue showroom or by mail order. Typically, addictive consumers experience feelings of great excitement and anticipation prior to and during the shopping experience, only to feel guilty and ashamed of themselves and their behaviour at the post-shopping stage.

COMPULSION OR ADDICTION?

This behaviour has been termed 'compulsive consumption' (Faber et al. 1987) or 'compulsive buying' (Valence et al. 1988) where the behaviour is seen as being under the control of an irresistible urge to buy. However, as Scherhorn (1990) points out, compulsion involves outside pressure to do something against the individual's will, whereas this behaviour is more accurately described as an addiction because it involves the development of normal behaviour into a pathological habit. Although 'buying', 'spending', 'purchasing' and even 'shopping' are often used to describe the addictive behaviour, the terms do not, in themselves, adequately encompass the whole experience. Holbrook and Hirschman (1982) argue that consumption phenomena include such experiential aspects as 'a primarily subjective state of consciousness with a variety of symbolic meanings, hedonic responses and aesthetic criteria'. Further, Holbrook (1995, p. 88) suggests that consumption includes the cycle of acquisition, usage and disposition of products. This definition of consumption acknowledges activities and states which extend beyond the rational information processing and decision-making stages of consumer behaviour. Although the conceptual distinctions between shopping, buying and spending have been pointed out by Nataraajan and Goff (1992) it is proposed here that all of these behaviours can be usefully subsumed under the term of consumption, and that the behaviour in question can be considered as addictive consumption which is used here to describe the total activity – from the pre-shopping anticipation and preparation, to the deliberation, selection and payment of goods (the 'shopping experience') to the post-shopping activities (secreting the goods and organising finances). But it may not involve all these manifestations of consumption for all people at all times. It also acknowledges that consumers may consume symbolic meanings as well as material goods (Mick and Buhl 1992). The definition of addiction, as it is used here, involves a habitual behaviour pattern which is often experienced subjectively as a strong urge to perform the behaviour and often associated with a feeling of having limited control. The behaviour is maintained despite severe personal consequences and attempts at control or abstention. However, this is not behaviour which is totally or almost out of control; but rather control of consumption behaviour is variable and limited, yet may still retain aspects of reasoned action (Nataraajan and Goff 1991).

DYSFUNCTIONAL BEHAVIOUR?

Much of the prior research has emphasised the dysfunctional aspects of this addictive behaviour and its consequences, but it also appears that the behaviour does fulfil some positive functions for the individuals concerned. A prime function served by addictive consumption is its ability to repair mood, even to the extent of helping some people cope with suicidal tendencies (Elliott 1994) and the mood repair function is also emerging as an important maintaining factor in other addictions (Gottheil et al. 1988). For women with adequate financial resources it may be that shopping to repair mood is less problematic than the use of the ubiquitous tranquillisers widely prescribed to women, who describe its use as helping them cope with the strains and role conflicts of being wives and mothers (Cooperstock and Lennard 1979). For women, therefore, shopping provides a socially acceptable alternative to alcohol or drugs for mood repair but, whilst it carries similar risks of addiction, has no visible marks, and the behaviour (both generally and during the shopping experience) is seldom noticeably bizarre or obvious to others.

THE SOCIAL CONTEXT AND RELATIONSHIPS

The social location of consumption behaviour has not been fully explored in previous studies which have tended to focus on individual psychopathology. However, in many other areas of problem behaviour, factors relating to relationships with significant others have been found to play an important role in maintaining the behaviour; e.g. agoraphobia (Gournay 1989), depression (Brown and Harris 1978), anorexia (Bruch 1974), problem drinking (Heather and Robertson 1981). Exchange theory suggests that individuals have a strong tendency to respond in kind to the behaviour they receive within a relationship. If satisfaction is received, they tend to provide rewards in turn; if dissatisfaction is received the response is to punish the other (Gergen 1969).

The exercise of power and control within a relationship has been conceptualised by Duck (1994) in a Model of Relational Challenges which identifies revenge and betrayal as characteristics of 'spoiling' relationships. When a previously satisfying relationship is spoiled by one partner's perception that they have been betrayed, then they may carry out acts of revenge. Betrayal in this situation can be defined as a failure to maintain the central element in a relationship, in particular the expectations upon which it is based (Jones and Burdette 1984). Perceived inequity in marriages leads to dissatisfaction (VanYperen and Buunk 1990) and to women, especially, feeling depressed and angry (Sprecher 1992). In relation to addictive consumption, it may be that in some cases the consumption may be conceptualised as an act of revenge on the partner by incurring debts, carried out in response to failures to fulfil the partner's expectations. In this case the behaviour may be partly out of control yet still retain aspects of reasoned action (Nataraajan and Goff 1992).

CREATING A SELF-IDENTITY THROUGH CONSUMPTION

Post-structuralist perspectives on consumption suggest that 'for most members of contemporary society individual freedom, if available at all, comes in the form of consumer freedom' (Bauman 1988). Existential-phenomenological accounts of the consumption experience suggest that even the mundane consumer choices made in everyday life can shape how consumers understand themselves and the lives they lead (Thompson et al. 1989; 1990). The practice of existential consumption through the act of choice allows individuals to exert some limited control over their environment and consciously engage in the development of a self-identity, in part through the shopping experience (Elliott and Ritson 1995). This creative act enables both small groups and individuals to define themselves and to express their identities through their consumption behaviour (Ritson et al. 1996), and is an important aspect of postmodern consumer culture (Brown 1995).

Discrepancies between the achieved self-identity and the ego-ideal have been found to lead to depression and anxiety (Higgins 1989) and this in part explains the behaviour in a substantial proportion of addictive consumers as they use consumption to repair their mood (Elliott 1994). However, the development of self-identity is a higher-order drive which is crucially dependent on pleasure as well as power and social participation (Csikszentmihalyi 1988). The concept of flow (Csikszentmihalyi 1975) describes an experience of the greatest pleasure where people act with total involvement which is charac-terised by a 'merging of action and awareness ... a centring of attention on a limited stimulus field'. Flow is dependent upon a sense of challenge coupled with a sense of control where people feel they can match their skills with opportunities for action where they can control their decisions. Many women experience flow during interactions with other people, especially their children, but also during creative activities (Allison and Duncan 1988). As shopping becomes increas-ingly central to our culture, many women find even mundane consumer actions such as looking in shop windows significant in their psychic lives (Bocock 1993). Addicted consumers may also be using their shopping behaviour as an opportunity for creativity and the con-struction and expression of self.

AN EMPIRICAL INVESTIGATION

As the exploratory stage of a larger study into addictive consumption, depth interviews were conducted with 46 women and 4 men selected from a sample of 265 people who volunteered to participate in the study after nation-wide media coverage. The majority were self-referred but 11 were referred by medical practitioners or counselling services. Informants were screened by informal use of the major constituent items from the Clinical Screener for Compulsive Buying (Faber and O'Guinn 1992) which included, for example, measuring how often respondents bought things even though they couldn't afford them; felt that others would be horrified if they knew of their spending habits; felt anxious or nervous on the days they didn't go shopping. Only those answering positively to at least two of the items were included in the study. Two of the women were from ethnic minorities (Afro-Caribbean and Middle-Eastern) and ages ranged from 19 to 74 years. Of the informants 34 were in full- or part-time employment, 5 were home workers and 11 unemployed or retired. Interviews were carried out across the UK to attempt to avoid regional bias.

In order to maintain the non-invasive nature of the interviews and avoid setting a quasi-medical framework around the discussion of the behaviour and its social location, phenomenological interviews (Thompson et al. 1989) were carried out. This gave informants the opportunity to 'tell their own story' rather than answer prescribed questions. In most cases, this was the first occasion informants had discussed aspects of their behaviour and private lives with anyone (let alone a stranger) and it was agreed amongst the research team that the interviews were likely to yield more depth and detail by being informant-led. Each interview was conducted in the informant's own home, and tape-recorded for later transcription. The interviews lasted from one to three hours and were largely unstructured (although certain topics were introduced into the conversation by the researcher).

The transcripts were analysed using pattern-coding methods (Miles and Huberman 1994) and emergent themes were identified. Quotations from informants are used to illustrate these themes and to build a rich picture of the individuals and their behaviour. Because of the publicity around addictive consumption, which sensitively highlighted the problem, many people acknowledged that this was the first time they had faced up to their behaviour and its consequences, having spent months or years keeping it a secret from others and denying its existence to themselves.

THE SOCIAL AND FINANCIAL CONTEXT

The incomes and backgrounds of the 50 informants were wide and varied and there appeared to be no regular pattern or 'type' of addictive consumer: 45 had an income in their own right, whether as a regular salary, an allowance or savings; 5 were on Income Support, Unemployment or Sickness Benefit and therefore had a small disposable income per week; 7 admitted to having been sexually, physically or emotionally abused as children, although at the other end of the scale, a few felt they had had privileged, loving and supportive childhoods. Only 2 of the interviewees were regular cigarette smokers, none admitted to be currently using non-prescribed drugs and most felt their intake of alcohol was moderate (that is, infrequent and mainly social). Of the informants 9 had suffered a bereavement in the past five years, 24 had been divorced or widowed and, out of that group, 9 remarried. Thirteen were or had recently been treated for depression and 4 were currently on Prozac. Of the women, 9 had pre-menstrual or menopausal problems, which included extreme stomach cramps or physical discomfort and noticeable mood swings.

However, the one commonality amongst the whole group was that they considered themselves to be addictive consumers. They all, to a greater or lesser degree, showed the same pattern of anticipation and excitement prior to and during the shopping experience, feelings of guilt and remorse afterwards and a desire to keep their behaviour and goods a secret from others. Of the others 22 either were or had been in debt (to an extent that caused them worry and hardship, bearing in mind that the level at which debt becomes a problem is relative to income); 9 felt that the main constraint on their addiction was their own sense of financial responsibility and, whilst they would spend up to their own pre-set limit, they could then (albeit with great difficulty and regret) avoid shopping until they next had disposable income available.

THE STAGES OF ADDICTION

All of those interviewed were at different 'stages' of addiction. Some felt that, due to external circumstances (losing a job, being declared bankrupt, becoming involved in a loving, supportive relationship) they had become less addicted to the shopping experience. They had faced up to their behaviour, come to terms with and explored the reasons they had become addicted and taken positive steps (usually with the support of a partner or professional) to break the addiction. Others, on the other hand, had only recently acknowledged to themselves that their behaviour had negative or unmanageable financial and social consequences; that it was yet another unresolved 'problem' in their life (alongside issues such as abuse, bereavement, loneliness, and so on) and that they were, in fact, addictive consumers.

REPAIRING MOOD

In general terms, all of the informants acknowledged that the shopping experience yielded short-term positive feelings. As an escape from depressive mood states and aversive self-awareness, the following comments are typical:

The only way to stop being depressed is to go shopping – but then it only comes back later. (Male: 51 years)

Shopping is the only time when I forget all the other problems in my life. (Female: 37 years)

Shopping makes me forget who I am – I feel I can get away from the real me. (Female: 48 years)

I don't think I like myself very much really – except when I'm shopping! Then I'm in my element. (Female: 30 years)

Likewise, the ability for the shopping experience to enable the addictive consumer to focus on the immediate pleasure was apparent:

It's like time stands still when I'm shopping. (Male: 42 years)

I don't really think about anything when I'm shopping – it's just like escaping into my own peaceful and trouble-free world. (Female: 67 years)

I'm aware of where I am – the surroundings and all the beautiful clothes – and nothing else seems to matter. (Female: 41 years)

I feel somehow set free – as if I can look at and buy all these things without it mattering. (Female: 33 years)

EXERCISING SOCIAL POWER AND CREATING SELF-IDENTITY

A previous study (Elliott 1994) suggested that distinctly separate groups of addictive consumers may exist, which were identified as falling into two groups, those people 'who are typically inadequate personalities struggling to cope with life' presenting themselves as generally 'sad people' and those 'who seem to manage their lives competently without problems apart from shopping' and are 'generally happy with life'. However, within this current study, a pattern began to emerge of the existence of previously unexplored aspects of the addictive consumption behaviour – those of revenge and existential choice. Analysis of the interview data suggests that in 9 cases, revenge played an important part, and in 10 cases informants were using shopping to create meaning for their lives. Of the remaining 31 informants, some of whom have been quoted above, 18 were profoundly unhappy individuals who either were or had been addicted to other behaviours or substances (e.g. eating disorders or alcohol) or were being treated for depression. Their consumption behaviour tended to be more spasmodic and manic. The remaining 13 informants appeared to be generally more content and able to cope with their lives, but were addicted to the consumption experience in order to aid mood repair.

To further elucidate the findings relating to social power and self-identity in addictive consumption, a short description of one of the informants from each category is detailed below (names are fictitious).

JANE: EXERCISING POWER IN A RELATIONSHIP

Jane is 36 years old, married and with three children (all females) under 12 years old. She lives in the Midlands area of the UK, in a large and elegant Victorian house. She was very spoilt as the youngest of four and admits that she was her 'father's favourite'. Her husband David is aged 43 and is a medical practitioner working long and irregular hours. Jane works part time at the local radio station. She is not in debt as her husband pays off the credit cards regularly and she has a small inheritance of her own. She buys clothes and accessories and is particularly interested in attending fine arts auctions. Jane and her husband appear to have a fairly stable and loving relationship, but she feels that he has taken over from her father as an indulgent father-figure:

> He says: 'Well, you were spoilt as a child and I suppose I will have to continue the tradition.'

About her husband she says:

> He loves to work and, in the early days when the children were very small and I was bringing them up practically single-handed, he would work

Saturdays and Sundays. I would resent that so I would think 'Right, if he's working, then I'm spending.' Now we're in a vicious circle – I'm spending and he's working. He says 'How can I cut down on work? I have to work to pay the bills.' In the early years we would have big rows about it.

and

If I think I'm being done out of weekend trips away and that sort of thing because my husband is a self-confessed workaholic, then [the shopping] is a way of getting back at him. I say 'Well, if you took more notice of me and more time off, then I wouldn't have to do it, would I?'

and

We don't seem to have the time to talk to each other any more – you know, about ourselves. I used to try and tell him what I wanted but he just didn't seem interested. I feel that things are very different now – I'm a mother and I'm trying to hold down a part-time job as well but he treats me exactly the same way as when we were first married. I just can't get him to understand that I've changed – I just don't know what to do any more.

At the same time, with regard to money, she feels he treats her as frivolous and incompetent:

Sometimes I get the Spanish Inquisition ... until recently, it would have been 'Show me your cheque book and explain where this money has gone' and I, trembling, would have to give him my cheque stubs. I've put a stop to that now but I still feel that he has control over me – at least, he thinks he has.

Jane herself seems to be in conflict between the child in her that wants to 'get back' at her husband, and the adult who has responsibilities as a mother and worker. About her shopping behaviour she says:

The sensible side of me says 'stop it – grow up!' whilst another little voice is saying at the same time 'I deserve it, and I want it, so it's mine.'

and

On average, I can spend up to £200–£300 a time on nothing. I suppose it's like sweetie money.

Jane considers herself to be generally happy and fortunate. She doesn't feel she shops to bolster low self-esteem or depression, but acknowledges it may sometimes be through boredom and is often a way of getting back at her husband (even though she acknowledges that he has no idea of the extent of her shopping and spending).

> Sometimes when I'm shopping, I see something I like and it's as if I think: 'Right, I'll show him!' Even though he doesn't know how much I'm spending, I feel that I am getting revenge on David for all the times he ignores what I want or isn't there when I need him. I don't think I could confront him any more, but I really can get back at him through shopping.

She and her husband rarely spend any time together, and he leaves the running of the household and bringing up the children mainly to her – which she generally enjoys but sometimes finds it lonely and boring. She has no other close confidants.

MARY: CREATING SELF-IDENTITY

Mary is 58 years old, twice divorced and now married to Mark, who is 15 years her junior. Her son committed suicide some 13 years ago, but she has a married daughter and grandson. She lives in a spacious modern house in the north-west of England. She works full time as an Administrator, but is due to retire soon. She is not in debt but has spent several thousand pounds of her own savings over the past few years to pay off credit cards and loans. She tends to buy goods in phases – a week buying handbags, a few days buying blouses, and so on. Mary is extremely energetic and she does not appear to need (or get) much sleep. She is extremely smartly dressed and presented and her house tastefully decorated and furnished. She describes herself as:

> ... a very, very fussy shopper. I go in to the shop and I've got to have a sweater. I weigh them all up; I measure them all out; I can't make up my mind about three of the same colour. I bring them all home and try them on until 2 a.m. or 3 a.m., until I find the one that is just right. Then, when I've found the right one, I have to go back the next morning and buy one of every colour in that. Then, they are forgotten. Probably just hung up in the wardrobe and never worn.

She describes these phases of buying particular items as 'missions':

> After I'd bought the whole of the Burberry range – coat, hat, scarf, bag – then that was that finished. But I couldn't settle, because my mind hadn't got a mission.

and

> When I knew I was going to retire, I went off sick for a couple of days. My next mission was something to wear in the house. So I bought track suits (indoor and outdoor), Reebok trainers (lightweight and silky), polo shirts in every colour. I know I'll be like a tramp in the house and just wear old jeans, but they are there, so at least I can think about what I could put on.

Apart from the purchases themselves, Mary finds the whole experience of going to the shops exciting and describes the experience of flow:

> I just love the feeling of excitement and wonderment as I go into the shopping mall. I love the buzz of people; the colour and displays; the whole atmosphere. I can just soak up that feeling at the beginning of my shopping trip – it's almost as if I say to myself 'OK, you're at home now, you can relax and enjoy yourself.'

Mary considers herself to be a very discerning shopper ('I do surveys on things, like which will wash the best') and will check each item to make sure it is perfect (that is has no snags or marks) and that the fit and cut are just right. She has a real 'eye' for colour and design, and can tell almost at a glance whether an item will match up with other clothes in her wardrobe. She admits:

> I will spend hours both in the shops and at home considering and comparing different items – invariably, buying more than one and, on many occasions, worrying at night about something I have seen that day in the shops but not bought.

On these occasions, she will arrive late for work in order to go back to the shop as soon as it opens the next day. Mary is not as secretive as some of the other informants about her shopping behaviour:

> I don't think I necessarily boast about my purchases, but I do feel a great pride when I find that 'perfect outfit' – even though I may have spent several days searching for it and it ends up, along with most of my other purchases either in the loft or hanging unworn in one of my four double wardrobes!

She feels she is seen by others as a 'canny shopper' (similar to the 'Market Maven' described by Feick and Price 1985) who often turn to her for advice on where to shop or how to coordinate an outfit. However, she goes shopping virtually daily:

> I get withdrawal symptoms and feel depressed if I don't go to the shops. I tried staying in on a Saturday last week and went for a long walk with Mark.

We got back at 4.20pm and I was sweating. I thought 'I have to go in to town' and I thought 'Well, what am I looking for? I don't need anything' but I can always see something.

By her own admission, Mary is:

... always looking. I love beautiful things but it's never just one item. Having bought a skirt, I have to go and search for things to go with it – everything matching. I suppose it's like painting a picture, isn't it? Building it all up until you've got the final complete thing.

About shopping generally, Mary is quite adamant about its importance in her life:

If ever there was anyone born to shop, it must be me! I have to say it's the most important thing in my life and gives me a real sense of purpose. Although I hate the fact that I can't break the habit, if I'm really honest, I don't want to – what else could I do that would give me so much pleasure and satisfaction?

REFLECTIONS

The case studies above demonstrate factors within the addictive behaviour which suggest that, for a number of addictive consumers, the terms 'addictive' or 'pathological' are not, in themselves sufficient to explain the totality of the complex behaviour. Whilst the behaviour before, during and after the shopping experience itself may be common to most addictive consumers, this study suggests additional reasons for the development and maintenance of the behaviour over a prolonged period – that is, the exercise of social power and the creation of self-identity.

Jane and other informants who showed elements of trying to exercise social control through their addictive shopping behaviour, all appeared to have feelings of lack of control in their relationship with their partner (and often, previously, their father). They felt undermined and patronised, and that their only responsibility was for 'mundane' tasks such as housekeeping and cooking. Comments such as 'he still treats me like a child' were common, even though the respondents themselves feel they have 'grown up' because of family or professional responsibilities. It appears therefore that they developed and maintain their shopping behaviour in order to have some kind of 'exciting' or even slightly dangerous control over a part of their personal lives and their finances. This in turn suggests some feeling of power (albeit secretive) over their partner. The fact that many partners appear to tolerate what they know or suspect about the shopping activities seems, if anything, to encourage the informants to take even greater risks and be even more outrageous in their activities. Building on Duck's (1994) Model of Relational Challenges, some consumers perceive themselves as victims of betrayal in a relationship, in that the partner has not fulfilled previously suggested or stated requests for the dynamics of the relationship to adapt to changes in external or family circumstances. Having taken overt action in the past to address the situation and found it unsuccessful, they adopt a more subversive, less overt method of 'getting back' at their partner – by developing and maintaining an addiction to consumption.

Some addicted consumers are creating a sense of meaning in their lives through their consumer choices, which for them involve an experience of flow. When making choices in the shop they are matching their skills as a consumer with the challenge of achieving the 'best' possible purchase, which takes them into the autotelic state described by Csikszentmihalyi (1975). This is not mere pursuit of pleasure however, but is part of a conscious process of self-development where the individual is seeking to create and maintain an identity which is founded upon skilful shopping behaviour. This is the reasoned behaviour described in the 'normal' population by Fischer and Gainer (1991) as being an integral part of the social construction of women's identity. Thus addictive consumption is not qualitatively different from 'normal' consumption (d'Astous 1990) but involves a more intensive behaviour carried out more frequently and with increased negative long-term consequences. However, the biphasic reinforcement effect which is characteristic of many addictions (Marlatt et al. 1988) means that the short-term benefits of the behaviour influence the behaviour much more powerfully than long-term negative consequences. The positive reinforcement provided by the achievement of flow and the construction of existential meaning suggest that this behaviour pattern will be very resistant to change.

This study suggests that addictive consumption is not a unitary phenomenon but has a number of subgroups, four of which are described above. This has implications for approaches to measuring the behaviour. The compulsive buying clinical screening scale (Faber and O'Guinn 1992) treats the behaviour as unidimensional, while the compulsive buying scale (Valence et al. 1988) posits that three conceptual dimensions underlie the behaviour. Both of these scales seem to perform reasonably well with each scale appearing to measure a different but related underlying construct (Cole and Sherrell 1995). Additional scale items relating to the use of consumption to exert influence within a relationship and to construct existential meaning may contribute to our ability to unpack the subtlety of addictive consumption which manifests as behaviours that share a common superficial appearance, but vary markedly in their motivations and the extent to which they can be thought of as reasoned actions.

CONCLUSIONS

It appears that far from being 'profoundly unhappy individuals trying to compensate for an enormous burden of negative feelings' (Scherhorn et al. 1990), some addictive consumers use the shopping experience not only as a form of self-expression and as an important element in the construction and maintenance of their self-identities but also as a means of having some control over a part of their own lives and having, or feeling they have, some control over their partner.

If addictive consumption is not qualitatively different from 'normal' consumption then it is reasonable to assume that some normal consumption is, in part, driven by these same factors of revenge within personal relationships and existential choice involving the flow experience. In that case, particularly in relation to revenge, the behaviour is not greatly influenced by marketing phenomena but is instead part of the interchange of power and influence within a relationship which has its own subjective dynamics. We see here the consumer consciously engaged in using consumption as a tool for social influence outside the confines of conventional economic relations. Although anthropologists of material culture such as Douglas and Isherwood (1978) and structural sociologists such as Bourdieu (1984) have pointed to the role played by goods in the creation and maintenance of social categories, relatively little work has explored the role of consumer goods within social relationships. Csikszentmihalyi and Rochberg-Halton (1981) discussed the use of material goods to differentiate the self and also to integrate with society, but as Lunt (1995) points out, we need to develop an understanding of how objects function as part of the dynamics of family relations, their use to provide sites of contestation and control and to punish and reward. By exploring the role of social relations within addictive consumption we may develop further insights into the 'social life of things' (Appadurai 1986) and the shopping experience. We may also derive insights into the phenomenology of emotions in the consumption experience by exploring the nature and frequency with which consumers achieve a state of flow through existential acts of choice whilst shopping.

REFERENCES

Allison, M. T. and Duncan, M. C. (1988) Women, Work and Flow. In M. Csikszentmihalyi and I. Csikszentmihalyi (eds) *Optimal Experience: Psychological studies of flow in consciousness*. Cambridge, Cambridge University Press.

Appadurai, A. (ed.) (1986) *The Social Life of Things*. Cambridge, Cambridge University Press.

Bauman, Z. (1988) *Freedom*. Milton Keynes, Open University Press.

Bocock, R. (1993) *Consumption*. London, Routledge.

Bourdieu, P. (1984) *Distinction*. London, Routledge and Kegan Paul.

Brown, G. W. and Harris T. (1978) *Social Origins of Depression*. London, Tavistock.

Brown, S. (1995) *Postmodern Marketing*. London, Routledge.

Bruch, H. (1974) *Eating Disorders: Obesity, anorexia nervosa, and the person within*. London, Routledge and Kegan Paul.

Cole, L. and Sherrell, D. (1995) Comparing Scales to Measure Compulsive Buying: An exploration of their dimensionality. *Advances in Consumer Research, 22*, 419–27.

Cooperstock, R. and Lennard, H. (1979) Some Social Meanings of Tranquillizer Use. *Sociology of Health and Illness, 1*, 331–47.

Csikszentmihalyi, M. (1975) *Beyond Boredom and Anxiety*. San Francisco, Jossey-Bass.

Csikszentmihalyi, M. (1988) The Flow Experience and its Significance for Human Psychology. In M. Csikszentmihalyi and I. Csikszentmihalyi (eds) *Optimal Experience: Psychological studies of flow in consciousness*. Cambridge, Cambridge University Press.

Csikszentmihalyi, M. and Rochberg-Halton, E. (1981) *The Meaning of Things*. Cambridge, Cambridge University Press.

d'Astous, A. (1990) An Inquiry into the Compulsive Side of 'Normal' Consumers. *Journal of Consumer Policy, 13*, 15–31.

Douglas, M. and Isherwood, B. (1978) *The World of Goods: Towards an anthropology of consumption*. Harmondsworth, Penguin.

Duck, S. W. (1994) Stratagems, Spoils and a Serpent's Tooth: On the delights and dilemmas of personal relationships. In W. R. Cupach and B. H. Spitzberg (eds), *The Dark Side of Interpersonal Communication*. Hillsdale NJ, Lawrence Erlbaum.

Elliott, R. (1994) Addictive Consumption: Function and fragmentation in postmodernity. *Journal of Consumer Policy, 17*, 159–79.

Elliott, R. and Ritson, M. (1995) Practicing Existential Consumption: The lived meaning of sexuality in advertising. *Advances in Consumer Research, 22*, 740–5.

Faber, R. J. and O'Guinn T. C. (1992) A Clinical Screener for Compulsive Buying. *Journal of Consumer Research 19*, 459–69.

Faber, R. J., O'Guinn, T. C. and Krych, R. (1987) Compulsive Consumption. *Advances in Consumer Research, 14*, 132–5.

Feick, L. F. and Price, L. L. (1985) The Market Maven. *Managing*, July, 10.

Fischer, E. and Gainer, B. (1991) I shop Therefore I Am: The role of shopping in the social construction of women's identities. In G. A. Costa (ed.), *Gender and Consumer Behavior*, Salt Lake City, Utah, University of Utah Press.

Gergen, K. (1969) *The Psychology of Behavior Exchange*. Reading, Mass., Addison-Wesley.

Gottheil, E. et al. (eds) (1988) *Stress and Addiction*. New York, Brunner/Mazel.

Gournay, K. (1989) *Agoraphobia: Current perspectives of theory and treatment*. London, Routledge.

Heather, N. and Robertson, I. (1981) *Controlled Drinking*. London, Methuen.

Higgins, E. T. (1989) Self-discrepancy Theory: What patterns of beliefs cause people to suffer? *Advances in Experimental Social Psychology, 22*, 93–136.

Holbrook, M. B. (1995) *Consumer Research: Introspective essays on the study of consumption*. London, Sage Publications.

Holbrook, M. B. and Hirschman, E. C. (1982) The Experiential Aspects of Consumption: Consumer fantasies, feelings and fun. *Journal of Consumer Research, 9*, 132–40.

Jones, W. H. and Burdette M. P. (1984) Betrayal in Close Relationships. In A. L. Weber and J. H. Hervey (eds), *Perspectives on Close Relationships*. New York, Allyn and Bacon.

Lunt, P. (1995) Psychological Approaches to Consumption. In D. Miller (ed.), *Acknowledging Consumption: A review of new studies*. London, Routledge.

Marlatt, A., Baer, J., Donovan, D. and Kivlahan, D. (1988) Addictive Behaviours: Etiology and treatment. *Annual Review of Psychology, 39*, 223–52.

Mick, D. G. and Buhl, C. (1992) A Meaning Based Model of Advertising Experiences. *Journal of Consumer Research, 19* (December), 317–38.

Miles, M. B. and Huberman, A. M. (1994) *Qualitative Data Analysis*. California, Sage Publications.

Nataraajan, R. and Goff, B. G. (1991) Compulsive Buying: Towards a reconceptualization. *Journal of Social Behavior and Personality, 6*, 307–28.

Nataraajan, R. and Goff, B. G. (1992) Manifestations of Compulsiveness in the Consumer-marketplace Domain. *Psychology and Marketing, 9* (1), 31–44.

O'Guinn, T. C. and Faber, R. J. (1989) Compulsive Buying: A phenomenological exploration. *Journal of Consumer Research, 16*, 147–57.

Ritson, M., Elliott, R. and Eccles, S. (1996) 'Reframing IKEA: Commodity-Signs, Consumer Creativity and the Social/Self Dialectic'. *Advances in Consumer Research, 23*, 127–31.

Scherhorn, G. (1990) The Addictive Trait in Buying Behavior. *Journal of Consumer Policy, 13*, 33–51.

Scherhorn, G., Reisch L. A. and Raab, G. (1990) Addictive Buying in West Germany: An empirical study. *Journal of Consumer Policy, 13*, 355–87.

Sprecher, S. (1992) How Men and Women Expect to Feel and Behave in Response to Inequity in Close Relationships. *Social Psychology Quarterly, 55*, 57–69.

Thompson, C., Locander, W. and Pollio, H. (1989), Putting the Consumer Back into Consumer Research: The philosophy and method of existential phenomenology. *Journal of Consumer Research, 16*, 133–46.

Thompson, C. J., Locander, W. and Pollio, H. R. (1990) The Lived Meaning of Free Choice: An existential-phenomenological description of everyday consumer experiences of contemporary married women. *Journal of Consumer Research, 17*, 346–61.

Valence, G., d'Astous, A. and Fortier, L. (1988) Compulsive Buying: Concept and measurement. *Journal of Consumer Policy, 11*, 419–33.

VanYperen, N. W. and Buunk, B. P. (1990) A Longitudinal Study of Equity and Satisfaction in Intimate Relationships. *European Journal of Social Psychology, 20*, 287–309.

10

Shopping for an Addiction

Mary Harris

The human animal is a beast that dies and if he's got money he buys and buys and buys and I think the reason he buys everything he can buy is that in the back of his mind he has the crazy hope that one of his purchases will be life everlasting! – Which it never can be ... (Tennessee Williams 1955, pp. 61–2)

INTRODUCTION

This chapter discusses some of the possible reasons that people shop addictively, its effects on individuals who practice this form of shopping, its relationship to family and gender issues, and its links to other types of addictive behaviours. The chapter also includes material from the author's work as a psychotherapist treating addictions and concludes with a case study which describes one woman's experience of and treatment for addictions.

In the play *Cat on a Hot Tin Roof*, the character 'Big Daddy' describes how his wife has '... bought more stuff than you could haul in a couple of boxcars ...' (Williams 1955, p. 59) in a vain attempt to avoid her fear of death and the emptiness of her life. In the same play, Big Daddy's son uses alcohol to avoid his sense of disappointment with his life and his daughter-in-law spends her time fantasising about sexual encounters in order to avoid facing the break-down of her marriage.

Like Williams's characters, some people use addictive behaviours as a way of avoiding painful feelings. Not confronting uncomfortable issues can result in practising not just one addiction, but multiple addictions at the same time or in substituting one addiction for another at various times. Shopping to excess, as well as the abusive use of alcohol, drugs or food, can increase the sense of alienation and desperation which the behaviours are initially meant to relieve. Shopping excessively can also create secondary problems, such as unmanageable debts and marital or family conflicts (Wilson Schaef 1987).

People who use activities or substances excessively may come from families with patterns of addictions which go back several generations. Within such a family, patterns of addictive behaviours may be linked to gender-role expectations; it is still more common for men to abuse alcohol and drugs and for women to overeat and to shop to excess. Moreover, families whose members practice addictive behaviours seem to have other commonalities, such as denial and dishonesty regarding family members' addictions, difficulty with expressing feelings appropriately, unrealistically high expectations of themselves and others, a need to control their own and other people's behaviours and colluding to protect each other from the consequences of their addictions. Kasl (1987) describes the addictive family as a system which serves to perpetuate and evoke addictive behaviours amongst its members.

For women particularly, shopping can move beyond an everyday necessity or a pleasurable activity and become a focal point of their interest and/or an expression of their identity. At the point where shopping begins to impact negatively on an individual's emotional well-being, relationships, or finances, it becomes an addiction (Johnson 1980).

SHOPPING IN RELATION TO WOMEN'S ROLE AND SELF-IDENTITY

Some authors describe the 'modernity of the late nineteenth and early twentieth centuries as a public stage from which women were excluded' and suggest that life in middle-class Victorian England existed in 'separate spheres' for men and women which resulted in 'the social and material exclusion of women from public life and urban areas' (Falk and Campbell 1997, p. 60).

Victorian social roles were challenged as increasing numbers of unaccompanied women began to travel freely in public. Whereas 'respectable' women had previously been confined mainly to their homes and to domestic activities, they began to pursue and experience greater social and personal freedom. As women's freedom of movement increased, shopping became central to the experience of many ordinary women. Department stores in particular were appealing because they provided a safe environment in which women could spend time and enjoy a variety of services such as supervised areas for children, restaurants and powder rooms (Falk and Campbell 1997, p. 67).

Shopping came to be seen as a 'pleasurable social activity' and a way to enhance women's social status. The home furnishing available in department stores became 'visible indicators' of status and, increasingly, reflected the shopper's identity. Shopping provided women with an anonymous, safe and socially acceptable public place where they could spend unsupervised time and exert financial control. Shopping was an acceptable domestic activity which allowed women relative freedom of movement and became an important aspect of modern female identity. Partly because of the shopping experience, women developed a new sense of the possibilities of modern life and began to discard the previous view of themselves as dependent, passive and retiring. Shopping helped women form a new definition of themselves and created 'a space for individual expression similar to men' (Falk and Campbell 1997, pp. 64–70). Since the beginning of the twentieth century, shopping has increasingly become a major leisure activity and '... significant form of self expression' and '... an important element in the construction ... of their self identities' for many women (Elliott 1994, pp. 159–60).

Shopping gave women increased freedom to spend money; it also fostered, in many women, a sense of identity, which could be expressed by buying fashionable clothes, available in shops. This experience came to be associated with an increased freedom to explore their sexuality. Women's pleasure in touching and trying on expensive material goods was seen as a kind of sensual experience. At the same time, men were experiencing a loss of authority over women's spending habits which came to be associated with a loss of control over women's sexual desires. As men felt more threatened and displaced by the advent of a mass culture and women's expanding independence, the balance of power within the family was gradually transformed (Falk and Campbell 1997, pp. 76–9). For many women, an increasing sense of their own power was closely linked to spending power; to shop for and purchase clothing and household goods gave them a sense of individuality which was otherwise lacking in their lives.

SHOPPING AS AN ADDICTION

For most people, shopping remains a normal and culturally acceptable behaviour. For a small percentage of the population shopping behaviour has become dysfunctional. Recent studies carried out in the USA, Canada, Germany and the UK identify a group of people who 'buy for motives which are not directly related to the actual possession of the goods'. Faber and O'Guinn (1992) maintain that 1–2 per cent of the population practice a pathological form of shopping behaviour. This group of people persistently repeat the behaviour despite its leading to severe financial and social consequences (Elliott, Eccles and Gournay 1996, pp. 355–6). This type of shopping is described as an irresistible urge to buy despite attempts to curb or inhibit the behaviour. Elliott believes that within this context, shopping 'is an addiction because it involves the extension of normal behaviour into a pathological habit' (1994, pp. 159–60).

WHEN A BEHAVIOUR BECOMES AN ADDICTION

In exploring shopping as an addiction, it seems useful to explore the term 'addiction'. Much early literature focused on alcoholism, as it was the first behaviour to be widely studied as an addiction. According to current thought, a person may become addicted to a substance, including alcohol, drugs, caffeine and nicotine, or may become addicted to an activity, such as shopping, exercising, eating, gambling or working. Wilson Schaef believes that

> An addiction can be any activity over which we feel powerless ... the behaviour has taken control of us, ... causing us to do and think things that are inconsistent with our personal values and leading us to become progressively more compulsive and obsessive. (Wilson Schaef 1987, p. 18)

In considering shopping as an addiction, it also seems useful to draw distinctions between normal activities and excessive behaviours and to identify points at which normal behaviours can become problematic and eventually be classified as an addiction. Craig Nakken describes behaviours as occurring on a continuum, which can progress from patterns and habits to compulsions and addictions. According to this model, a pattern of behaviour is a practice or activity which helps us to structure our lives and is not destructive or harmful. A pattern remains flexible; we may, for example, say that we like to have breakfast at 9.00 a.m., but we are not upset or bothered if it is necessary to have breakfast at a different time. A habit is a more individualised behaviour and is frequently associated with words such as always or usually. Thus, when I say that I like to eat breakfast at 9.00 a.m., I am describing a pattern, and when I say that I always have toast for breakfast, I am describing a habit. Patterns are fairly easy to change, while habits are more difficult to alter. Giving up a habit may cause a temporary sense of discomfort, but the feeling is usually short-lived (Kasl 1987).

Behaviours which are damaging to us go beyond patterns or habits and, depending on their severity or the damage they cause to our health, finances or relationships, may be defined as either a compulsion or an addiction. A compulsion is different from a pattern or habit in that it is based on a need to reduce tension or anxiety, often brought about by feelings which the person wants to avoid or control. Compulsions are usually associated with a sense of urgency or need and words such as 'have to' or 'must'. When I say that I have to eat breakfast at 9.00 a.m., I am describing a compulsion. According to Nakken,

> There is often a frantic feeling associated with the behaviour until it is completed. When a person is unable to carry out the compulsive behaviour, feelings of agitation and distress may continue for hours or days, until the compulsive urge is met ... (Kasl 1987, p. 31)

Such behaviours are often carried out in a trance-like state. Compulsions are more difficult to discard or alter than habits, but they can usually be managed or accommodated without causing undue disruption to a person's life. Compulsive behaviours may be harmful but do not seriously impair functioning. Compulsions may damage but do not usually destroy relationships (ibid.)

Addictions are seen as more destructive than compulsions. The damage which an addiction can cause to our emotional or physical health, our relationships and to our financial or professional functioning is denied. 'Addiction involves the words powerlessness and unmanageability, both of which the person denies' (Kasl 1987, p. 31). It is at this point that the addictive shopper spends money beyond his or her means and denies the consequences of the behaviour. According to Wilson-Schaef, 'A sure sign of an addiction is the sudden need to deceive ourselves and others – to lie, deny, and cover up. An addiction is anything we feel tempted to lie about' (p. 18).

Another definition of addiction focuses on the impact of the behaviour on the person's life. Vern Johnson (1980) suggests that an addiction involves behaviours which negatively affect any one or more of the following areas of functioning: the person's physical, emotional, spiritual, personal, or professional existence. This definition of addiction was formulated to describe substance abuse; although a behaviour such as shopping doesn't directly affect a person's health, it can cause serious damage in other areas of life. Shopping behaviour can have a negative impact on emotional functioning, interpersonal relationships and economic circumstances.

TWO KINDS OF ADDICTIONS

Addictions can be divided into two major categories: substance addictions and process addictions. Both are said to function similarly and to produce essentially the same results. Substance or ingestive addictions involve taking alcohol, drugs or nicotine, among other substances, into the body in order to avoid or deny painful feelings or to induce pleasant feelings. This kind of addiction may lead to increased physical dependency on the substance. A person who becomes addicted to a process does not experience the physical dependency associated with a substance addiction, but may become addicted to a set of behaviours. An addiction to a process is similar to a substance addiction in that both serve to help people look for solutions to their problems outside themselves and to avoid or deny painful feelings. This kind of addiction can involve excessive shopping, gambling, exercise, work or sexual activity. According to Wilson-Schaef, 'The characteristics and dynamics of any addiction are similar to those of any other addiction' (1987, p. 26).

THE PURPOSES OF AN ADDICTION

When a person is 'practising' an addiction, he or she knows at one level that the behaviour is harmful or damaging. In order to continue the addiction, the person must feel that he or she is experiencing a reward or benefit; the addiction must serve a purpose. The purpose of an addiction can be an attempt to fill a void or avoid painful feelings and to feel better about ourselves. Wilson Schaef (1987) sees the addicted person as experiencing loneliness or emptiness in his or her everyday life; the addiction is meant to provide a magic panacea to fill the void and to remove painful feelings. Kasl describes this experience as a person 'searching for something to help her feel complete, but she doesn't know how to find it' (p. 5). Frequently, the sense of emptiness is experienced as feeling unloved. According to Kasl,

> The underlying intention of addictive behaviour is to find love and to feel good. Such behaviour actually comes from a desire to fill a profound emptiness, anesthetize pain, and stay away from feelings. (p. 12)

The attraction of shopping, as with other addictive behaviours, is that the effect is immediate; the emotional pain stops at once. As is the case with other addictions, 'We do not have to deal with our anger, pain, depression, confusion, or even our joy and love, because we do not feel them, or we feel them only vaguely' (Wilson Schaef 1987, p. 18). Although the initial relief is eventually replaced by the original painful feelings, the immediate relief reinforces the behaviour. 'It is so seductive because it works immediately' (Kasl 1987, p. 96).

Some believe that addictive behaviours are driven by an underlying sense of shame on the part of the individual (Bradshaw 1988). Feeling ashamed of one's normal, human failings can slowly become a generalised sense of shame which takes over our self-identity. According to Bradshaw (pp. vii–viii), 'To have shame as an identity is to believe that one's being is flawed, that one is defective as a human being.' It is this core sense of shame which Bradshaw believes drives all compulsive/addictive behaviours and is an attempt to heal a ruptured sense of self; to avoid feelings of loneliness and hurt. He believes that, 'Each addictive acting out creates life-damaging consequences which create more shame' (p. 15). The persistent sense of shame fuels a cycle of addictive behaviours.

The person whose sense of self is shame-based is in constant pain. Bradshaw believes that this feeling is experienced as chronic loss and mourning for the authentic self which, in turn, creates a need for relief. Any behaviour which takes away the 'gnawing discomfort' will become the individuals' only priority and their most important relationship. He says that, 'Whichever way you choose to mood alter will be the relationship that takes precedence over all else in your life' (Bradshaw 1988, pp. 95–9).

THE COSTS OF AN ADDICTION

An addiction may temporarily help someone deny painful feelings or avoid facing uncomfortable issues, but the long-term effects of the addictive behaviour are damaging. An alcohol addiction may cause individuals to experience severe, irreparable damage to their health and may harm their professional functioning; these are consequences which the addictive shopper is unlikely to experience. Like the alcoholic, however, the addictive shopper may experience harmful consequences such as a loss of contact with the self. According to Wilson Schaef,

> As we lose contact with ourselves we also lose contact with other people and the world around us. An addiction dulls and distorts our 'sensory input' and costs us the 'ability to become intimate with others'. (1987, pp. 18–19)

The person 'practising' an addiction often experiences a sense of alienation not only from his or her significant others but from the self. Addicts may feel intense and contradictory feelings which they are incapable of expressing in appropriate ways. Eventually, many addicted people lose the ability to differentiate among feelings which may all begin to feel the same. By this point, the addict may experience no feelings except numbness or generalised anxiety. The experience of any feeling can seem threatening and can trigger the addictive behaviour (Wilson Schaef 1987; 1990).

For many addicted people, the experience of losing touch with a deeper self results in chronic, mild depression. Kasl (1987, pp. 150–1) believes that the depression associated with an addiction covers a cluster of feelings and attitudes about the self which include 'learned helplessness, anger turned inward, loss of self-esteem, lack of connectedness to others, and negative, inaccurate, self-defeating beliefs'.

The depression which is often associated with addictions may also be linked to the addict's need for control. Wilson Schaef believes that

> The illusion of control is a setup for depression. When we believe that we can and should be able to control our world and it turns out that we cannot, we experience failure, and this is depressing. We then try even harder to gain control and fail even more miserably. (1987, p. 45)

The addict's attempts to control the addiction may be seen as an attempt to avoid painful thoughts and feelings by focusing on attempts to control the addictive behaviours rather than on the self (Wilson Schaef 1987, p. 43). People who are addicted often believe that they should be perfect and are unable to live up to their own expectations of themselves. At the core of the addict's view of the self is a belief that they are failures and that nothing they do can ever be good enough. The desire for perfectionism can serve to both trigger and reinforce the addictive behaviour (p. 68).

People who believe that they should be perfect experience any failing as proof of their inadequacy. Their thinking becomes dualistic; either I am perfect or I am worthless, completely good or bad, either in control or totally out of control. Their view of the self becomes black or white with nothing in between. Addicts experience themselves as 'bad': regardless of their accomplishments or achievements, they never see themselves as good enough or worthwhile as people (Wilson Schaef 1987, p. 112). In describing this process, Kasl says that

> When a person becomes addicted, the personality splits into two distinct parts, each denying the existence of the other. It is as though the person has two sets of values. Addiction is like having two sides – the addict side and the healthy side – engaging in a life and death struggle to control the inner world. While people derive temporary feelings of pleasure through their addictive behaviour, harmful consequences are sure to follow. She falls more and more under the control of an unknown force within. (1987, pp. 29–32)

MULTIPLE ADDICTIONS

An addiction may be an attempt to deny painful truths and multiple addictions may become a way of life. Kasl describes this process as

> a constant state of strife, split between our perceived reality and the buried reality. Because addiction is the psyche's way of seeking escape from buried feelings and easing the inner strife, the addictive agent can be almost anything, alcohol, sex, cigarettes, religion, caffeine, TV, anger, depression shopping, cleaning, eating ... (1987, pp. 2218–19)

Some people practice serial addictions and substitute one addiction for another, such as replacing smoking cigarettes with overeating. Others practice addictions simultaneously, such as shopping and overeating, or drinking and smoking. Kasl believes that two addiction can be 'ritualised' together; most commonly sex and alcohol or drugs, and almost as frequently, sex and food (1987, p. 197).

Wilson Schaef describes addictions to alcohol, drugs, nicotine, food, relationships, and sex as secondary addictions; the primary addiction is the person's sense of 'powerlessness and nonliving' which the addictive process both masks and perpetuates (1987, p. 16).

Another view of addictions, whether to a substance, process or relationship, suggests that all addictive behaviours represent a core issue in the addict's life. Lefevre believes that,

> We suppress our natural feelings by using something artificial in order to overcome the human response of feeling emotional pain when we do damaging things to ourselves and to our relationships. (Lefevre 1988, p. 4)

Lefevre also believes that addictions are a symptom of the 'addictive disease', which is in the person, and not just about a substance or a behaviour. In order to treat the underlying disease, he stresses the need to recognise the commonalities among all forms of addictions, regardless of the particular addiction being practised at any given time. Treating one addiction on its own usually results in the substitution of yet another addiction and fails to address or treat the root problem underlying the addictive process (Lefevre 1988).

PEOPLE AT RISK OF BECOMING ADDICTED

People who practise addictions as adults often experienced abuse or neglect as children. Kasl (1987, p. 83) reports that between 50 and 80 per cent of the women she treats for chemical dependency were survivors of abuse and that within her therapy groups for incest survivors, almost half of the groups' members have also been treated for drug or alcohol abuse. Although the divergence between 50 and 80 per cent is unaccounted for, other therapists also describe the high incidence of clients who have experienced abuse as children and who, as adults, practise multiple addictions. In treatment programmes for eating disorders, 80 per cent of women treated described themselves as survivors of sexual abuse (Kasl 1987, p. 214). Robin Norwood makes the link between eating disorders and family patterns when she says that '... nearly every woman I have seen with an eating disorder has been the daughter of either one alcoholic, two alcoholics, or an alcoholic and a compulsive eater' (Norwood 1985, p. 165). In describing possible links between childhood abuse and multiple addictions, Kasl says that

> In many instances, misuse of food, sex, alcohol, work and money either occur together or interchangeably as an individual desperately tries to quell an inner emptiness created by some form of childhood abuse or neglect. (1987, p. xiii)

ADDICTIVE FAMILY SYSTEMS

Individuals who practice addictions frequently come from families whose members have been addicted to substances or activities, sometimes over the course of several generations. Therapists who describe the family as a system believe that the principle of homoeostasis is at work within families, causing its members to seek balance over change in their interactions with each other, even when the balance is harmful or destructive and change could be positive (Satir 1972). Change in one member of a family 'will lead to a compensatory change in another family member' (Stafford 1992, p. 68). In disturbed families, change of any sort is often seen as threatening, and family members strive to restore or maintain equilibrium through the maintenance of rigid patterns of behaviour. According to Bradshaw, 'a dysfunctional family uses the members to maintain its equilibrium. The more dysfunctional the system, the more closed and rigid are the roles it assigns' (1988, p. 59).

When one person is addicted, he or she may be expressing or acting out the distress of the family. Fossum and Mason believe that addiction is always a 'family disease' and is the 'central organising principle of the system – maintaining the system as well as the shame' (Bradshaw 1988, p. 96). Within an alcoholic system, the patterns and behaviours used to hide the addiction also serve to maintain it and eventually affect all its members. According to Wilson Schaef, 'Any addictive system is contagious, and those who live within it become infected with the disease sooner or later. The dynamics and patterns are the same for those infected as they are for the alcoholic' (1987, p. 13).

Families whose members practice addictions frequently deny that they are experiencing difficulties and, simultaneously, feel deeply ashamed of their underlying problems. Describing alcoholic families, Stafford says that, '... shame and denial dovetail to become guardians of the addiction, and how roles are created to maintain the stability of the family' (1992, p. 84). Bradshaw calls this sense of shame 'toxic' and believes that it is multigenerational; passed from one generation of addicts to the next. He believes that

> Shame-based people find other shame-based people and get married. As a couple each carries the shame from his or her own family system. Their marriage will be grounded in their shame-core. The major outcome of this will be a lack of intimacy. It's difficult to let someone get close to you if you feel defective and flawed as a human being. Shame-based couples maintain non-intimacy through poor communication, nonproductive circular fighting, games, manipulation, vying for control ... (Bradshaw 1988, p. 25)

This sense of shame, according to Bradshaw becomes the basis of the family's dealings with each other. He states that

> Shame has been called the master emotion because as it is internalised all the other emotions are bound by shame. Emotionally shame-bound parents cannot allow their children to have emotions because the child's emotion triggers the parents' emotions. Repressed emotions often feel too big, like they would completely overwhelm us if we expressed them. (1988, p. 54)

Attempting to avoid or deny the addictive family's feelings of shame may create characteristic patterns of communication. Such families may develop rules which stifle open communication in order to maintain the illusion that the family is 'normal'. 'Unwritten rules keep communication rigid. Family members do not talk about anything which draws attention to the alcoholism, they deny or ignore strong feelings' (Stafford 1992, p. 75). This type of communication circumvents open, honest discussion which could confront the alcoholic with the consequences of his or behaviour and disrupt the system's homoeostasis. 'So long as the family remains in denial, illusion and shame, the drinking continues, and the happy family facade is maintained in the face of overwhelming contradictory evidence' (ibid.).

Family members may also lie about the addictive behaviour to protect each other from outside sanctions, such as one person's lying about another person's drinking to protect the alcoholic from losing his or her job. Over time, persons within this system may find it easier to lie 'gratuitously', even when telling the truth would have no negative repercussions (Stafford 1992, p. 91).

When family members consistently avoid direct communication, the family becomes a 'closed system', whose members avoid spontaneous or genuine communication and become rigid, both in responses to each other and to the outside world. A closed system may intensify and reinforce addictive behaviours. According to Virginia Satir (1972), troubled families use four characteristic patterns of communication in their interactions with each other: by blaming others for their problems, by excessively apologising or placating others, by responding to others' feelings in a cold, rational, logical manner, or by distracting others from serious issues by changing the subject.

Bradshaw describes the addictive family as needing to control communication among its members by enforcing a 'no talk' rule which 'prohibits the full expression of any feeling, need or want ... no one speaks of his loneliness and sense of self-rupture' (1988, p. 40). This becomes a major defence strategy which both protects and stifles family members.

The need to control in others can extend beyond controlling communication among family members and can become generalised into other aspects of the family's interactions. An individual's inability to control one's own addictive behaviours can be denied by focusing on controlling the behaviours of other family members. What we cannot control in ourselves may become the basis for a need to control others. According to Bradshaw,

> We need to control because our toxic shame drives us outside ourselves ... We objectify ourself and experience ourself as lacking and defective. Therefore, we must move out of our own house. The striving for power flows from the need to control ... Achieving power is a direct attempt to compensate for the sense of being defective. When one has power over others, one becomes less vulnerable to being shamed. (1998, p. 89)

In addictive families, spontaneous behaviour may become so inhibited that all interactions, communications, and behaviours become rigid and controlled, reflecting the family's need to present a 'perfect' front to the outside world, masking the flaws within the family. The need for perfectionism is pervasive in addictive families, and becomes a way of coping with and avoiding a deeper sense of failure and imperfection. Family members develop a sense of shame around addictive behaviours and learn to deny 'normal' human failings and limitations. According to Bradshaw, 'Perfectionism is a family system rule ... which denies healthy shame ... by assuming we can be perfect. Such an assumption denies that we will make mistakes' (1998, p. 61).

Family members taught the need for perfection experience a sense of being measured from the outside by an externalised source and of never being able to measure up.

Attempts to present a perfect image to outsiders may result in the addicted family's need to conform to and enforce rigid role expectations. The family's expectations of its members may be based on gender; men may be expected to be decisive and unemotional, while women may be expected to be acquiescent and caretakers for others (Bradshaw 1998). Other family therapists who work with addicted families believe that children are assigned roles by their parents which both protect and perpetuate the dysfunctional system. One child may take on the role of 'family hero' who is expected to solve the family's problems, while another child takes on the role of the 'enabler', who covers up the addictive members' behaviours and protects the addicts from the consequences of their behaviours. Addictive families may also include a 'mascot', who acts cute or helpless to attract attention, a 'scapegoat', who is blamed for the problems in the family, and a 'lost child', who withdraws from the family completely (Wegscheider-Cruse and Cruse 1990).

The roles learned by children raised in addicted families often become the basis for their adult behaviour and affect their relationships as adults. Speaking about alcoholic family systems, Stafford believes that

> ... the roles that it assigns to its members and how these roles are carried over into adult life ... [affect] the quality of life and the capacity to achieve fulfilment. The characteristics which adult children of alcoholics develop are, in fact, a function of the family system and an attempt to maintain stability within that sick system. (1992, p. 68)

Whether the addiction is to alcohol or shopping, the addict is unable to take care of his or her own unmet needs and often marries someone who holds out the promise of meeting their partner's sense of emptiness. When this happens,

> Each looks to and expects the other to take care of and parent the child within him or her. Each is incomplete and insatiable. The insatiability is rooted in each person's unmet childhood needs. When two adult children

meet and fall in love, the child in each looks to the other to fill his or her needs. (Bradshaw 1988, p. 44)

Being unable to meet a partner's needs may result in parents projecting their own needs and expectations onto their children. Such children experience themselves as not having their own childhood and as having been expected to function as adults from an early age. Bowlby, writing in the 1940s, said that

> in alcoholic families, the alcoholic parent is seeking the care and attention which was lacking in her childhood and attempts to obtain the missing parenting from her own child. Thus she is ... 'inverting the normal parent–child relationship by requiring the child to be the parent figure and adopting the role of child herself'. (cited in Stafford 1992, p. 82)

Bradshaw also describes this process when he says that

> By taking on the role of supplying his shame-based parents' narcissistic gratification, the child secures love and a sense of being needed and not abandoned. This process is a reversal of the order of nature. Now the child is taking care of the parent's needs, rather than the parents taking care of the child's needs. (1988, p. 44)

The process of children parenting their parents is handed down to the next generation as the adult children of alcoholics seek to fulfil their own needs either by taking on addictive behaviours themselves and/or by creating relationships based on being useful to others at the cost of their own needs and feelings (Norwood 1985).

BREAKING THE CYCLE

Effective treatment of one addiction may involve the individual's recognition of other addictions. Treating someone for a shopping addiction is only successful if it addresses the underlying needs and feelings which trigger the addictive behaviour. Failing to do so often results in giving up one addiction and replacing it with another. Successful therapy involves first identifying the person's addictive tendencies. One instrument used to identify addiction is 'The PROMIS Questionnaire' (Lefevre 1988) which was designed to identify a range of potentially addictive behaviours. This questionnaire asks respondents to answer questions involving their behaviours in relation to eleven categories: alcohol, nicotine, recreational drugs, caffeine, gambling and risk taking, work, relationships, sex, shopping, spending or stealing, exercise, prescription drugs and food. Each category contains thirty questions related to the particular substance or behaviour. In interpreting the results of the questionnaire, one to nine positive answers in any one category are said to indicate a possible addiction, which may not be of great concern, an area with ten to nineteen positive answers indicates a cross-addiction, and an area with twenty or more positive answers indicates a primary addiction. Lefevre recommends that treatment should first address the primary addiction or addictions and eventually address minor cross-addictions. Failure to identify and treat all of the person's addictions is seen as treating symptoms or behaviours rather than the root addiction and may result in relapse or substitution of another addiction for the original addiction.

Lefevre (1988) describes this as treating the addict, rather than the addiction, and sees treatment recovery and relapse prevention as consisting of three stages: beginning with an initial state of actively practising an addiction, entering treatment for the addiction and entering recovery. In the initial stage, the addict has an overriding sense of emptiness, a need to and an inability to control his or her addictive behaviours, a preoccupation with the addictive substance or behaviour, difficulty in focusing on other people's needs or feelings, and a tendency to blame personal difficulties on external events or circumstances, rather than taking responsibility for his or her own actions and decisions.

According to Lefevre's model (1988), when an addict enters treatment, he or she needs to practice full abstinence from the addictive substance, or behaviour, and learn to face and accept personal responsibility for his or her choices and actions. Lefevre also believes that successful treatment involves active participation in a Twelve Step Programme, which follows the steps and principles originally laid out in the Alcoholics Anonymous Programme. Successful recovery, according to this model, includes accepting one's inability to control the addiction through will-power and logic and accepting a higher power outside or greater than one's self (Johnson 1980).

Treating addictive behaviours also involves facing the denial surrounding the behaviour and addressing the underlying needs that the addiction is meant to compensate for. Part of the work involved in breaking addictive patterns also involves the person facing his or her own 'humanness' and acknowledging parts of the self which have been disowned. Not accepting a less desirable part can reinforce an addictive pattern. Wilson Schaef believes that

> If we flee from our shadow side, judge it, or hate it, it will come back to haunt us ... Under every addiction is a longing for self and for love. Facing

rather than avoiding our flaws can help to release the needs which fuel addictive patterns. (1987, p. 35)

According to Kasl,

We break through the addictive miasma by connecting with our truths and releasing our buried feelings and healing our tired bodies. We must recognise and heal the inner split. Anger, directed at the appropriate source, is often the wakeup call ... When we connect with ourselves deeply, we calm the conflict that leads to addictive and compulsive behaviour. (1987, p. 219)

The original sources of the addict's pain may be out of his or her awareness. Helping the client to recognise and acknowledge the pain he or she experiences in the present often serves as the starting point. This process allows the person to begin experiencing and integrating the deeper feelings which trigger the addictive behaviours.

Psychotherapy frequently involves changing addictive patterns by confronting feelings which have been denied as well as learning to let go of the need to be perfect and to demand perfection from those around us. Ironically, letting go of the need to control ourselves as well as others creates a stronger sense of being in control of one's life. Wilson Schaef (1987, p. xv) describes this as '... restoring one's relationship to oneself and others'.

Reconnecting with one's self in the present means learning to recognise and respond to a current need rather than reacting addictively to an unaddressed need from the past. Addicts describe the point where the addiction takes over as a feeling almost like an hypnotic state and speak of coming out of a 'trance' to realise that they have been practising their addiction/s. In treatment, they gradually learn to identify the feeling which the addiction masks and learn better ways of coping. Wilson Schaef describes this when she says, 'When you are sleepy, sleep; when you are hungry, eat; when you are sad, cry', and adds, 'When you need comfort, find someone to comfort you; when you are lonely, learn to experience your loneliness as one of many human emotions' (1987, p. 4).

Some current treatments for addictions stress the need not only to connect with a deeper level sense of self, but to learn to distance ourselves from our sense of attachment. One tradition advocating this stance is Buddhism which sees peace and contentment as an outgrowth of relinquishing attachments. When this attitude is applied to psychotherapy, according to Wilson Schaef,

We are advised not to purge our desires from our lives, but to let them pass through our awareness and to observe the experience of them, without madly seeking them or becoming bound to them. (1987, p. 18)

Recovering addicts often find that learning some form of meditation helps them to let go of the addictive needs and describe connecting, at this point in treatment, with a spiritual part of themselves which assists them in letting go of their addictive drives. Wilson Schaef describes this when she says,

We can become attached to substances, wealth, ideas, opinions, theories, beliefs, sense pleasures and even the concept of nonattachment ... When we become enslaved by our 'thirsts', we lose our connection to our spiritual center. (1987, pp. 17–18)

Learning to disengage gradually from attachments such as addictions involves accepting the inevitability of life's disappointments without needing the artificial highs and lows which addictions can temporarily provide.

THE AUTHOR'S EXPERIENCE OF ADDICTIVE CLIENTS

As a psychotherapist who has worked with addictions in both clinical and private settings, my experience both confirms and contradicts current therapeutic beliefs and practices. The clients who have come to me wanting treatment for their addictive behaviours often have much in common with each other. The treatment which seems to be effective with one person, however, may not be helpful for another person; some individuals seem capable of stopping their addictive behaviours with little or no psychotherapeutic support, while others continue practising an addiction regardless of its negative effects and in spite of therapeutic interventions.

In my experience, people who seek treatment for an addiction, whether to a substance or a behaviour, come from families with a history of addictions. Clients who come for treatment often initially deny or fail to recognise the presence of an addiction, either in themselves or relatives. Admitting that a behaviour has become out of control in their own lives is often coupled with the discovery that several generations of family members both practised and denied practising various forms of addictions. I remember asking a client who had come to me for treatment of alcoholism whether there were any alcoholics in her family. Her initial response was a firm no, followed, when she returned the next week, by her statement that she had realised in the intervening week that twelve of her relatives had also been alcoholics. Such insights are painful but necessary in helping clients begin taking responsibility for and changing their own addictive behaviours. I have also found that addictive behaviours can often 'skip' a generation: clients may discover that their own parents are free from addictions, but that their grandparents were addicted to a substance or a behaviour.

Addictions also seem to be influenced by gender factors. More men than women come to me for treatment for alcoholism, while more women than men seek treatment for excessive shopping, eating disorders, and addictions to prescription drugs. Several female clients have described addictive shopping as offering them a sense of revenge in response to feeling powerless in their marriages. One woman came to therapy initially for help in coping with her alcoholic husband. In therapy, she realised that she had used tranquillisers for years to avoid painful feelings and often swallowed her feelings of frustration by overeating. For her, successful change meant focusing on her own feelings and gradually learning to express her needs, rather than trying to help her husband with his addictions.

Clients seeking treatment for addictions often realise that they have practised several addictions simultaneously or have given up one addiction in favour of another at various times in their lives. The client who has stopped smoking may begin addictive shopping. The need, in this case, is to explore the underlying causes which the addiction helps to mask. I worked with a client who described that, when she was not involved in a romantic relationship, she starved herself and shopped for clothes addictively, in order to attract a man. Once in a relationship, she overate and drank excessively until the relationship ended; a pattern which she had repeated for years. In her case, therapy involved exploring the feelings underlying her need for and fear of an intimate relationship which the addictions help her to avoid facing directly.

Much of the initial work in therapy involves clients recognising and admitting the role that addictions have played in their lives. Clients describe how addictions both protect them from and, at the same time, reinforce their sense of inadequacy and pervasive feelings of sadness. One of the core beliefs that they describe is an internal judge, telling them that they should be perfect and reminding them, each time they resort to the addiction, that they are failures, and unable to curb the behaviour through the use of will-power alone. One of my clients described herself as a devout Christian; she often talked about her inability to tolerate other people's shortcomings. For her, being able to stop addictive behaviours came about as she explored the idea of forgiving herself for not being perfect.

People in treatment for addictions also describe parents who were often critical in spite of or perhaps because of their own inadequacies and addictive behaviours. Needing to prove their own worth, such parents taught their children that they were worthless. Clients describe the effects of years of physical, emotional and sexual abuse as children, which their own addictions help them to deny.

Clients in treatment for an addiction invariably describe never having been able to discuss their deeper feelings within their families and the fear that showing their feelings will cause them to be ridiculed. Talking openly and non-defensively about feelings is often experienced for the first time in the safe environment that therapy provides.

For some clients, successful treatment for addictions does involve years of painful exploration of childhood trauma in individual therapy; others have learned to change addictive patterns in therapy or self-help groups. I no longer believe that the client has to hit rock bottom, or join a twelve-step group or to accept a Higher Power in order to change, although for many clients, all of those may be effective. I now believe in using an integrative approach to therapy. For some clients, successful therapy involves catharsis and insight; for others, effective treatment involves cognitive and behavioural approaches. Help and change take different paths for each person. What is needed is to explore the hidden pain and sense of shame which the addiction masks and perpetuates. Each client needs to find a way of working towards a healthier goal as opposed to focusing on curbing an unhealthy practice. Stopping smoking is possible, for example, by focusing on an increased ability to breathe rather than focusing on not being able to have a cigarette. Permanent change is accompanied by a shift in self-worth and acceptance, rather than by using force or will-power which focuses on an addictive behaviour by itself.

I have also given up trying to predict which clients will succeed at mastering their addictions. I remember working with a man who had tried to quit drinking alcohol for most of his adult life; he had gone to individual and group therapy and Twelve Step Programmes for years. I initially felt pessimistic regarding the likelihood that, this time, he would succeed. And yet, he did just that; eight years after his last drink, he said that he was finally ready to quit.

CASE STUDY

The following case history is not unusual for people who experience shopping as an addiction. The woman presented in this case study, although not a client of mine, agreed to be interviewed regarding her addictive behaviours. She describes herself as having been addicted to alcohol and a compulsive over-eater, in addition to shopping addictively. She also describes several generations of her family members as having multiple addictions and as exhibiting many of the characteristics of 'troubled' families discussed in this chapter. In my work with compulsive shoppers, clients often describe their shopping behaviour as one of several addictions and relate family patterns similar to those discussed in this case study.

Linda (not her real name) describes both her parents as having been alcoholics who managed to function successfully in spite of their frequent drinking bouts. From an early age, Linda learned to 'parent' her own parents, protecting them from the consequences of their drinking from the outside world, as well as 'parenting' her younger sister, by preparing meals for her and bathing her when their parents had been drinking.

Linda recalls that her paternal grandfather died when her father was three. Her father recounts that his mother abandoned him several times during his childhood; once, he claimed, leaving him by himself in an hotel room for several days when he was eighteen months old. Linda describes her grandmother as a compulsive over-eater who, according to her father, sexually abused him by arranging and watching friends engage in sexual activities with her young son.

According to Linda, her father grew up to become an alcoholic and, in Linda's words, a 'sexual addict'. She describes him as having had frequent extramarital affairs and sexual liaisons. Linda remembers the 'sexual energy' surrounding her father and the sexual innuendoes and comments which made up his interactions with her and her younger sister. He made his living writing and publishing pornographic books.

Linda says that her maternal grandfather sexually abused his daughter, Linda's mother, and later sexually abused both Linda and her younger sister. Her maternal grandmother, according to Linda, dealt with her husband's sexual behaviour by compulsive overeating and compulsive shopping.

Linda described herself as having felt empty and lonely for most of her life. When she went to university, she sought to avoid the pervasive sense of loneliness by drinking excessively and having frequent sexual affairs. At that point in her life, she restricted her eating behaviours to the point of anorexia and restricted spending money by buying second-hand clothing. Although she could have afforded new clothing, she felt driven to hoard food and money, out of a fear of 'having nothing left' if she spent any money. After leaving university, her first job paid enough money for her to have credit cards. She describes a 'switch' in her attitude about spending at this point. She could afford to buy expensive clothing and, shopping on credit, she could avoid thinking about her mounting debts. Shopping made her feel really good about herself during and after clothes-buying sprees; she felt powerful and attractive.

Linda describes the next several years of her life as revolving around addictive sexual and alcoholic behaviours and periods of over-eating and severely restricting her eating in order to lose weight. At this point, compulsive shopping was not the primary addiction in her life, although she sometimes went on 'shopping binges' when she had been drinking. During these times, shopping gave her a sense of freedom and made her feel 'exhilarated'; the feelings of guilt and anxiety came later when faced with mounting credit-card debts. Shopping itself was 'fun' and gave her a 'high' without the 'hangover'.

Linda's drinking eventually caused her to seek inpatient treatment for alcoholism. She says that the initial treatment addressed her alcohol addiction, but not the underlying issues which had caused her to drink to excess or to practise other addictions. Although she managed to stop drinking, she continued to overeat and her shopping addiction intensified. She began to feel as out of control around her spending patterns as she had previously felt in regard to drinking. She describes her shopping as 'binges' which occurred when she went out intending to buy 'one practical item for the house', usually groceries, and ending up buying dozens of items, usually of clothing, which she didn't need, feeling 'unable' to stop herself.

Linda recounts that the binge shopping often consisted of buying items of clothing which were too small, planning on dieting to be able to wear them. She often bought the same item, two sizes too small, in every available colour and ended up eventually discarding the never-worn clothing. She sometimes shopped by herself and, at other times, went shopping with friends who 'enabled' her out of control shopping behaviour. She also 'binged' by mail, ordering some items of clothing in several different sizes and all the available colours, which she either returned or kept without ever having worn. She describes one 'shopping binge' which lasted for six months. By not looking at or paying the bills on her credit cards, she was able to avoid facing the enormous debts she was incurring.

Finally, Linda's GP suggested that she consider getting treatment for the 'stress' and 'exhaustion' which had begun to affect her health. Entering inpatient treatment for a second time, she was able to identify the multiple addictions which she practised at times simultaneously and at other times alternating between one addiction and another. She reports that she began to see herself as being addicted to compulsive shopping as well as alcohol, nicotine and over-work. At this point, she explored the addictions which she practised as a pattern which she had seen modelled by her parents and grandparents, and gradually learned to identify the 'secondary gains' which the addictive behaviours afforded her. She became more aware of using addictive behaviours to avoid experiencing painful feelings and using one addiction to help her avoid facing the consequences of another.

Over the next several years, Linda recounts that she participated in individual therapy and attended Twelve Step Programmes on a regular basis. As she learned healthier coping responses, she was able to recognise and express the feelings of emptiness, despair and the constant sense of 'shame' which triggered the addictive behaviours.

At this point in her life, Linda says that she continues working towards gradual, positive changes in her life, rather than expecting 'immediate' perfection in herself which, paradoxically, had often led to her out-of-control behaviour around shopping, drinking and overeating. Although she has not drunk alcohol in a number of years, she still sometimes eats and spends 'too much'. She is, however, now able to recognise the feelings and events which trigger these behaviours as they come up and is able to stop herself much sooner without experiencing the shame which accompanied previous relapse. Progress, for her, lies in reducing the problematic behaviours and in feeling better about herself. The emptiness and shame which she used to experience frequently are slowly being replaced by contentment.

REFERENCES

Bradshaw, J. (1988) *Healing the Shame that Binds You*. Deerfield Beach, Florida, Health Communications Inc.
Elliot, R. (1994) Addictive Consumption: Function and fragmentation in postmodernity. *Journal of Consumer Policy*, 17, 159–79.
Elliott, R., Eccles, S. and Gournay, K. (1996) Revenge, Existential Choice and Addictive Consumption. *Psychology and Marketing*, vol. 13, no. 18, 355–6.
Faber, R. J. and O'Guinn, T. C. (1992) A Clinical Screener for Compulsive Buying. *Journal of Consumer Research*, 19, 459–69.
Falk, P. and Campbell, C. (eds) (1997) *The Shopping Experience*. London, Sage.
Johnson, V. (1980) *I'll Quit Tomorrow*. New York, HarperCollins.
Kasl, D. C. (1987) *Women, Sex and Addiction*. London, Mandarin Press.
Lefevre, R. (1988) *How to Identify Addictive Behaviour*. London, Promis Books Limited.
Norwood, R. (1985) *Women Who Love Too Much*. London, Arrow.
Satir, V. (1972) *Peoplemaking*. Palo Alto, California, Science and Behavior Books.
Stafford, D. (1992) *Children of Alcoholics*. London, Piatkus.
Wegscheider-Cruse, S. and Cruse, J. (1990) *Understanding Co-dependency*. Deerfield Beach, Florida, Health Communications, Inc.
Williams, T. (1995) *Cat on a Hot Tin Roof*. Harmondsworth, Middlesex, Penguin.
Wilson-Schaef, A. (1987) *When Society Becomes an Addict*. San Francisco, Harper and Row.

11

Shame on Credit

Fiona Murray

I had been working with my male Jungian therapist for over a year before I was able to overcome my shame sufficiently to talk about my compulsive shopping habits. I had been aware for some time that my shopping had become as out of control as my drinking had been.

I had arrived at his consulting room overloaded with carrier bags filled with expensive clothes which I had to leave outside the door because I felt ashamed to make the extent of my addiction so obvious. I might have left the bags behind but the shame crossed the threshold with me.

As I talked I felt the panic, fear and self-loathing physically overwhelming me to the extent where I felt almost paralysed. My therapist became someone to be feared. He might take my credit cards away and I feared this prospect just as I once feared being told that my drinking had to stop.

A particularly disturbing incident had happened a few days prior to this session. It was my birthday and I had been aware that I might use this as an excuse to spend money more recklessly than usual. Throughout that morning I had managed to control the urge to spend, but as I passed one of my favourite shops a jacket caught my eye and I immediately surrendered to an irresistible compulsion to buy it. I made the purchase as if I were in a trance and left feeling intoxicated.

By the time I arrived home feelings of shame, panic and bewilderment had replaced the elation. I began to feel depressed and fearful as I realised the undisclosed extent of my debts. I felt as if I were going mad, and at this stage had not realised that I had become as addicted to shopping as I had once been to alcohol. I could not bear to admit that I was being affected so powerfully by another manifestation of addiction. In the full awareness of just how difficult the last battle had been I could scarcely tolerate the thought of another struggle.

Life without shopping seemed a very bleak prospect and for some time I would continue to shop in quiet desperation knowing that I would not be able to sustain either the level of financial indebtedness or the sense of shame and guilt. I could no longer use alcohol to alter my emotions, but shopping had become just as potent. The despair when addictive behaviour reasserts itself cannot be underestimated. I had almost lost my life as a result of an addiction to alcohol and had put an enormous amount of energy into my recovery. It became impossible even to contemplate telling those I loved and myself that I was again addicted.

'I shop, therefore I am' describes the existence of a shopping addict and brings into stark focus the reality of an emotional, psychological and spiritual process almost totally preoccupied with the next purchase.

The first part of the chapter tells the story of my life before I gained my current understanding of addiction. My insight and self-awareness grew over seven years through a process of AA, Jungian Analysis, Integrative Therapy and academic study which helped me to understand and live with my addictive behaviour.

The story is set in the context of loss and emotional deprivation over four generations of women. My grandmother died when my mother was born and her father's brother and his wife subsequently adopted my mother. She recalled that she was well looked after, to the extent that she was clothed and fed, but she cannot remember being cuddled or shown affection.

It was inevitable that my mother, without the nurture and connectedness with her mother, was emotionally unavailable for me. My mother lost a son when she miscarried. I was conceived later and I believe that from the moment of my birth I was always designated as 'second best' because of my gender.

I gave my daughter, the only child born to me, away for adoption over thirty years ago when I was nineteen.

I cannot remember my childhood as being happy. What I can remember are frequent illnesses, particularly when I contracted pneumonia because of a neglected chest infection. My mother admitted to me that the doctor was extremely angry with her more than once for not looking after me properly. It seems that there was little real concern for my welfare.

There is a deep appreciation in the field of psychotherapy for the hidden nature of childhood wounding which can be caused by unhealthy dynamics in even the most normal of families by a pervasion of 'toxic nonempathic responsiveness, manipulation and instability that later manifest in the compulsions, violence, and empty lives of the adult children' (Firman and Gila 1997, pp. 3–4).

My mother and father argued violently and on several occasions my mother left me with my father and returned to her home in Scotland where she stayed for several days at a time. On her return I was always given a present. Once it was a pet tortoise, another time it was an Easter rabbit full of little chocolate eggs. On reflection it seems that I was given presents in atonement or in an unspoken need for absolution. My mother seemed to be saying, 'I love you. Forgive me.'

Throughout my adult life I would seek this reparation for myself in the form of alcohol or shopping whenever I felt hurt, isolated or abandoned. I also understand why I once felt compelled to buy others presents when I felt that I had displeased or hurt them. I was looking for absolution in the same way that my mother had once sought it from me.

My mother worked and was able to give me a substantial sum for weekly pocket money which I initially spent on clothes for my favourite doll and later on cosmetics for myself. She always took me to buy beautiful clothes on my birthday and at Christmas with the money given to me by my grandmother who lived in Scotland. I have a sense now that my mother would never have dared disobey the edict from my grandmother that the money was to buy me something pretty.

I experienced the euphoria of shopping at the early age of eight or nine for it represented one of the few occasions where I was the recipient of some meaningful female attention, even if it was only the sales assistant fussing over me.

However, this euphoria was in sharp contrast to the humiliation I experienced when forced to wear some of the ugly second-hand clothes given to my mother for me to wear. It seems that what I was permitted to wear depended on my mother's current perception of her maternal role, and, as I grew older, her acknowledgement of my sexuality and femininity, and whether both should be praised or punished.

Family life was described by my mother as a series of 'hungers and bursts'. My father's career as a contract engineer meant that there would be periods when he earned a great deal of money and the family environment felt comparatively safe. The atmosphere at home was one of celebration and I can remember money being spent quite indiscriminately, as if tomorrow did not exist and there would never have to be a 'day of reckoning'. Inevitably the contract would end and we would be living on unemployment benefit, a way of life that felt fearful, unsafe and restrictive.

There was always a feeling of immense relief and euphoric anticipation of the good times to come whenever my father started work again. Now I recognise that these feelings were replicated every time I took out yet another line of credit, or had managed to consolidate my debts to release more disposable income to spend. A 'burst' became possible again and I believed I had found a way of controlling the cycle. There would be no more 'hungers'.

I was nine years old when my parents gave me a Cherry-B. I loved the flavour and it was my first experience of the potent mood-altering effect of alcohol. I remember after that how I would look forward to my regular Saturday night drink. I loved the warmth and the 'high' that alcohol brought. Jacobs writes that:

> ... a key sign that one is dealing with this particular sub-class of persons (Jacobs, 1984) is the striking clarity and completeness with which they recall their very first experience ... that led to their discovery that they could change the unhappy conditions they had resigned themselves to endure. Apparently it is the striking contrast between their aversive, unhappy, non-fulfilling resting state and its dramatic alleviation that creates such a novel, intense and well-remembered experience. (1986, pp. 172–3)

In therapy I could clearly remember what was bought and when, the time of year, the interior of the shop and the euphoria associated with those early shopping trips. I can also remember my first adult shopping 'high'. Shortly after being given my first-ever wages earned from a Saturday job I bought a bright pink jumper I had been wanting all week. My mother was angry because I had not taken my very first pay packet straight home to her, as she had once been forced to do by her mother.

I believe that financial habits are learned from the example set by the parents. When I left school and started work as a civil servant I dutifully handed an agreed sum to my mother on payday 'to pay my keep'. Whatever remained was for bus fares, clothes and entertainment. However, during the course of the month my mother would reimburse me with most of what I had paid her plus some of the money that she had earned herself.

My mother told me once that what she most feared was to be disliked or unloved. I now believe that she met her own needs by giving her own hard-earned cash to my father and me. Money for beer would get my father out of the house and into a good mood; giving me money and buying me beautiful clothes would allow her to feel like a good mother, especially if I were feeling depressed. Every time I went out she put money into my hand. I feel certain that this act formed the basis of my 'magical thinking'. If I wanted something enough the money would always appear, rather like the 'magic' of instant credit.

This behavioural mood-altering effect of shopping was, for me, as powerful as alcohol and came

... as if from heaven, the miracle of the pharmocogenic pleasure-effect ... A magical movement of the hand introduces a magical substance, and behold, pain and suffering are exorcized, the sense of misery disappears and the body is suffused with waves of pleasure. (Rado 1997, p. 57)

I find it very difficult to reconcile my mother's seeming financial generosity with her apparent lack of concern for my welfare. It seems as if the greater my suffering, the more she could feel like a 'good mother'. My second therapist, a woman, suggested that my mother might have seen my existence as a threat to her survival. I reached the conclusion that she could only love me if I were disempowered through suffering.

Whilst I was recovering from a major operation eleven years ago I could not understand why I felt so disturbed at the thought of having her at home to look after me whilst my husband was away on a business trip. Perhaps I feared her compassion because it had always been earned with my pain.

She was regarded as something of a saint in the village where we lived, and yet the suffering I experienced as the result of a stammer was disregarded. I believe it was caused by my Scottish father constantly berating me for speaking with an English accent. Every time I opened my mouth I expected to be ridiculed and it became impossible for me to speak in class at school. As a result I was severely bullied and neither my parents nor my teacher did anything to intervene.

I felt neglected, humiliated and very lonely until I was fifteen and became my father's 'drinking buddy' (Forward 1989, p. 82). My mother constantly refused to accompany him on his visits to the local pub. I earned his approval because I could hold my drink and he attracted many compliments for having a beautiful daughter. This under-age drinking with my father now seems like a desperate attempt to form a relationship with him. Forward writes of:

... a special and often secret bond between parent and child. This particular type of conspiracy feels like camaraderie to a child. It is often as close as the child can get to something approaching love and approval. (1989, pp. 82–3)

My father appreciated fine clothes and I would often accompany him on these shopping excursions. When we shopped and drank together I felt so proud, excited, needed and important. Alcohol magically lifted my mood and the thrill of shopping with my father reinforced the belief that I had found the cure for all the emotional pain that I had ever suffered. Jacobs

... places primary emphasis on the presence of two interrelated sets of *pre-disposing* factors that are held to determine whether or not an individual is at risk of maintaining an addictive pattern of behaviour. The first of these two sets is: a unipolar physiological resting state that is chronically and excessively either depressed or excited. This lifelong persistent state of either hypo- or hyper-arousal is believed to predispose the individual to respond only to a rather narrow 'window' of stress-reducing but potentially addictive substances or experiences, and to make the person resistive to other kinds of addictive behaviours.

The second set of predisposing factors is of a *psychological* nature. These reactions arise from social and developmental experiences in childhood and early adolescence, and convince these persons that they are inferior, unwanted, unneeded, and/or generally rejected by parents and significant others ... one of the essential reinforcing qualities that maintains the chosen addictive pattern is that, while indulging in it, the individual can escape from painful reality and experience wish-fulfilling fantasies of being an important personage, highly successful and admired. (1986, p. 168)

I believe that I became addicted to alcohol very quickly. The more I drank, the more sexually available I became to the men I met in bars. Sadly, this seemed a way of gaining acceptance amongst a cynical group of people. I mistook sexual availability for genuine popularity and the greater the promiscuity, the greater the shame, so the more I drank to cope. I enjoyed drinking enormously and the benefits would outweigh the costs for at least fifteen years.

Inevitably, without contraception, I became pregnant with my daughter when I was eighteen and deeply involved with a married man who then wanted no further involvement with me. I felt that I had no choice but to give her away for adoption when she was ten days old.

My parents, my father in particular, expected me to pretend that the whole shameful business had never happened. I coped with my feelings by relying on alcohol and tranquillisers prescribed by my doctor.

Then to gain the confidence to return to my previous employment in the media I bought clothes. I needed to re-invent myself and buying a new wardrobe, according to the women's magazines, was the most effective way of achieving this goal. I could hide my shame under a mantle of confidence and try to convince the world and myself that I had recovered from my ordeal. I had spent a great part of my life feeling isolated, mocked, humiliated and full of shame; I could cover this with clothes and make-up. I dressed so that the vulnerable, hurt aspects of myself should not be seen.

And the Weaver said, Speak to us of
Clothes.
And he answered:
Your clothes conceal much of your
beauty, yet they hide not the
unbeautiful.
        Kahlil Gibran (1926, p. 46)

In the early 1970s I joined a major airline as an air stewardess and was able to hide inside my uniform. I could dress up and play my part in what seemed a most glamorous profession. I was safe from derision and mockery. But alcohol was cheap, plentiful and available with very little censure and my drinking escalated. The clothes took a great deal of my money and the alcohol began to erode my health and dignity. My income was considerable and I discovered that shopping under the influence of alcohol increased the euphoria. Perhaps, with hindsight, I was trying to recreate the times when I went shopping with my father.

Acquiring what was momentarily fashionable filled the criteria for membership to a desired social grouping. I had found a way of becoming whom I wanted to be, a person of perceived wealth, taste, power and status. This desire to 'belong to the club', has been potently expressed in a recent car advertisement. 'Well how do you expect to be taken seriously if you're not a member!?'

By the late 1970s my drinking was out of control and I was very concerned but unable to voice my fears, even though I knew that the airline would be sympathetic. It became clear after one incident whilst on duty abroad that my career was in serious jeopardy. I resigned and two weeks later was married.

It was then that the true extent of my drinking became apparent to those who had, for their own reasons, chosen to ignore it. I lost three jobs in rapid succession, my health was suffering and my recent marriage was threatened. I knew that I needed help and I sought out the local branch of AA. It was not for another eighteen months that I managed to stop drinking. The toll on my mental and physical health, relationships and employment prospects was immense. I stopped drinking the very year that my father died.

Once I began to feel physically better I again became concerned about my appearance. I again made a conscious decision to present a polished image to the world to detract from the shame of being an alcoholic. I had never considered the extent of my clothes shopping to have been a problem until I had stopped drinking. When I had plenty of disposable income I saw shopping as a harmless pastime. I had an account at several well-known retail outlets and the monthly payments were manageable.

However, now there were other disruptive financial and emotional issues weaving a complex web. I began to resent the financial burden imposed on my income by my stepchildren's school fees and maintenance to my husband's first wife. Despite my husband's reassurance that I was the most important person in his life, I felt betrayed, insignificant and 'second best'.

> To build on Duck's (1994) model of relational challenges, some consumers perceive themselves as victims of betrayal in a relationship, in that the partner has not fulfilled previously suggested or stated requests for the dynamics of the relationship to adapt to changes in external or family circumstances. Having taken overt action in the past to address the situation and found it unsuccessful, they adopt a more subversive, less overt method of 'getting back' at their partner – by developing and maintaining an addiction to consumption. (Elliott et al. 1996, p. 667)

The purchases began to feel like a compensation for the resources I was being forced to relinquish, a way of getting even. I had lost drink as a source of comfort, but buying clothes had become a way of comforting myself. Shopping made me feel good. I believed that I could buy a state of emotional security but I did not realise the true cost. Stephen King wrote:

> Something for everyone,
> Something you really had to have.
> And always at a price you could just about
> Afford. The cash price that is.

> Because there was always another price.
> There always is when your heart's most secret
> True desire is for sale.
> (1991, p. 802)

Although buying, hoarding and even hiding goods provided relief from the feeling that I would not survive a period of 'hunger' the deceit became soul-destroying. I had tried to repress the guilt and shame, which I dare not feel because I knew then that I would not be able to continue with the addictive behaviour which appeared to make my life worth living.

I was conscious of stockpiling, for if I were not able to shop, at least I would be able to turn to my 'larder' – my wardrobe. Seven years later a very expensive handbag remains unused at the back of a shelf.

Clinical observations strongly collaborate the concerted, innovated attempts of addicted persons to ensure that they will not be long without the wherewithal necessary to maintain their chosen addictive pattern. These persons have developed ingenious methods for 'stashing' substances, so they will be on hand for an emergency. They also squirrel away specially earmarked and otherwise inviolate money (or other negotiables) to purchase same. Similar forms of hedging against the phobic-like anticipatory fear of being without are seen amongst non-substance abusers who demonstrate other types of addictive behaviour, for example, compulsive gamblers (Jacobs 1986, p. 177).

I was able to hide my addiction for as long as my own financial resources would allow. Even whilst my husband and I were both earning substantial salaries I realised that there was something disturbing about my physical and mental agitation whilst shopping. I shopped alone as I once drank alone. The greater I sensed the disapproval might be the more exciting it became. I felt pampered, secure and omnipotent. I could have anything in the world that I wanted without having to undergo the humiliation of asking. There was a feeling of precarious excitement in the knowledge that I could demonstrate my independence whilst punishing my husband for daring to believe that he was a generous and all-powerful provider. Elliot et al. reported that:

> ... informants who showed elements of revenge in their addictive shopping behaviour appeared to have feelings of lack of control in their relationship with their partner (and often, previously, with their father) ... It appears therefore that they developed and maintain their shopping behaviour in order to have some kind of 'exciting' or even slightly dangerous control over a part of their personal lives and finances. This in turn suggests some feeling of power (albeit secret) over their partner. The fact that many partners appear to tolerate what they know or suspect about shopping activities seems, if anything, to encourage the informants to take even greater risks and be even more outrageous in their activities. (1996, pp. 666–7)

At the onset of the recession in 1991 I coped with the prospect of a severe reduction in our income with an act of sheer defiance. I opened a charge account in an expensive shoe shop and immediately spent hundreds of pounds on four pairs of shoes and two handbags in an attempt to ward off the fear of another 'hunger'. This shop was a branch of the chain where my father during a 'burst' bought my first pair of 'grown up' shoes. It was as if a fearful little girl had dragged me into the store and was screaming at me 'More! Buy more! More!' until I began to panic, overwhelmed by the extent of her need for gratification. Smiling sadistically and temporarily replete, she led me to the door where I was abandoned with the sense of powerlessness and guilt. Jacobs writes that:

> ... the heretofore overlooked feature of anticipatory fear of a *future* 'catastrophic' event is common, even central, to all types of addiction. It is seen as the prime mover that stokes the crescendo of frantic, unmodulated indulgence at the later downhill stages in substance abusers and addicts. (1986, p. 178)

Every new line of credit created a 'high' out of all proportion to the act. It felt powerful and at the same expressed my pain and anger: 'I could manage on my own, thank you very much!' It allowed me to reject in the present those in the past who had ignored my needs or witnessed my pain and still left me abandoned.

Reflecting on the psychoanalytic concept of transference, I prefer to think of it not necessarily onto a person, but onto a situation, or a place in time. There are two situations which resonate from the past to the present of which I am now consciously aware. One is a place, the shoe shop; the other is the immense relief I once felt when opening a new credit agreement which reminds me how I used to feel when my father found a job. Patrick Casement describes how:

> ... because there is no sense of time in the unconscious, anything in an overlap of past and present experience can be seen as unconsciously belonging equally to the past or the present ... previous experience and related feeling are transferred from the past and experienced as if they were in the present. (1985, p. 7)

This overwhelming feeling that I must provide for myself because I could trust no other person may have originated during a 'hunger' from the past. That I could not find words to express it suggests that I was too young to speak at the time. In the present I wanted to punish and I wanted revenge.

Shopping enabled me to express my rage and fear and to feel avenged for past deprivations. The act of shopping took on a significance out of all proportion to the exchange of money for goods. It was as if the addiction had become a parody of a 'good parent' who could be magically summoned up at the swipe of a credit card.

I deliberately tried to ignore the fact that I was getting into debt. I saw the credit limit as a credit, not a debit. It did not occur to me to save money and then spend it. I wanted immediate gratification and saving would have taken far too long. Credit was the means to an end and I was desperate to have enough to buy what I wanted. I needed the subversive energy of my Shadow to liberate the manipulative part of my psyche so that I could plot, scheme and lie in order to satisfy my addiction.

The defence mechanisms of denial and rationalisation meant that I was mostly protected from feelings of panic and shame until the early hours of the morning when I was forced to stop running and face the fact that I was seriously in debt.

> It is generally said that a miracle never lasts longer than three days. The miracle of the elation only lasts a few hours. Then, in accordance with the laws of nature, comes sleep, and a gray and sober awakening, 'the morning after'. (Rado 1997, p. 57)

When my husband was forced to retire early I was forced to admit the extent of my indebtedness. My husband behaved like a benevolent father when confronted with the result of my excesses and paid my debts without a word of censure. I remember feeling very young, as if I had been a naughty girl and been forgiven on the condition that I behaved, so if I bought anything, I had better not let him find out. I went to great lengths to make sure that shopping was locked in the boot of the car until he was out. Then I would have to get rid of all the bags as I once had to get rid of all the bottles. I dreaded his scrutiny of my spending which only intensified the need to hide my purchases.

I could manage to control my addiction for months at a time, but rather like the alcoholic for whom 'one drink is never enough and a thousand too many' I found that once I had started to shop for clothes I could not stop. I began to cram clothes into my wardrobe as a bulimic would cram food into her mouth.

Elliott writes:

> The suggestion that compulsive buyers and adolescent shoplifters are both victims of the consumer age was proposed by Cox and Moschis (1990), and the possible comorbidity between addictive consumption and bulimia (Kreuger, 1988) and between bulimia and shoplifting (Norton, Crisp, and Bhat, 1985) was suggested by Faber and O' Guinn (1992). (1994, p. 176)

An anorectic will often turn to bulimia as a 'cure' for her illness. It means that she can eat, or at least be seen to be eating, without having to retain the unwanted intake. For me a similar strategy developed. I could now have the thrill of shopping without having to keep the clothes. As the bulimic empties her stomach, so I returned my purchases to the stores for refunds until the 'hunger' returned.

An addict needs a 'fix' just as much as an infant needs immediate gratification of its hunger to alleviate inner discomfort and the resulting tension and anxiety:

Psychologically, addictions represent a chronic and compulsive need for intake: to gratify oral-incorporative needs. They also involve a physical craving or body need, which may have a constitutional, organic or biochemical origin. (Lowe 1972, pp. 29–30)

I craved alcohol and, later, the moment of purchase to provide a 'rush' of comfort so intense that it eventually became addictive. It was as though I was unconsciously recreating the cycle of 'hungers and bursts'. A ritual compulsion repeated over and over again can tell a therapist a great deal about how the patient was treated when little.

Freud observed that in children there was an apparent compulsion whereby situations which the child could not tolerate were symbolised and constantly re-enacted ... Freud recalled analyses of patients who appeared compelled to relive the anxiety-provoking situations of their childhood, without insight, transference or resolution occurring. (Stafford-Clark 1965, p. 158)

He also observed that sometimes the repetition compulsion could be an application of the pleasure principle where the child repeatedly sought pleasure from a familiar activity. But where the activity was obviously far from being pleasurable he interpreted it as the working through of an instinct for self-destruction, the death instinct (Thanatos).

The activity of the death instinct can only be deduced indirectly in most people. It is seen at its most obvious in the urge to self-destruction seen in compulsive and repeated suicide attempts, in destructive habits such as unnecessary risk taking, in alcoholism or drug addiction, or in the psychopathic pattern of the lives of individuals who bring destruction upon themselves and everyone closely associated with them. (Stafford-Clark 1965, pp. 158–9)

Gustave Flaubert wrote the tragic mid-nineteenth-century story of Madame Bovary, a beautiful woman driven to suicide because she was unable to face the insurmountable debts incurred by her compulsive spending. Her widower died as a result of the devastating grief he felt caused by the manner of her death (she ate arsenic), and his indebtedness. Their orphaned daughter was sent to work in the cotton mills.

Emma Bovary shopped as an antidote to her misery – 'a sharp pain ... which she knew would never end'. The brief experience of how life might have been if she were rich had left her feeling intolerably deprived and dissatisfied. She longed for romance and excitement:

How far away the ball already seemed! What was it that so completely severed this evening from the day before yesterday ... She resigned herself to the inevitable, however, and reverently locked away in the chest of drawers the lovely dress which she had worn, and the satin slippers with their soles still stained with the yellow beeswax of the dance floor. Her heart was like them: the touch of wealth had stamped it with a sharp pain, which would never end. (Flaubert 1981, p. 52)

The title of a recent television programme on addictive shopping, *She's Gotta Have It*, describes how the id responds directly to the instincts, those needs which arise from the body, for example, the biologically based needs for food, warmth and sexual gratification. There is a degree of excitement in addictive shopping and a tension which demands immediate relief. However, the subsequent intense pleasure following the purchase is quickly negated by profound self-disgust.

Stafford-Clark describes one of Freud's last works, *An Outline of Psychoanalysis* (1939), where he discusses his formulated theory of 'The Psychical Apparatus' – the id, the ego and the superego, 'as one of the most interesting he ever wrote' (1965, p. 109).

The id, governed by the Pleasure Principle, seems to have been in control whenever I shopped without being able responsibly to consider the effect on the family finances. Rational thought had no power against the urgency of the need to buy for my infantile id (the little child in the shoe shop), was totally unaffected by logic or reason. I had to buy because it was the only way I could relieve that painful tension. Why suffer the discomfort of deferred gratification and self-denial when your craving can be satisfied by 'Instant Credit'? Sales professionals instinctively recognise the customer's desire for gratification and manipulatively close a sale by offering instant credit. 'Of course you can afford it!'

This demanding infant rendered my ego, the supposedly rational, decision-making, planning and logical part of my personality, completely impotent. I was incapable of postponing the demands of my id because my ego had no power to intervene and allow any consideration of the thoughts, feelings and reactions of others. Afterwards my punitive superego would threaten my ego in the form of guilt and shame for my self-indulgent behaviour.

Given my early experience, conflict between the id and superego was inevitable. My ego would eventually be caught in the middle of these opposing sets of demands and become the battleground on which these opposing factions would fight for control. I could feel the battle wage inside me as my weakened ego struggled to convince me that I had already overcome one addiction and could win again. My id won consistently and I would become depressed by the misery of guilt inflicted by my punitive superego. I became frightened that I would not be able to contain this state of psychic warfare for long. I began to suffer physically with tension headaches, rashes and stomach upsets. A sense of reality and common sense could never survive, crushed as they were between the screaming child and the punishing parents. To quote Freud:

> An action by the ego is as it should be if it satisfies simultaneously the demands of the id, the superego and of reality – that is to say, if it is able to reconcile their demands with one another. The details of the relation between the ego and the superego become completely intelligible when they are traced back to the child's attitude to its parents ... the id and the superego have one thing in common: they both represent influences from the past ... (1939, pp. 152–4 in Stafford-Clark 1965, p. 112)

I began to understand this conflict when I started therapy again whilst studying for my Diploma in Counselling. My second therapist, a woman, helped me to understand that I had made a very early decision that my survival was my responsibility and I would not, indeed could not, feel guilty unless I were found out. The consequences of this were that I felt cast-out and miserable. I would overcompensate by investing a great deal of energy into being a most perfectly behaved child in order to win back the love and approval which I believed I had lost.

Freud believed that every behaviour is a compromise, which can take three major forms – defence mechanisms, neurotic symptoms and dreams.

'Freud said that all dreams were meaningful. Not only does the dream have a meaning but the meaning of the dream is the cause of the dream' (Stafford-Clark, 1995 p. 57) and that:

> An important but long-past and buried memory or idea is represented in the dream by a recent and relatively different impression. This is the most complex type of displacement, and occurs relatively more frequently in the dreams of those who are already exhibiting symptoms of emotional disturbance in their emotional life. (Stafford-Clark, 1995 p. 61)

I have had several potent dreams, which I have explored in therapy and which have given a symbolic understanding to my deeper motivation to purchase.

In one dream I was in a relationship with a man whom I have long desired in reality. We had stayed away together for the night and as we tidied up the room and folded our nightwear away in a drawer, he deliberately hid the delicate, pale pink nightdress he had given me under a pair of plain white cotton pyjamas. In the dream I felt very excited that I had finally consummated my physical desire, together with a great sense of loss that I would not be able to wear the beautiful nightdress again. I felt humiliated and guilty at the disapproval of the religious couple who owned the house and left a bible in plain view on the table as I left.

The pink nightdress could be interpreted as my femininity that had been repressed by my mother's insistence that I wore second-hand clothes and shoes which were as unflattering as the white cotton pyjamas. As a teenager, how I longed to be the recipient of the admiration and even envy of my peers instead of the mockery and ridicule I received every day because my shoes were ugly and unfashionable. It seems significant now that my father bought me my first pair of elegant 'grown-up shoes' for I sense that he did not always approve of my mother's attitude towards me and tried to console me.

My sexuality must have been as repressed as my femininity and just as ripe for punishment, otherwise why would the two punitive Calvinistic figures have been present as a form of superego? A friend once described my father as 'a Calvinist' because of his tendency to be strict and strait-laced. In the dream it seems that I was not only being punished for committing adultery, but for also daring to have any sexual feelings.

It seems as if my mother forced me to deny my femininity and it became as inaccessible as the pink nightdress locked in the drawer. In this context clothes buying becomes a ritualistic means of claiming what had been denied to me earlier in life. It would seem to be strongly motivated by anger, revenge and a powerful desire to make those who once mocked me feel insignificant in the presence of my beauty. I am very aware that I dressed to attract attention or provoke desire and jealousy.

For many years I yearned for beautiful jewellery to the extent where I would buy it for myself. I could never understand the reason for this until this dream.

I was in a beautiful water meadow walking alongside a man whose face I could not see but who I sensed to be older than I am, benevolent, powerful and charismatic. He led me towards a marble counter where there was a rich display of jewellery. He carefully removed the earrings from my pierced earlobes and gently replaced them with the diamond earrings, holding my cheek tenderly as he did so. On waking I was still deeply affected by the tenderness of his bestowing me with this magnificent gift. I felt like a goddess.

Months later I was watching a television play where a man was tenderly presenting his mistress with a pair of beautiful earrings. My husband turned to me and said 'I wish I could afford to do that for you.' Rather than feel touched by the fact that he seemed sad, I was aware that I felt angry and deprived.

Another of my dreams featured my mother and I only felt recently that I had even begun to understand it.

The setting was a heavily wooded area in a lush green clearing where a scaffold was erected with the noose showed up clearly against the trees. There was to be an execution. My mother walked calmly across to the steps of the scaffold like a martyr powerless over her fate. She turned to me, held out her hand and dropped into my outstretched palm a ring which my father had had made for her in the Middle East. She turned away from me and went almost willingly to a death which, in the dream, seemed like a sacrifice.

I remember the occasion in waking life when she gave me that very ring with the same gesture and felt that I never really understood her motivation. It felt like a reward for finally becoming the kind of daughter she always wanted – I was a 'good girl'. Later, as in the dream, it felt like a request for absolution, suggesting that was the purpose of the gifts of clothes and money. The act was as wordless as expressions of her love.

There was no executioner in the dream. So was this an act of self-sacrifice? Was she trying to show me the silent sacrifices she had made without my ever knowing it until it was too late? Or was it that the value of the ring was meant to shift a balance so that I was the one left feeling guilty? Was I then in her debt?

The dream now seems prophetic because she died without ever telling me how ill she really was. I can only think that she did not want to overly concern me. I feel confused for on one hand I feel guilty for not taking a more active part in her care towards the end of her life. On the other hand I am angry with her for expecting me to be equally self-sacrificing. I dream of her often now and when we meet it is in the spirit of love and reconciliation where we speak the words which we were never able to say when she was alive.

I feel now that I tried to parent myself through the act of consumerism. If I bought myself beautiful things I could not only avoid the fear of the 'hungers', but also make myself feel as precious and as prized as I had in the dream where I was given the earrings. I am also aware of the early extent of Oedipal rivalry between my mother and myself.

Dreams can be rich in symbols and worked with creatively in the context of my personal myth have been of great therapeutic value and have brought underlying life issues into consciousness.

Jungian therapy showed me how dreams can be an important route to the reconciliation of opposites, the transcendant function. I would consider these opposites to be a princess and Cinderella (the morning after the ball). The therapeutic goal was for me to find a place somewhere in the middle where I could be 'normal', which could be neither 'regal' nor 'robbed', not enduring 'bursts' or 'hungers' – I wanted to feel 'ordinarily content'.

Carl Jung based his approach to therapy not only on his own experience and studies of his patients, but also on an extensive study of myths, comparative religion and mythology, in an effort to discover universal truths which would be valid for all human beings. These studies gave rise to Jung's idea that all mankind has shared experiences throughout our ancestral past at the level of the Collective Unconscious, a reservoir of primordial images or archetypes.

A potent archetype for addiction is the vampire, its predatory aspect being as powerful as it is compelling and seductive. Contemporary cinematic interpretations of Dracula portray him (or her) as an irresistible lover who is terrifyingly welcome. The window is left open as an invitation. He usually seduces the victim into an ecstatic state of surrender, not unlike the first drink swallowed by the alcoholic or the moment when the addictive shopper chooses to buy.

However, the vampire resembles addiction in its relentless, remorseless and merciless capacity eventually to destroy any positive self-perception because:

> ... some of our life force – the stuff that allows us to perceive our own beauty, talent, and worth – has been bled out of us by the vampire and we now have an insufficient amount to maintain a healthy self-perception ... Whenever we experience this feeling of shameful insufficiency, we have been the victim of a psychic vampire. (Hort 1996, pp. 15–16)

Faced with a mesmerising display of clothes and accessories I would feel an overwhelming and mindless need to consume. Barbara Hort explains how:

> ... if we are not clear about exactly what we have lost, then we are likely to go about it in any old way that occurs to us. The yearning for replenishment is the second symptom of having encountered a psychic vampire and is usually experienced as a hunger for more ...
> More. No matter how much we have had, it's never enough. Since we've been bled of what counts, our hunger for everything else is bottomless. We feel driven to consume goods, experiences, and people as if we were starving, as if those substitutes for life force would somehow fill the void. (1996, p. 16)

The inner psychic vampire relentlessly compels its victim to search compulsively for that which will satisfy the unremitting hunger. This yearning for more 'is distinctly different from simple human aspiration.

It is not born of finite ambition, but of the bottomless, shame-driven hunger that alerts us to the vampire's presence' (Hort 1996, p. 17). Hort explains how obsession and compulsion are:

> ... the inevitable step-children of a psyche bent on control ... over time it seemed that she, who was the master of her obsessions and compulsions, became their slave, and she found herself labouring endlessly to meet their demands. Never rich enough, nor thin enough, nor loved nor safe nor accomplished enough. She felt she was never, never enough. Just one more deal, just one more pound, just one more conquest, just one more finished list. Then she would be the best. Then she would truly be loved. Then she would be truly the best. Then she would finally be perfect. The sad truth for this woman, as for us all, is that when the vampire drives us, there is no satisfaction in whatever we compulsively seek, no refuge from what we compulsively fear. There is only the momentary illusion of control and the inevitable return of the terrified hunger. (1996, p. 197)

I had been attempting to fill my inner void with drink, drugs, and/or the pursuit of material things in an attempt to find wholeness. In reality the 'fix' only brought me transient relief from the nagging sense of futility, despair and emptiness. To be an addict is never to be free of a gnawing sense of dissatisfaction, resentment and hunger. Over the years I have invested a terrible amount of my energy into being 'extraordinary' for being 'ordinary' would make me 'dead', 'invisible'. I would no longer exist.

Jung considered that the personality as a whole is the psyche, the soul. An individual is seen as whole from the moment of birth with the personality already there, not acquired through learning and experience. The psychic struggle is to maintain that wholeness and Jung saw the role of therapy as helping a person to recover lost wholeness and strengthen the psyche. He made important contributions to the AA Twelve Step Programme with an emphasis on lost wholeness and the need to replace what has been lost through addictive behaviour.

Jung stated that addiction was a 'thirst for wholeness' (Sparks 1993, p. 24) and that no psychology could heal an addict; there needed to be 'a radical re-arrangement of consciousness' (p. 300), a spiritual awakening where something more than thoughts were changed.

The spiritual awakening and insight began with my second therapist and my unexpressed need for a warm, accepting, non-judgmental mother figure was met. Greater self-awareness initially resulted in the pain of disillusionment as it became apparent that addiction had never been successful in gaining satisfaction, nor was it likely to be.

Julian David (1997) maintains that:

People coming to a therapist are looking for a relationship and they have a right to it. That is perhaps Jung's single greatest principle, they have a right to it. The fact that it is transference does not alter that. All relationships are partly transference and the further we go into the unconscious the larger that element becomes; and since therapy must be an entry into the unconscious, to make a better and more nourishing relationship with it, so there is no avoiding the transference. Moreover the positive transference has been shown by studies done recently in America to be the healing factor. In the container that it creates, the most negative and shameful material can be worked with.

My therapist enabled me to:

... learn to sit in the pain. That, if it can be done, is the healing. The wounder heals.
    ... If one is assuaged by strong affect of any sort, it may be grief or shame, or rage, or intense unassuageable need, the best way is to sit in it, as in a bath. If it is powerful, it will be like a highly abrasive chemical retort. Or it may be shame, and the alchemical retort is smelly and disgusting and we want to get out of there; but it is far better just to sit and smell and feel everything to its utmost. Then it is difficult to describe what happens, but something happens. There is a change of consciousness, similar to that with which people emerge from deep depressions, if they have suffered them honestly. What seemed intolerable becomes tolerable, even the way into some new insight, some new source of energy, because of new conscious- ness. Great suffering brings great understanding if we bear it, that is to say, positively, deliberately, freely, bear it. (David 1997)

Therapeutic struggle enabled me consciously to reconcile the opposites of need and reality in order to be free of the guilt of the overdraft. My impulsive behaviour eventually came under control as I realised that managing both cravings and money did not necessarily lead to a life of deprivation, but to one of greater financial and emotional security.

I can no longer afford to allow the vampiric inner voice of my addiction to lure me into shops with the reassurance that 'You're quite safe. You're only going in to have a look.' I want to be free of the grip of an obsession which might last for days and finally drive me into a purchase just to be free of the craving.

I realise now that for a number of years I had believed that the glossy magazines were portraying how life should be and that I was in some way deficient if I did not live up to their unrealistic standards. Rosalind Coward argues that female desire is crucial for a consumer society. This desire is constantly courted:

... in the kitchen, on the streets, in the world of fashion, in films and fiction
... Everywhere it seems female desire is sought, bought, packaged and
consumed ... If only you could achieve these personal improvements,
everything could be transformed, you'll almost certainly feel better ...
constantly we are made to feel a desire for something more – dissatisfaction
is displaced into desire for an ideal ... (1992, p. 116)

Lowe explains how our early needs are inevitably frustrated and that
we must accept the inevitability of remaining psychologically
vulnerable regarding those needs for the rest of our lives:

> ... our measure of vulnerability may show in our responsiveness to modern
> advertising. Advertising depends on creating a demand, or, in psychological
> terms, deliberately arousing needs. Advertisements become much more
> effective if they can arouse those basic and universal needs which in our
> normal development are inevitably left unsatisfied. The principle itself is
> simple. The advertiser first reactivates our earlier needs, then attempts to
> demonstrate that his product will satisfy them. Our response to such
> advertising is not so much rational as emotional: in fact because the
> persuaders are so well hidden, we are often not aware that we have been
> manipulated. (1972, p. 21)

The psychological obsession with an object of desire created a
craving which compelled me, beyond reason, to buy. This compulsion
which drew me to the stores eventually proved just as hard to defeat as
alcohol. I would conjure up a fantasy of how I would dazzle people at
an event, which could be months away. I would then dedicate my time
and energy into making this fantasy into a reality. The sole focus of
my existence became the search for the dress, the hat, the shoes, the
bag, the scarf, the tights, and the perfume. Reality became distorted
and the rest of my life was to be endured until the day when I could
become the focus of everyone's attention.

It is small wonder that this particular manifestation of addiction is
complex and paradoxical. It made me look good whilst feeling bad. I
had resource to anther kind of 'cocktail' – one of revenge, power,
acceptance and beauty, all heavily endorsed by a consumer society
unhampered by the shame of debt and easy availability of credit.

Alcohol and addictive shopping have manipulated me and lied to
me. Like bad parents they held out the promise of warmth and connectedness but left me full of shame and almost dead, emotionally,
physically and spiritually. I have loved the very things which almost
destroyed me and I still feel a sense of betrayal and anger. It has been
extremely difficult to hold in awareness just how much love, trust and
energy I poured into the people, substances and behaviours which have

brought me such pain. Any 'parent' would do: even a bad one was better than nothing. Perhaps I believed I deserved nothing better. I was after all a girl, born a second child – born second best. My therapist helped me to understand the roots of my addictive behaviour and learn to forgive myself. Now I can dare to be ordinary in the full knowledge that I am more than the sum of what I buy.

REFERENCES

Casement, P. (1985) *On Learning From the Patient*. London, Tavistock/Routledge.
Coward, R. (1992) Female Desire and Sexual Identity. In R. Bocock and K. Thompson (eds) *Social and Cultural Forms of Modernity*. Cambridge, The Open University/Polity Press.
David, J. (1997) From: The Roots of Addiction. C. J. Jung Lecture, Bristol, 11 October.
Elliott, R. (1994) Addictive Consumption: Function and Fragmentation in Postmodernity. *Journal of Consumer Policy* 17, 159–79. Holland, Kluwer Academic Publishers.
Elliott, R., Eccles, S. and Gournay, K. (1996) Man Management? Women and the use of debt to control personal relationships. *Journal of Marketing Management*, 12, 657–69.
Firman, J. and Gila, A. (1977) *The Primal Wound*. Albany, New York, State Univesity of New York Press.
Flaubert, G. (1857). *Madame Bovary*. Oxford, Oxford University Press (1981).
Forward, S. (1989) *Toxic Parents: Overcoming their hurtful legacy and reclaiming your life*. New York and Toronto, Bantam Books.
Freud, S. (1939) *An Outline of Psychoanalysis*. S. E. XXIII, pp. 152–4. In D. Stafford-Clark (1965) *What Freud Really Said*. London, Pelican Books.
Gibran, K. (1926) *The Prophet*. London, Penguin Books.
Hort, B. (1996) *Unholy Hungers: Encountering the psychic vampire in ourselves and others*. Boston, Massachusetts, Shambala Publications Inc.
Jacobs, D. F. (1986) A General Theory of Addictions: A new theoretical model. In D. L. Yasilove (ed.) *Essential Papers on Addiction*. London and New York, New York University Press.
King, S. (1991) *Needful Things*. London, Hodder and Stoughton.
Lowe, G. (1972) *The Growth of Personality*. London, Penguin Books.
Rado, S. (1997) The Psychoanalysis of Pharmacothymia. In D. L. Yasilove (ed.) *Essential Papers on Addiction*. London and New York, New York University Press.
Sparks, T. (1993) *The Wide Open Door*. Center City, Minnesota, Hazleden Educational Materials.
Stafford-Clark, D. (1965) *What Freud Really Said*. London, Pelican Books.

DEDICATION

To Ellen

Afterword

Adrienne Baker

As editor, I am taking the privilege of making the final comment, sharing it with the words of one of our many participants:

> I can't understand why I keep going back to that store when I know there's nothing there I really like. I mean I know that whatever I buy isn't going to make a difference to my life. How could it? It's not about clothes, I know that; it's about loss. There've been lots of losses. There's such a sadness around this ... You reach a certain age where you see the value of possessing just the minimum, but why do I bring the clutter into the house then to get rid of it? I can't bear the clutter of possessions. It's such a relief when I take things back. (Woman, 60)

In a way, taking things back completes a circle. The urge to have, to fill an emptiness, has to be given in to – as if, each time, there is an element of renewed hope. The returning becomes, perhaps, almost an act of purification. The point is that each time the shopping is turned to, there *is* a rekindled cycle of hope, as if the human spirit, despite everything, is determined to survive.

This book has been a process, too. The gathering together of contributors and participants, of papers and books, of thoughts and theories, of narratives and experiences, has in itself been almost addictive. I don't know how I'll feel when I hold all our chapters and take them out of my room. Each one seems laden with feelings and filled with the desire to communicate.

I hope it has given space for people to say, 'This is what it's about', that it no longer needs to be a secret addiction, that in learning about it we can understand. Perhaps the insights of people who have told their stories will help them, and others, to resist the clutter of a tempting society. Perhaps it will help us all to get a heart of wisdom.

Index

Compiled by Sue Carlton

women
  and addictive shopping 3, 17–19,
    22, 200
  'adjusted' woman 18
  and advertising 120
  ageing 119–20, 124
  attractiveness 118–20, 123, 129–30
  clothes shopping 114–15, 120–30
  cultivating the self 119
  and development 23
  and kleptomania 66–7
  'natural' shoppers 120
  as the 'other' 136–7
  and power 201
  role of 162, 200–1

self-esteem 5, 121
self-identity 18, 119, 200–1
and sexual power 117, 128
and shoplifting 61–2, 63, 67
and space 134
stereotyping 17–18
and stress 38
visibility 127–8
Woodman, M. 157–8, 177–8
Wright, Kenneth 45, 49
Wurm, C. 76

Yalom, Irvin 78, 86, 87, 93, 129

Zola, E. 57, 58, 67